The Certainty of the Pre-Tribulation Rapture
First and Second Thessalonians Commentary

By Marianne Manley

The Certainty of the Pre-Tribulation Rapture
First and Second Thessalonians Commentary
© Copyright 2020 by Marianne Manley

All scripture references are taken from the King James Bible. Permission is granted to copy all contents of this book.

Acknowledgments

To God be the glory for helping me write this book! I am grateful for the support of my dear husband Chuck and my children during this time. I would like to thank some of the many grace pastors and teachers who have helped me understand God's word rightly divided: Les Feldick, Richard Jordan, Tom Bruscha, Rick Jordan, David Reid, David O'Steen, Paul Lucas, and others. I was helped by Shawn Brasseaux's informative articles on Forwhatsaithscriptures.org. I thank LeighAnn Mycko, Aaron Howay, and others for their memes. I am grateful for Maureen Parker, Patty Carlson, Lynn Wellborn, and Aaron Howay for proofreading. In preparing these books, I primarily read and study the word of God over and over again until the Holy Spirit helps me to understand His word better, but I also listen to sermons, read articles, and many other books.

The First and Second letters to the Thessalonians are in this book. The Bible commentary is printed within brackets after the Bible text which is printed in bold. *Author's note: when some verses are found in the book I may leave off the book and write (2:5) instead of (1 Thess. 2:5).

How to use this book: read it using a ruler and a pen, when you find a great cross reference or comment you can mark it in your Bible, circle important words (color some of them), make notes, so that you have them next time you read that passage. I recommend the Scofield Study Bible III in the King James Version. It is wise to get a leather cover for it that holds a pen and zips.

<u>**This book is designed to guide and help the reader get the sound doctrine in Paul's letters into their inner man (spirit and soul)**</u>**. I recommend reading** <u>***God's Secret A Primer with Pictures for How to Rightly Divide the Word of Truth***</u> **before this book. It is an overview of the Bible in 100 pages and covers the basics of right division (available on Amazon). Then the rest of the commentaries that I have written in the order that they appear in the Bible.** <u>***Through the Book of Books***</u> **by Lori Verstegen is also helpful.**

Table of Contents

Three Steps to Understanding the Rapture 5

Two Groups: Peter's and Paul's 6

Book Ends 10

Why Right Division is REALLY Important! 12

Edification Process 16

The Key Verse 2 Tim. 2:15 17

13 Letters Written by Apostle Paul (order, structure, and purpose) 18

Dispensation Defined 20

Why God Kept the Mystery a Secret 21

Timeline 23

Rightly Dividing 101 24

The Pre-Tribulation Rapture is Certain 25

Preface 26

Introduction 28

First Thessalonians Outline 32

First Thessalonians Chapter Review Sentences 33

In a Nut Shell 34

1 Thessalonians Chapter 1 The model Church. 35
    The Paulicians an Abbreviated History 46

Several helpful Maps follow. 48

1 Thessalonians Chapter 2 The Model Minister (Paul) and his reward. 53

One Year Extension of Mercy for Israel 63

1 Thessalonians Chapter 3 A Model brother (Timothy). 64
    What the Old Testament Prophets Saw 73

1 Thessalonians Chapter 4 A Model Walk and the Rapture 74

Detail Drawing of the Three Sounds at the Rapture 83

The Rapture was a Mystery given to Apostle Paul 84

Second Coming of Christ to Earth in Prophecy 85
    Christ the Lord is Risen Today (hymn) 86

1 Thessalonians Chapter 5 The Model Walk and the Day of the Lord 88

1 Thessalonians Chapter Summaries 98

When Will the Rapture Occur? 99

Three Days and Three Nights Timetable 102

When Did Jesus Die? 103

Torah Calendar for Nisan (Abib) 34 AD 104

Seven Thousand Years 105

Explanation of Torah Calendar Abib in AD 34 106

Second Thessalonians 108

Second Thessalonians Outline 109

Second Thessalonians Introduction 110

2 Thessalonians Chapter 1 Patience and faith despite persecution 112

2 Thessalonians Chapter 2 "Shaken in mind" by false doctrine 121
    The Seven Years of Tribulation was Prophesied 135
    The Signs in heaven where all prophesied. 136

2 Thessalonians Chapter 3 Follow us in word and work 139

Second Thessalonians Chapter summaries. 148

Cain and Abel 149

Two Seed-Lines 150

The Order of Events After the Rapture 155
    Be Still, My Soul (hymn) 156

Rapture Verses 158

The Second Coming Verses 160
    One Day (hymn) 163

Our Walk in the Body of Christ (Romans to Philemon) 164

Appendix 165
    Why I Use the King James Bible 165

About the Author 171

Other Books by Marianne Manley 172

Three Steps to Understanding the Rapture
(1) <u>We must be saved and have His Spirit.</u>

Before we can understand the Rapture we must understand the Bible. Only saved people can understand the Bible; because it cannot be understood unless we have God's Spirit in us to help us. When we believe the gospel we receive His Spirit.

How are we saved? We hear the word, and trust the gospel of our salvation. "In whom ye also TRUSTED, after that ye HEARD the word of truth, the GOSPEL OF YOUR SALVATION: in whom also after that ye BELIEVED, ye were sealed with that holy Spirit of promise,

What is the gospel of our salvation?

Salvation is by grace through faith in Christ alone (Jesus paid it all and we added nothing to our salvation).

We must believe: "how that [by crucifixion] Christ [the Son of God] DIED for OUR SINS [all who live in mystery] according to the scriptures; And that he was BURIED, and that he ROSE AGAIN the third day according to the scriptures" (1 Corinthians 15:3, 4).

(2) <u>We must believe that God has preserved His word to us</u>. If you are NOT a King James Bible believer, then please read the helpful article provided in the Appendix. One Bible helps us to all say the same thing.

(3) We must understand that Christ from heaven made Paul "the APOSTLE of the Gentiles" (Romans 11:13) to reveal the MYSTERY to the body of Christ in the DISPENSATION OF THE GRACE OF GOD (Ephesians 3:1-9).

"Paul, an apostle, (not of men, neither by man, but by Jesus Christ, and God the Father, who raised him from the dead;) . . . But I certify you, brethren, that the gospel which was preached of me is not after man. For I neither received it of man, neither was I taught it, but by the revelation of Jesus Christ" (Galatians 1:1, 11, 12).

When we understand Paul's distinctive ministry to the body of Christ then we are "rightly dividing the word of truth" (2 Timothy 2:15).

Two Groups: Peter's and Paul's

When I understood that God had <u>two groups of people</u> in the Bible then I began to understand the Bible so much better. <u>The Bible became so fascinating that I just can't get enough.</u> One group will live "eternal in the heavens" (2 Corinthians 5:1). The other group will live in the kingdom on earth forever (Matthew 19:28, 29; Isaiah 60:19-21; Revelation 22:5).

Peter and Paul preached a different gospel (good news) to different groups of people. <u>Peter</u> preached the <u>gospel of the circumcision</u> to the believing remnant of Israel, while <u>Paul</u> preached the <u>gospel of the uncircumcision</u> to the body of Christ. Peter's group will live on earth, and Paul's group will live in heaven.

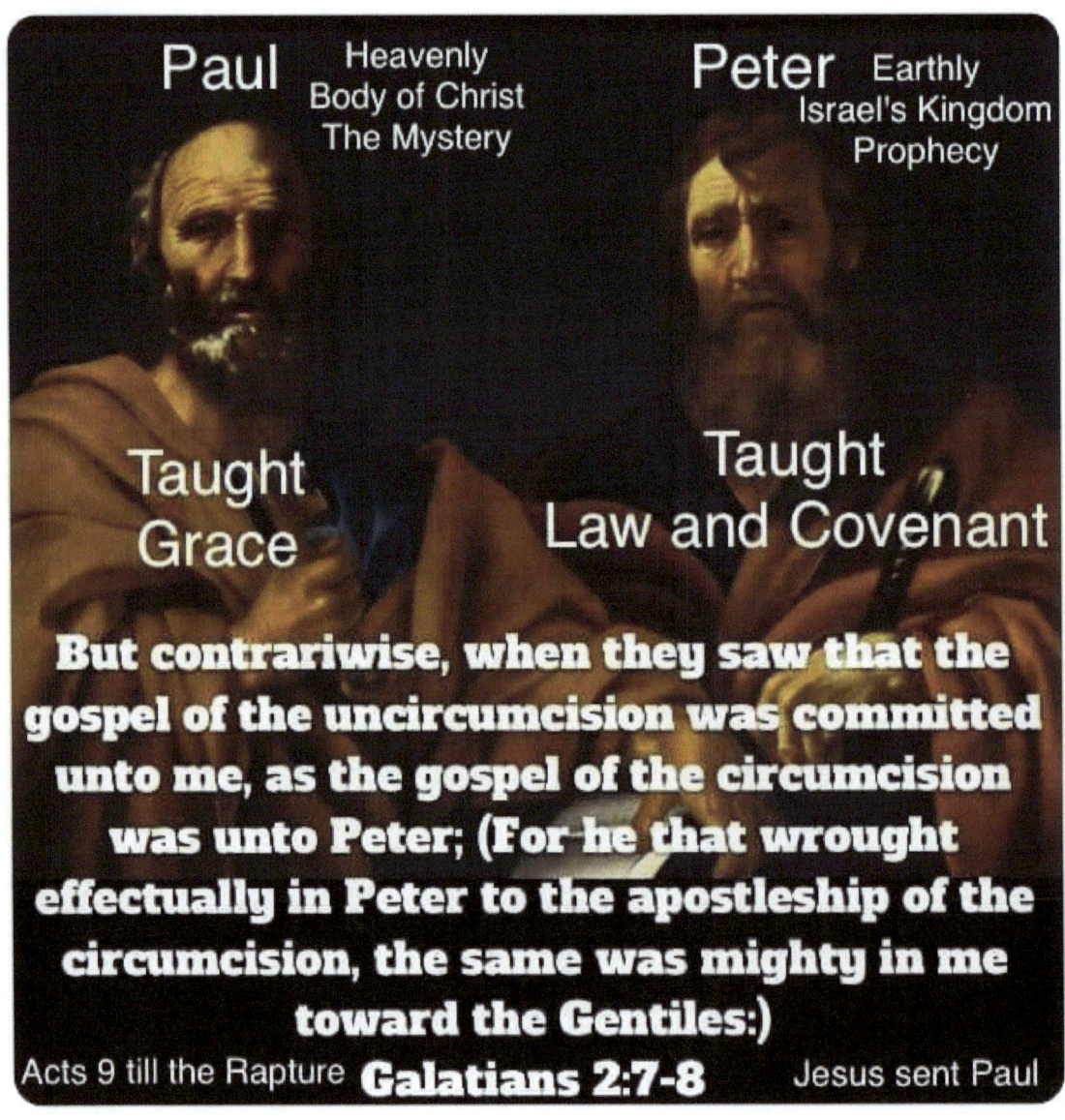

The order of Paul's Acts epistles including when and where they were written:

Galatians	1 Thess.	2 Thess.	1 Cor.	2 Cor.	Romans
Acts 15:35	Acts 18:5	Acts 18:11	Acts 19:10	Acts 20:1	Acts 20:3
Antioch	Corinth	Corinth	Ephesus	Macedonia	Corinth
AD 52*	AD 53	AD 53	AD 56	AD 57	AD 58

*approximate dates

The Two Ministries of Christ
By Paul M. Sadler

Earthly Ministry (Four Gospels and Early Acts)	Heavenly Ministry (Paul's Epistles and Mid-Acts)
King of Israel—John 1:49	Head of the Body—Col. 1:18
Declaration: The Law and the Prophets (coming wrath)—Matt. 5:17,18	Declaration: Grace and Peace—Phil. 1:2
Gave Himself a ransom for the sins of His people—Matt. 20:28; Luke 1:68,77	Gave Himself a ransom for the sins of the world—I Tim. 2:5,6
Seated at the right hand of the Father until His enemies are made His footstool—Acts 2:34-36	Seated at the right hand of the Father in a position of exaltation over all things to the Church—Eph. 1:20-23
Called 12 Apostles on the earth—Matt. 4:18-22; 10:1-5	Called one Apostle (Paul) from heaven—Acts 9:1-4; 26:13,19
Christ commands the 12 Apostles to confine their ministry to Israel—Matt. 10:5,6	Christ appoints Paul the Apostle of the Gentiles—Rom. 11:13
Instructs the 12 to carry out the Great Commission—Mark 16:14-18	Instructs us to carry out the Commission of Reconciliation—II Cor. 5:18,19
Gospel of the Kingdom proclaimed—Mark 1:14,15	Gospel of the grace of God proclaimed—Acts 20:24
Terms of salvation: Repent, believe on His name, submit to water baptism—Mark 1:15; 16:16; John 3:16; 20:31	Terms of salvation: Believe Christ died for your sins, was buried, and rose again—Acts 16:31; I Cor. 15:1-4
Earthly hope and calling—Matt. 5:5	Heavenly hope and calling—Col. 1:5
Christ's visible return to the earth—Matt. 24:29,30; Acts 1:10-12	Christ's invisible return in heaven—I Thes. 4:13-18
Eternal reign from the New Jerusalem on the New Earth—Rev. 21	Eternal reign with Christ from the New Heavens—Eph. 1:10; 2:6,7

As members of the Body of Christ we are responsible to proclaim, defend, and stand for the heavenly ministry of Christ.

GOD HAS TWO DIFFERENT PEOPLE

WITH TWO DIFFERENT AND SEPARATE PROGRAMS

All saved people, saints of all ages, are IN CHRIST.
However, apostle Paul was the first to be saved and sealed
IN THE BODY OF CHRIST. To say that the 12 are IN THE BODY, is to say
the 12 are not part of Israel's covenants and that they will
not be able to function according to prophecy in order to reign
with Christ in the Millenium Kingdom as part of a
Kingdom of priests. But, that's simply not what the KJV Bible
rightly divided teaches us.

Book Ends

The Bible can be pictured as a sentence with a parenthesis in the middle.
_____(body of Christ)_____ .
If we take the parenthesis out of a sentence, we still have a complete sentence.

_____ .

We are living in a GIANT PARENTHESIS between two book ends. These book ends are the <u>two appearings</u> of Christ to the body of Christ. The firsts <u>appearing</u> of Jesus Christ was in the air to apostle Paul on the road to Damascus, and His last appearing is to the body of Christ at the Rapture.

Both appearings are found in Titus. "For the grace of God that bringeth salvation hath <u>appeared</u> [to Paul on the road to Damascus] **to all men, teaching us that, denying ungodliness and worldly lusts, we should live soberly, righteously, and godly, in this present world; Looking for that blessed hope** [the Rapture], **and the glorious <u>appearing</u> of the great God and our Saviour Jesus Christ" (Titus 2:11, 13).**

To reiterate:

The book ends of the Dispensation of Grace are the two appearings in Titus 2:11, 13. The Lord Jesus Christ, first appeared to Paul on the road to Damascus in Acts 9 (Paul's salvation and commission as the apostle to the Gentiles, Acts 9, 22, 26; and Rom. 11:13). Then last when "the fulness of the Gentiles" (Rom. 11:25) comes in and the body of Christ is Raptured (1 Thess. 4:16, 17). <u>When the parenthesis (mystery) is removed at the Rapture, God will continue what He began on earth almost as if the parenthesis never was.</u>

To understand the Rapture, we must <u>rightly divide mystery from prophecy</u>.

RIGHTLY DIVIDING THE WORD
II TIMOTHY 2:15

Questions to ask when studying Scripture . . .

1. Who is speaking?
2. To whom is this Scripture directed?
3. Does this concern individuals or nations?
4. What is the context?
5. Does this concern spiritual or physical matters?
6. Is this passage literal or figurative?
7. Does this Scripture deal with temporal or eternal matters?
8. Is this passage conditional or unconditional?
9. Does this agree with Paul's writings?
10. Does this passage deal with my standing or my state?
11. Does this concern the first or second coming of Christ?
12. What does the rest of the Bible say about this?

*Notice that the Bible is laid out: PROPHECY – MYSTERY – PROPHECY

Why Right Division is REALLY Important!

You will never understand your Bible.
You may have believed the wrong gospel
You will not understand what God is doing today.
You will not understand who you are in Christ.
You will not be a good ambassador for Jesus Christ.
You may be sharing the wrong message to the world.
You will not know how the Holy Spirit is working through His word.
You may be following doctrine that is not meant for you, which makes that doctrine false.
You will not know God's plan and purpose for mankind.
You will not understand how the life of Christ is manifest in your mortal flesh.
You may not be fit "for the master's use, and prepared for every good work" (2 Tim. 2:21).
When it is all over you will be ashamed and not a workman for God.
You will be un-approved unto God not "rightly dividing the word of truth" (2 Tim. 2:15).
You need to know right division so that you can believe it (not oppose yourselves) and get out of the "snare of the Devil" and believe the truth, not a lie (2 Tim. 2:25, 26).

(Gleaned from a YouTube teaching by Pastor Tom Bruscha, Jan. 21, 2017)

Differences between Rapture and Second Coming

- Church saints meet Christ in the clouds.
- Occurs before the wrath of God is poured out.
- Christ returns to heaven with church saints.
- Imminent
- After the rapture, believers are removed and only unbelievers remain.

- Christ descends to the Mount of Olives.
- Occurs after the wrath of the Day of the Lord.
- Christ descends and stays on earth.
- Preceded by signs.
- After the second coming, unbelievers are removed and only believers remain.

Mystery   **Prophecy**

The Catching Away Of The Church The Body Of Christ

RAPTURE

In Your Bible Studies, Keep In Mind That From Genesis Up To Acts 9 No One Had Ever Heard Of The "Body Of Christ," Much Less About The Rapture.

It Was A Complete MYSTERY Hid In God From Genesis To Acts 9, And Not Revealed To Anyone Until Jesus First Revealed It To Our God-Appointed Apostle Paul. Paul Was Made A Minister Of The Dispensation Of The Grace Of God. Why? To Preach Among The Gentiles The Unsearchable Riches Of Christ And To Make All Men See What Is The Fellowship Of The MYSTERY.

LEARN MORE ABOUT THIS MYSTERY:

Eph 3:1-10; 1Co 2:6-8; 1Ti 2:57; Col 1:19-27;
Ro 11:25; 1Co 15:51-52; Ro 16:25 KJV

> **NOW TO HIM THAT IS OF POWER TO STABLISH YOU ACCORDING TO MY GOSPEL, AND THE PREACHING OF JESUS CHRIST, ACCORDING TO THE REVELATION OF THE MYSTERY, WHICH WAS KEPT SECRET SINCE THE WORLD BEGAN, BUT NOW IS MADE MANIFEST, AND BY THE SCRIPTURES OF THE PROPHETS, ACCORDING TO THE COMMANDMENT OF THE EVERLASTING GOD, MADE KNOWN TO ALL NATIONS FOR THE OBEDIENCE OF FAITH: TO GOD ONLY WISE, BE GLORY THROUGH JESUS CHRIST FOR EVER. AMEN.**
> **ROMANS 16:25-27 KJV**
>
> **ROMANS THRU PHILEMON SOUND DOCTRINE**

"Now to him that is of power to stablish you according to my gospel, and the preaching of Jesus Christ, according to the revelation of the mystery, which was kept secret since the world began, But now is made manifest, and by the scriptures of the prophets, according to the commandment of the everlasting God, made known to all nations for the obedience of faith" (Rom. 16:25, 26).

Paul says believers are saved, established, and stabilized:
(1) According to "my gospel" [Justification by faith (imputed righteousness) which Christ revealed to Paul (Rom. 3:22-28, 4:5, 23-25; 1 Cor. 15:3, 4)].

(2) "preaching of Jesus Christ, according to the revelation of the mystery, kept secret since the world began, but now is manifested," [Christ's ministry from heaven to us through Paul, the doctrine in Romans to Philemon.]

(3) and "by the scriptures of the prophets" [all the rest of the Bible from a Pauline point of view], according to the commandment of the everlasting God, made known to all nations for the obedience of faith" [to all] (Rom. 16:25, 26).

Edification Process

God is the builder of the spiritual edifice of sound doctrine in our spirit and soul. God builds the edifice of wisdom, knowledge, and understanding in us. God gave the blueprint of the edifice to Paul, His masterbuilder for us. **Paul's thirteen letters to the body of Christ builds sound doctrine into the soul of the believer.** An edifice is a building. We can picture Paul's thirteen letters as a two-story house. The first foundation is Romans. The Corinthian letters and Galatians form the walls of the first story. The <u>foundational doctrine in Romans</u> must be understood before proceeding to the <u>advanced doctrine</u> of <u>Ephesians</u>. The foundation of the second story is Ephesians. Philippians and Colossians form the walls of this level. Then the Thessalonian letters put the roof on top with the hope of the First (1 Thess.) and Second Coming of Christ (2 Thess.). *All of Paul's epistles were written after the Jerusalem Council.

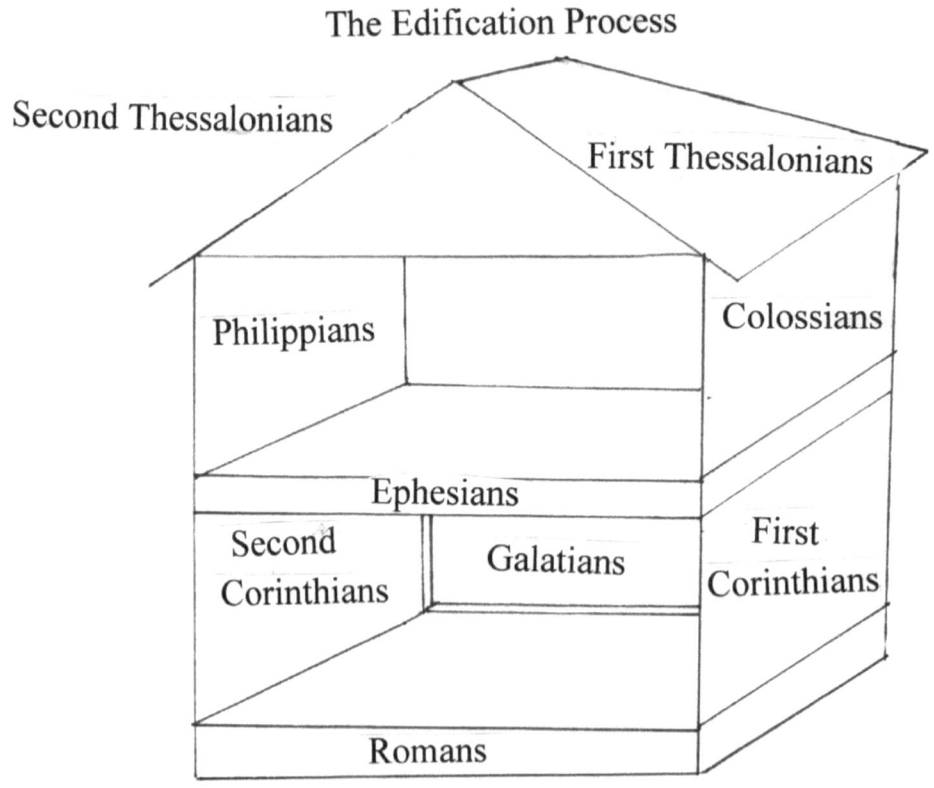

The Edification Process

Then First and Second Timothy, Titus, and Philemon are related to grace living with respect to the local church. They are how to live in the house.

Romans <u>doctrine</u> is related to our salvation (justification). FAITH
Ephesians <u>doctrine</u> related to the body of Christ (sanctification). CHARITY
Thessalonians <u>doctrine</u> related to Christ's coming (glorification). HOPE

The Key Verse 2 Tim. 2:15

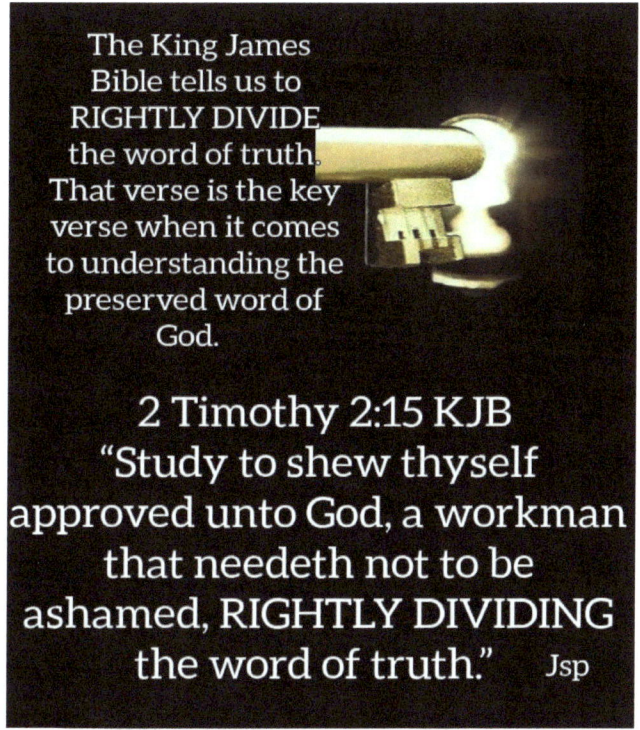

To understand the Bible, we must study God's word God's way. God tells us how to study His word: "<u>Study</u> to shew thyself approved unto God, a workman that needeth not to be ashamed, <u>RIGHTLY DIVIDING THE WORD OF TRUTH</u>."

Mandate (command): Study.

Motive: to shew thyself approved to God, a workman that needeth not to be ashamed (at the judgment seat of Christ).

Method: Rightly dividing the word of truth (making the divisions that God makes in His word).

All the Bible is truth. We are to divide truth from truth, not truth from error. Some truth is for the body of Christ (Romans to Philemon) who will live "eternal in the heavens" (2 Cor. 5:1), while the rest of the Bible is for the people who will live in the kingdom on earth.

<u>The goal is to understand ALL of the Bible from a Pauline perspective</u>. "Consider what I say; and the Lord give thee understanding in all things" (2 Tim. 2:7).

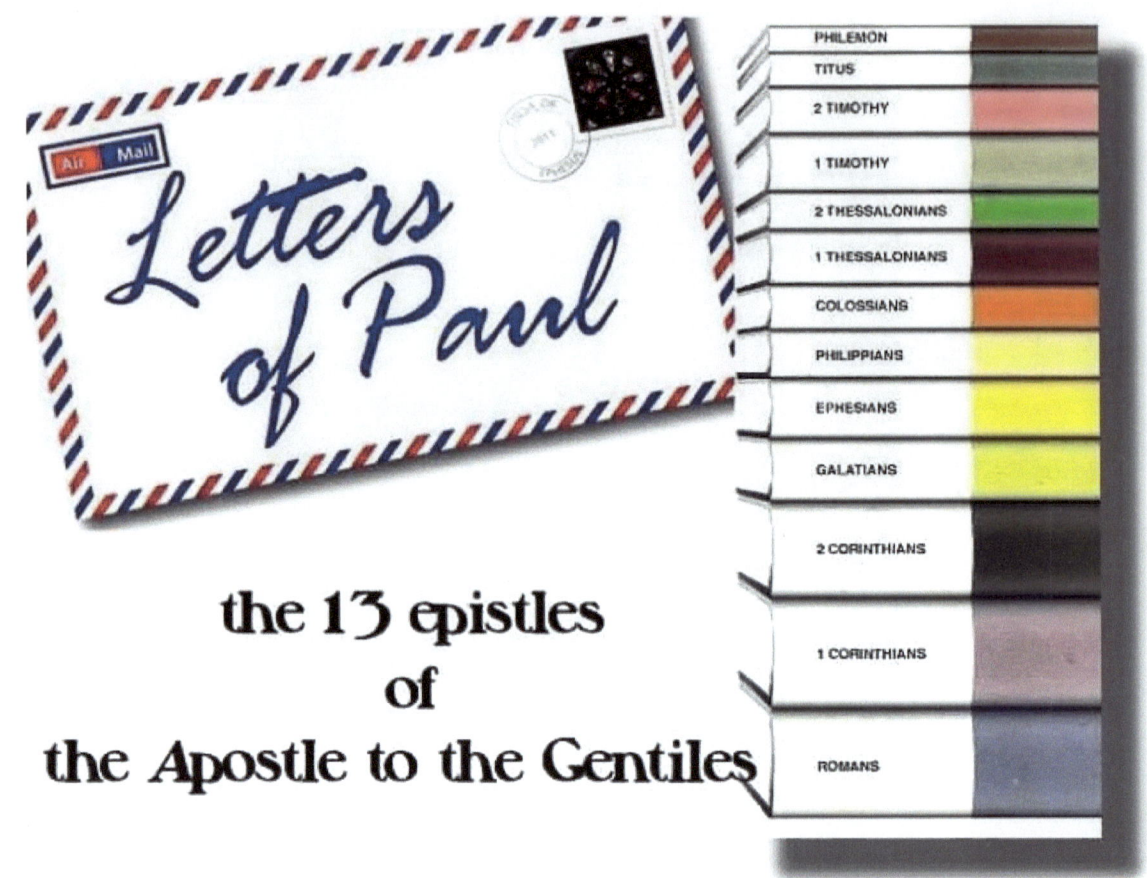

*Please notice that the order of the books begins at the bottom with Romans.

13 Letters Written by Apostle Paul (order, structure, and purpose)

Philemon a letter of appeal to a friend – demonstration (intercession)
1 & 2 Timothy and Titus letters to individual church leaders – utilization (exhorts)
1 & 2 Thessalonians letters to a questioning church – expectation (encourages)
Colossians a letter to a wavering church – culmination (admonishes)
Philippians a letter to a giving church – subordination (servanthood)
Ephesians a letter to a stable church – exaltation (identification)
Galatians a letter to a legalistic church – liberation (correction)
1 & 2 Corinthians letters to a carnal church – sanctification (reproof)
Romans a letter to stabilize a church far away – justification (explained)
(The above is written with help of Dr. W. Edward Bedore of Berean Bible Institute, P.O. Box 587, Slinger, WI 53086.)

<u>Each of Paul's letters builds on the other and is designed to edify our inner man.</u> So that we go from being spiritual babies to mature useful sons of God. "That the man of God may be perfect, throughly furnished unto all good works" (2 Tim. 3:17).

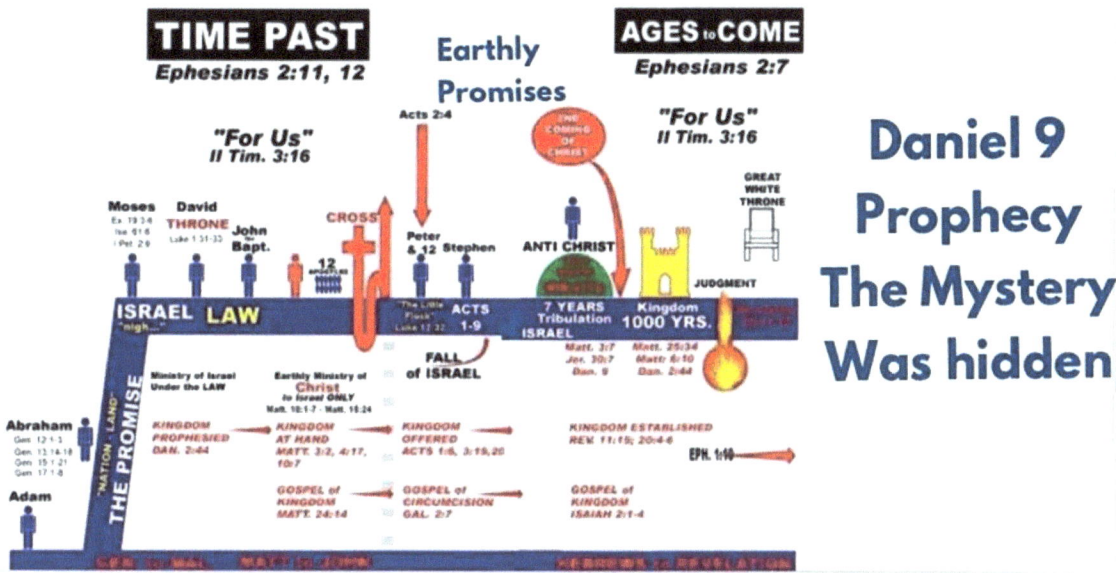

Do you know that the "But now" (Eph. 2:13) began in Acts 9, with Paul "the apostle of the Gentiles" (Rom. 11:13) salvation on the road to Damascus?

The dark stormy clouds of the horrific Tribulation were brewing on the Horizon in Acts 7, but God interrupted prophecy and inserted the mystery. God now offers us grace and peace (the middle part). For us it is glorious sunshine. Believers can relax and enjoy the grace and peace He is dispensing today, but unbelievers are still under the law and will be judged by it.

We must love God's word. "They received not the love of the truth, that they might be saved . . . but had pleasure in unrighteousness" (2 Thess. 2:10-12).

Dispensation Defined

> 1 Corinthians 9:17 For if I do this thing willingly, I have a reward: but if against my will, a dispensation of the gospel is committed unto me.
>
> Ephesians 1:10 That in the dispensation of the fulness of times he might gather together in one all things in Christ, both which are in heaven, and which are on earth; even in him:
>
> Ephesians 3:2 If ye have heard of the dispensation of the grace of God which is given me to you-ward:
>
> Colossians 1:25 Whereof I am made a minister, according to the dispensation of God which is given to me for you, to fulfil the word of God;
>
> the word DISPENSATION 4 times in the KJV

Paul uses the word DISPENSATION four times. Bible study needs to be both Biblical and dispensational. Dispensation means dispersing or distributing. A gas station dispenses gasoline and a pharmacy dispenses medications. In the Bible, it means God is dispensing a set of instructions for people to believe and obey. A dispensation is not a period of time, but rather it is **God's method of distributing or dispersing His will in a given age.**

We need to study God's word God's way. We are commanded to: Study to shew thyself approved unto God, a workman that needeth not to be ashamed, **rightly dividing the word of truth" (2 Tim.2:15). We divide our truth from the rest of the Bible.**

Why God Kept the Mystery a Secret

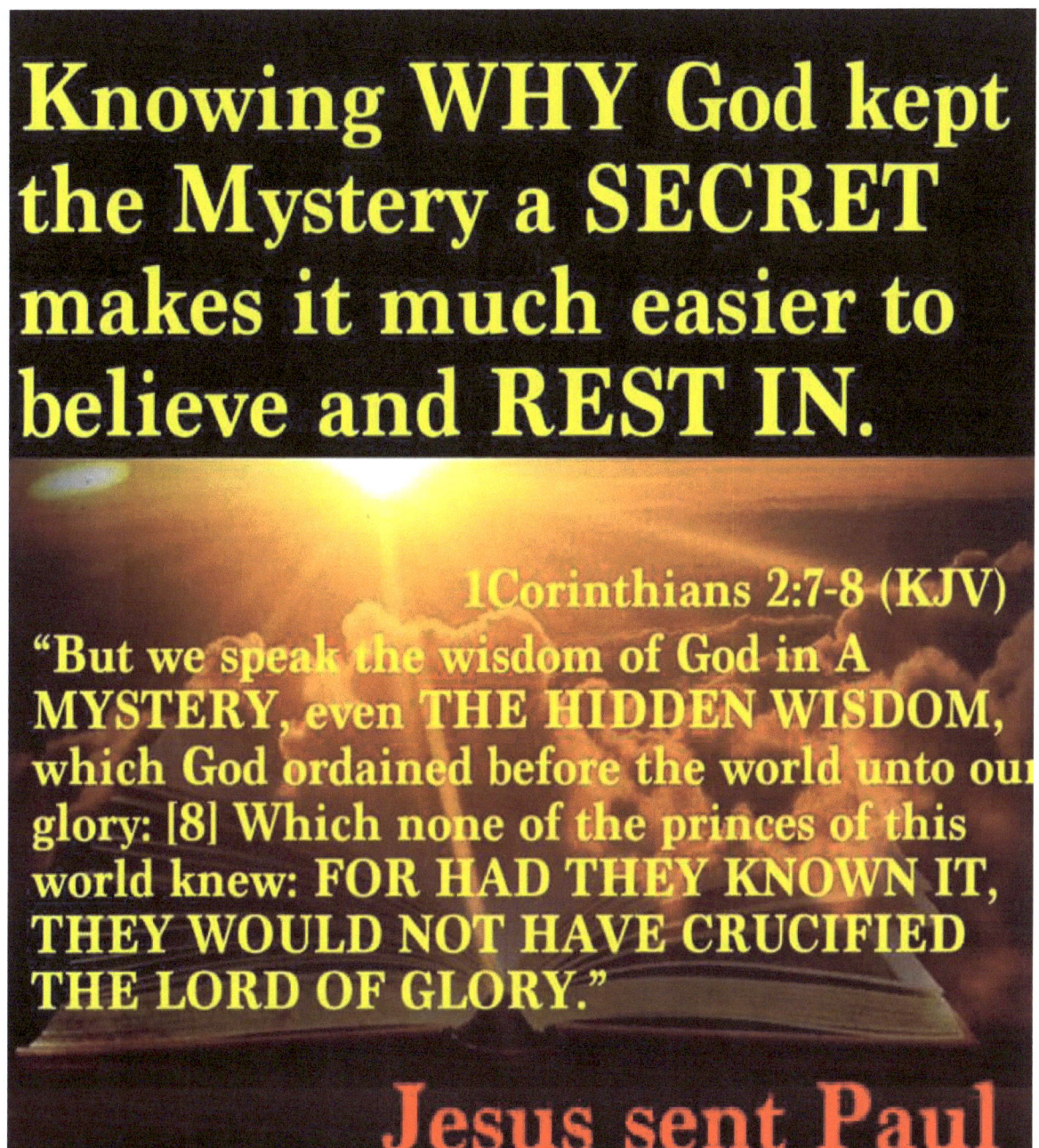

In the Bible, a "mystery" is a divine secret. The truth for this dispensation of grace was not revealed in the Old Testament, nor at the time of Christ and his twelve apostles; it was first revealed by Christ to His one apostle Paul.

If Satan had known that he lost both heaven and earth when Jesus Christ died on the cross for mankind, he would not have allowed Him to be crucified.

Satan attacks the mystery and the doctrine of our blessed hope (the Rapture).

Satan had attacked this truth in Thessalonica. Paul had to write two letters to defend it. In the first letter Paul focuses on the Rapture. In the Second letter Paul focuses on the day of the Lord to let them (and we) know we are not in it.

Satan knows that if we have a clear understanding of when the body of Christ began and when we will be taken up to heaven, that we will have stable minds. We counter Satan's lies with God's truth, rightly divided.

Timeline

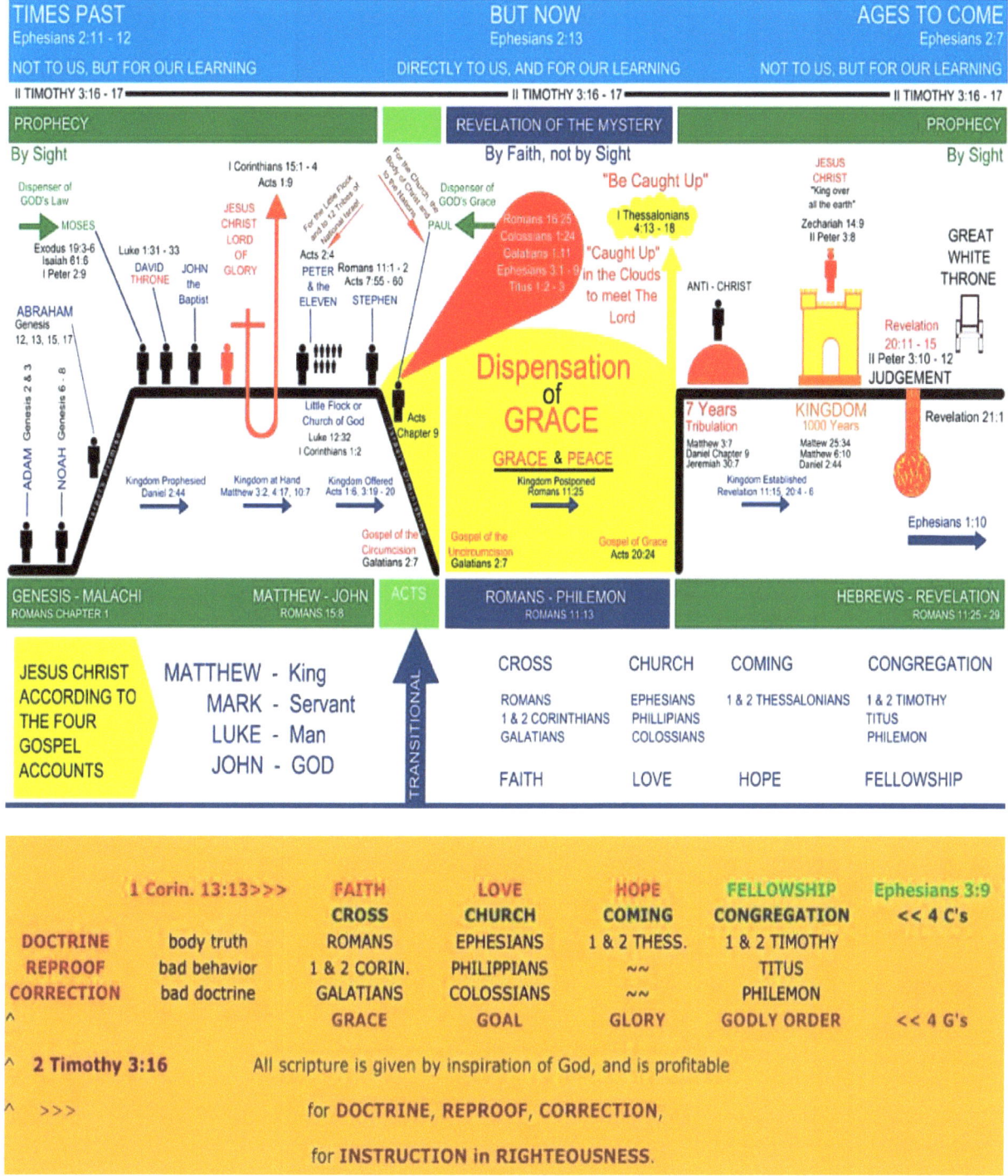

After Thessalonians we will be in heaven, so there is no reproof or correction.

Rightly Dividing 101

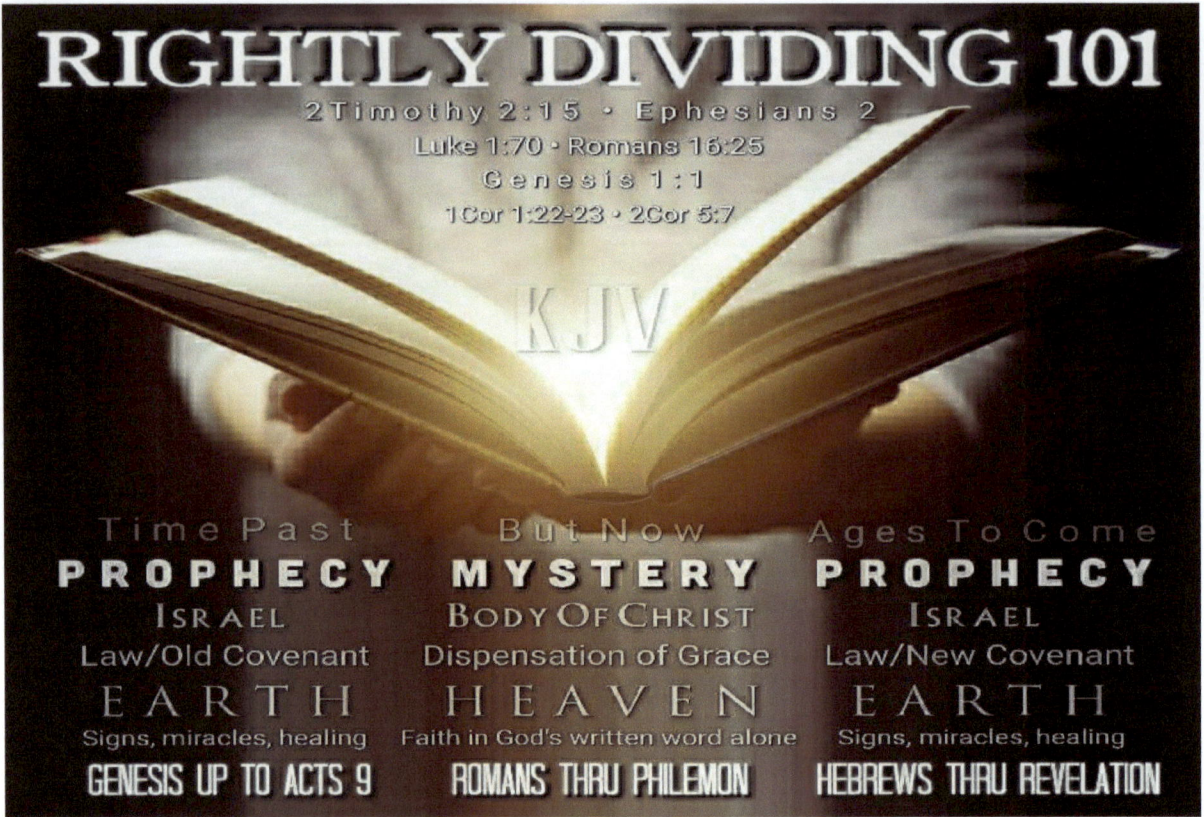

*Notice that the Bible is divided according the Divine order of the books.

The basic division of the Bible is Prophecy – Mystery – Prophecy.

Everything hinges on the true word of God, the KJV. The basic divisions of the Bible are "laid out" in the order of the books of the Bible. All the Bible is truth. The key is to rightly divide truth from truth (2 Tim. 2:15). The word of God is divided into **Time Past** (Eph. 2:11, 12), **But Now** (Eph. 2:13), and **Ages to Come** (Eph. 2:7). God spoke to the kingdom on earth believers by prophets "since the world began" (Luke 1:70). But God gave Paul "the mystery, which was kept secret since the world began" (Rom. 16:25) for the body of Christ, the heavenly kingdom believers. From the beginning, God had a plan for both the Heaven and the Earth (Gen. 1:1). The people of Israel walk by sight (1 Cor. 1:22), but the members of the body of Christ walk by faith (2 Cor. 5:7). We have "all spiritual blessings in heavenly places" (Eph. 1:3).

Christ crucified and risen again is the major foundation for both groups of people. Other people have died on a cruel cross, but only the Lord Jesus Christ resurrected. Jesus is God. Salvation is 100% God, and 0% man.

The Pre-Tribulation Rapture is Certain

> **SAVED FROM WRATH**
>
> And to wait for his Son from heaven, whom he raised from the dead, even Jesus, which delivered us from the wrath to come. (1 Thessalonians 1:10 KJV)
>
> For God hath not appointed us to wrath, but to obtain salvation by our Lord Jesus Christ, (1 Thessalonians 5:9 KJV)
>
> Much more then, being now justified by his blood, we shall be saved from wrath through him. (Romans 5:9 KJV)
>
> **SEALED TILL THE RAPTURE**

The "wrath" is the Tribulation, (70th week of Daniel), or Jacob's trouble.

- "So that ye come behind in no gift; **waiting for the coming of our Lord Jesus Christ (1 Cor. 1:7)**
- "For our conversation is in heaven; from whence also **we look for the Saviour, the Lord Jesus Christ**" (Phil. 3:20).
- "And the Lord direct your hearts into the love of God, and into the **patient waiting for Christ**" (2 Thess. 3:5).
- "**Looking for** that blessed hope, and **the glorious appearing of the great God and our Saviour Jesus Christ . . .**" (Titus 2:13).
- "For they themselves shew of us what manner of entering in we had unto you, and how ye turned to God from idols to serve the living and true God; And to **wait for his Son from heaven**, whom he raised from the dead, even Jesus, which **delivered us from the wrath to come**" (1 Thess. 1:9, 10).
- We will be saved from the Trib. "**For God has not appointed us to wrath, but to obtain salvation by our Lord Jesus Christ**, who died for us, that whether we wake or sleep, we should **live together with him** (1 Thess. 5:9).

Preface

The purpose of this book is to relate the certainty of the Pre-Tribulation rapture by understanding God's word in the Thessalonian letters. Have you ever asked yourself why the legs of Nebuchadnezzar's image (Dan. 2:31-35) are so long? Have you ever wondered why the atrocities of Hitler in World War II are not mentioned in the Bible? Yet, we know that other future events have been prophesied such as the Lord Jesus Christ's Second Coming to stand on the Mount of Olives (Zech. 14:4). The answer to these questions are really simple once you understand that we are living in the un-prophesied time period, when God is not fulfilling prophecy, known as the dispensation of grace. The key is "rightly dividing the word of truth" (2 Timothy 2:15). We have to divide the Bible where God divides it. God divides the books of the

Bible written by Paul, from the rest of the Bible. The birthday of the true Church, the body of Christ, was not the Jewish holy day of Pentecost in Acts 2, but Paul's salvation in Acts 9. Everything outside of Paul's letters is known as prophecy, because it was prophesied in God's word. The Bible is laid out Prophecy – Mystery – Prophecy. Once we have this understanding, verses that we thought contradicted themselves no longer do. The Bible becomes even more fantastic once we learn to rightly divide the truth. With so much clarity we will not be able to get enough of God's exciting and fascinating word.

If there is anyone who is not certain that the Rapture of the Church, the body of Christ, will occur before the Tribulation, the study of these two epistles will bring them great comfort and put their minds at rest. These letters should convince anyone that the Rapture is before the Tribulation or WRATH.

The Rapture is limited to only Church members. <u>The Rapture is exclusively found in Paul's letters because it was a mystery that Christ only revealed to Paul.</u> Paul was the first member in the Church, the body of Christ (1 Tim. 1:16). Both the Dispensation of Grace and the body of Christ began with his salvation on the road to Damascus in Acts 9. Paul repeats his salvation testimony to the Jews in Acts 22, and to the Gentile King Agrippa in Acts 26.

My goal is to share the truth of what Christ tells us through Paul in a concise and interesting way, so that readers will understand the word of God better. My hope is that the reader will learn how to rightly divide the truth and have more of value at the Judgment Seat of Christ. The many pictures and great maps help to give visual understanding of key concepts.

Knowing God's word increases our faith and helps us to grow spiritually so Christ in us can be glorified. The only thing we can take with us when we die, or are Raptured, is the doctrine that is stored up in our inner man.

I used to wonder <u>why the legs of the image in Nebuchadnezzar's dream were disproportionately too long for the rest of the body</u>? I found the answer when I learned how to rightly divide. God delayed destroying the feet.

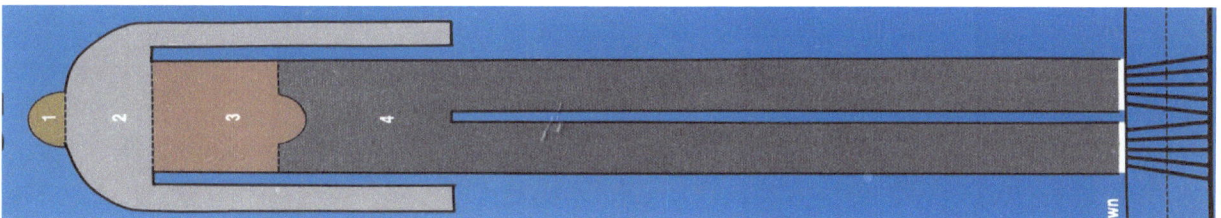

Introduction

The capital city of Thessalonica in Macedonia was founded in 315 BC by Cassander (one of the four Greek generals who divided up the empire of Alexander the Great). It was located on the Egnatian Way, Rome's greatest highway. The city was first named Therma because of the hot springs. He renamed the city in honor of his wife Thessalonike, a half-sister of Alexander. It was a military and commercial city known for its wealth and its vices.

When I visited the city in 1977, I went to a large cave in a big rock with torches along the walls and a spring of water in the middle of it. I was told that this had been a meeting place for Paul's church.

Paul and Barnabas had separated prior to his second apostolic journey. Paul took Silas (Silvanus) with him, and along the route he picked up Timothy and doctor Luke. Paul has joy, excitement, and approval concerning the Thessalonians. Their faith, love, and lives proved how successful the preaching of Paul, Silas, and Timothy had been among them.

Paul preached in Thessalonica for less than a month (it was a very young local church). In that short time, he not only organized a local church, but he also managed to teach the great doctrines of the faith to these eager learners. Paul says that they are a model church, "ensamples" (or examples) not only to the other churches in Macedonia and Achaia but "every place your faith to God-ward is spread abroad; so that we need not to speak any thing" (1:8).

The Thessalonians letters were probably written in <u>AD 53</u> from Corinth by Paul. There are five short chapters in First Thessalonians <u>which all end with a reference to the coming of Christ to rapture the body of Christ</u>. There are three chapters in Second Thessalonians. They are very rich in doctrine. These letters were written while sign gifts were still in effect. Sign gifts ceased in Acts 28:28 (1 Cor. 13:8-13). The occasion for Second Thessalonians was Silas and Timothy's return from checking on the spiritual welfare of the Thessalonian church. How do we know that Silas went with Timothy? Paul's sending of Timothy is recorded in 1 Thess. 3:1, 2 and their return in Acts 18:5. Paul was thrilled by his splendid report of their love for him and wrote a cheerful, charming, and comforting letter. Second Thessalonians was probably written within a few months after the first letter (Acts 18:11) after Paul heard about the forged letter that had shaken them up and made them fearful.

Paul presents the Rapture in relation to different aspects at the end of each of the five chapters of First Thessalonians:
Our salvation by Christ and our deliverance before the tribulation (1:9, 10);
Reward for service at the Judgment Seat of Christ (2:19-20);
Christ's presentation of the body of Christ to the Father in glory (3:13);
The details of our Rapture (4:13-18);
Christ's work to keep, sanctify, and preserve believers (spirit, soul, and body) and the confident expectation of the Rapture before the wrath (5:8, 9, 23).

The Thessalonian church letters are the last ones in the order of Paul's epistles in the canon of scripture, although they were probably written after Galatians. This is because the mature church depicts the goal of the believer's sanctification, thinking, conduct, departure, and destination. The Rapture ends the dispensation of grace, the opportunity to believe Paul's gospel, and join the body of Christ. The Rapture is "the redemption of the purchased possession, unto the praise of his glory" (Eph. 1:14). We will be "caught up" to meet the Lord in the air (1 Thess. 4:17). Interestingly, Paul had already been "caught up" to the third heaven (2 Cor. 12:2-4).

Paul wrote thirteen letters: nine to churches and four to individuals. These are often called the __Pastoral Epistles__. The __Pre-Prison__ Epistles, Romans to Galatians, are about the __cross__. Romans is foundational doctrine and explains the cross, Corinthians are about the preaching of the cross, and Galatians mentions the cross in every chapter. The __Prison Epistles__ are about the __Church__, the body of Christ. Ephesians is advanced doctrine for the body of Christ. Philippians is advanced edification for the body of Christ. Colossians is about holding Christ as the Head of the body of Christ and equal to the other Persons of the triune Godhead. The Thessalonian letters are about the __coming__ of Christ in the air to "catch up" the __body of Christ__ and are also about the Second Coming of Christ to the ground to establish His earthly kingdom with Israel.

Romans is __foundational doctrine__.
Corinthians is __reproof__ for not obeying the doctrine in Romans.
Galatians is __correction__ for being removed from the doctrine in Romans.

Ephesians is __advanced doctrine for the body of Christ__.
Philippians is __reproof__ for not holding to doctrine in Ephesians.
Colossians is __correction__ for not holding Christ as the Head according to Ephesians.

The Thessalonian letters are <u>doctrine concerning the coming of Christ</u>. There is <u>no more reproof or correction</u> after the Thessalonian letters because the body of Christ will be in heaven.

Why are the Thessalonian letters last in the order of the church epistles (but before the pastoral epistles)? The order of Paul's letters is designed to take us from milk to meat. If you studied them in <u>God's order</u>, then they will do for you what they are designed to do. This is why the books are not in a chronological order but an order of sanctification (spiritual growth) following the pattern in 2 Timothy 3:16, 17: doctrine, reproof, correction.

Several times in his letters <u>Paul approves</u> of what the Thessalonians are doing (5:11). Paul encourages the Thessalonians to <u>stand fast</u> in the doctrine they have believed and to <u>abound more and more</u> (1 Thess. 1:8, 3:8, 4:10, 5:1, 11; 2 Thess. 2:15; 3:4). Paul repeats the gospel of their salvation several times in this letter (1:10, 4:14, 5:10). <u>Paul would have liked for all the churches to understand the message of grace like this church had</u>. They turned from paganism, worshipping idols, dead gods, to worshipping the true and living God. Often persecution produces spiritual growth. Paul encourages them to continue in holy living.

The Thessalonians were able to operate and function the way God intended them to because they understood the "mystery" that Christ gave to Paul. The word of God was able to work effectually in them. "For this cause also thank we God without ceasing, because, when <u>ye received the word of God which ye heard of us</u>, ye received it <u>not as the word of men</u>, but as it is <u>in truth</u>, <u>the word of God, which effectually worketh also in you that believe</u>" (1 Thess. 2:13). <u>The Spirit of God uses the Word of God to work in us.</u>

God is able to make an ordinary man or woman extraordinary in their understanding of the Bible if they study it rightly divided and believe what God says in it.

When we come to Second Thessalonians, Paul will clear up the wrong division that had crept into the church. By a forged letter someone had moved the Rapture, saying that it was past and they were in the Tribulation awaiting the Second Coming of Christ. They said that the reason for their persecution was that they were living in the Tribulation. This false doctrine and wrongly dividing of the word of truth had shaken up the members of that church (and many believers today).

There will be many fascinating things discussed in these letters, particularly the <u>mystery of iniquity</u> (2 Thess. 2:7), but we must keep in mind that these letters go together. We will look more closely at the false redefining of terms that was going on in the forged letter when we get to that epistle. We will also examine Christ's coming to the earth to set up His kingdom in greater detail. There is a difference between waiting for the Church <u>to go</u>, and waiting for the kingdom <u>to come</u>. Paul expects us to understand the second letter in light of the first. The two epistles naturally link themselves together because <u>the main theme in both is the coming of Christ</u>. Therefore, we need to study these documents verse-by-verse as a pair.

Paul gives a clear description of the Pre-Tribulation (pre wrath) Rapture. He mentions "the gospel of God" and "the gospel of Christ" these gospels will be defined. The Apostle knew that he wrote by inspiration. Several years elapsed before Paul could return to the Thessalonians on his third apostolic journey.

The Judgment Seat of Christ (Rom. 14:10; 1 Cor. 3:10-17; 2 Cor. 5:10) is after the Rapture. Any blemishes or false doctrine will be burnt off of the believers there. Then Christ will present the "glorious church" to the Father. It will be "holy and without blemish" (Eph. 5:27).

Finally, in Genesis 3:15 God mentions two seed-lines when speaking to the serpent. Satan's evil seed-line began with Cain. We will investigate this further when we explore the <u>mystery of iniquity</u> in 2 Thess. 2:7.

Theme: Living life with the Rapture in view. Be the model church, continue with your work of faith, labour of love, and patience of hope until the coming of our Lord.

Key Verse: "<u>Remembering without ceasing</u> your <u>work of faith</u>, and <u>labour of love</u>, and <u>patience of hope</u> <u>in our Lord Jesus Christ, in the sight of God and our Father</u>" (1 Thess. 1:3).

The **Gospel of the Grace of God**
"Christ died for our sins according to the scriptures: and that he was buried, and that he rose again the third day according to the scriptures."
1 Corinthains 15:1-4 KJV

First Thessalonians Outline

The model church that the Thessalonians were is what we should be.

I. Model church.

A. The three tenses of the believer.
- 1. "Work of faith" (saved) past.
- 2. "Labor of love" (examples evangelizing) present.
- 3. "Patience of hope" (salvation from the wrath to come) future.

II. Model minister and preacher (Paul) and his reward.
- 1. Pure motive.
- 2. Genuine love (as a mother and father).
- 3. The result: genuine faith.
- 4. They are Paul's reward, his joy, and crown.

III. Model brother (Timothy) and his good report and love.
- 1. Why he was sent to them.

1V. Model life (walk) of the believers in relation to the Rapture.
- 1. Walk in holiness (4:1-8).
- 2. Walk in Love (4:9, 10).
- 3. Walk in honesty (4:11, 12).
- 4. Walk in hope (4:13-18).

V. Model life (walk) in relation to the Day of the Lord.
- 1. Walk in light (5:1-11).
- 2. Walk in gratitude (5:12, 13).
- 3. Walk in obedience to God's will (5:14-28).

The purpose of 1 Thessalonians: Paul answers the question of what happens to those who are dead and believed in Christ when the Rapture occurs? Paul wants to encourage the new believers in the young church. Paul answers questions about (1) whether or not they should quit their jobs and just preach while they wait for Christ, (2) he assures them that saints that have died will take part in the Rapture, and (3) the Rapture will occur before the wrath of God, the Tribulation. (4) Paul urges them to be sure not to defraud (rip off, cheat) another person by allowing that person to worship idols instead of the true God. (5) He wants them to live a responsible and holy life serving God. (6) He warns them of Pagan immorality, fornication. (7) They are to honor and follow the leaders in their assembly. (8) He wants them to work and preach to the lost and saved as he did.

First Thessalonians Chapter Review Sentences
(The review sentences are so simple because these letters are so well organized, clear, and concise.)
(1) Model church.
(2) Model minister (Paul).
(3) Model brother (Timothy).
(4) Model walk and the Pre-Tribulation Rapture.
(5) Model walk because they are NOT in the day of the Lord.

Each chapter in First Thessalonians ends with a reference to the Rapture:
Chapter 1 The Rapture in relation to our salvation from sin and deliverance from the wrath to come.
Chapter 2 The Rapture in relation to rewards at the Judgment Seat of Christ.
Chapter 3 Christ's next presentation of the body of Christ to the Father.
Chapter 4 Details concerning the Rapture, our comfort and hope.
Chapter 5 That the God of peace would preserve us wholly blameless in spirit, soul, and body until the Rapture.

Great doctrines Paul taught in First Thessalonians
Godhead (Trinity) (1:3, 3:11).
Holy Ghost and Holy Spirit (1:5, 6, 4:8, 5:19).
Power and assurance (1:5).
Election of the body of Christ (1:4).
Justification (1:9, 2:12, 5:24).
Sanctification and Brotherly love (4:3, 9, 10, 5:15-23).
Glorification our "catching up" and resurrection (4:14-18).
Life of personal holiness pleasing to the Lord (2:12, 4:1, 7).
Christ's Coming to save us from the wrath to come (1:10, 2:19, 3:13, 4:14-17, 5:8-10, 23).
Day of the Lord (5:1-3).

Second Thessalonians Outline
(1) Persevere despite persecution.
(2) Corrects false doctrine, the day of the Lord explained (we are not in it).
(3) Lazy busy bodies should go back to work and Paul's trademark signature.

Second Thessalonians Chapter Review sentences
(1) Rest with us.
(2) Gathered with us.
(3) Follow us in word and work.

In a Nut Shell

In clear orderly, logical letters Paul explains the Rapture. It is the result of their receiving the gift of salvation by grace through faith alone in what Christ has done: Justification, Sanctification, and Glorification (at the Rapture).

In both letters Paul corrects confusion about the Rapture. Paul understood both prophecy and mystery. He shares details about Christ coming for the body of Christ in the air at the Rapture and Christ's Second Coming to earth. The day of the Lord is particularly prominent in his second letter.

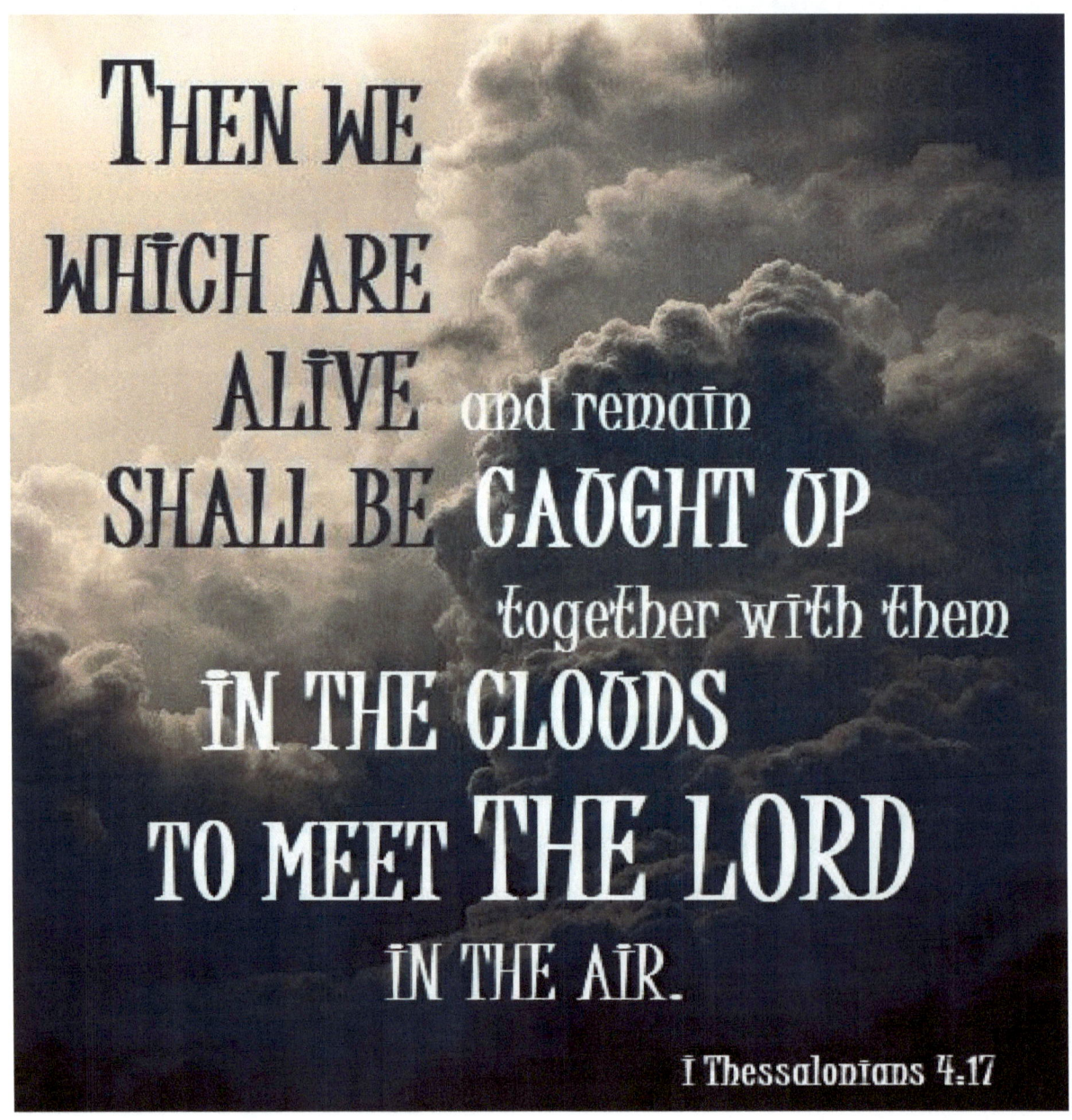

1 Thessalonians Chapter 1 The model Church.
1:1-5 Elect Church, the body of Christ predestined to live in heaven.
1:6-7 Ensamples to others.
1:8 Enthusiastic sharing of the truth.
1:9, 10 Expectant waiting for His Son, who saved us from the wrath to come.

Although Paul had only preached to the Thessalonian church over a period of three Sabbaths, they were "ensamples" (1:7). A model church not only to the other churches in Macedonia and Achaia but "every place your faith to Godward is spread abroad; so that we need not to speak any thing" (1 Thess. 1:8).

On the other hand, Paul marveled that the Galatians (the territory where Paul had gone on his first apostolic journey) had been quickly <u>removed</u> from the faith Paul had taught them. The Judiazers wanted them to live by keeping the law (Gal. 1:6-9, 3:1-5). In contrast to the Thessalonians, the Corinthians (to whom Paul preached for more than a year and a half) were carnal and babes in need of spiritual milk. Paul had to reprimand and rebuke them because they followed 10,000 instructors from among themselves, and many failed to follow their one apostle and spiritual father, Paul (1 Cor. 4:15, 11:1, 14:37).

In contrast, for the Thessalonians Paul was often a cheerleader. He tells that they were already doing the right thing. He has nothing but praise for this model church. These saints in Thessalonica clearly understood the mystery and the distinctive ministry of apostle Paul. This is why, in the very first verse, they are the only ones that God's spokesman greets as "in God the Father and in the Lord Jesus Christ." They were all the way "in" the truth of God.

Paul calls them beloved (1:4) cherished (2:7) desired (2:8) dear (2:8) brethren (2:14) his hope, joy, crown of rejoicing (2:19) glory and joy (2:20) children of light and the children of the day (5:5).

<u>In view of the imminent Rapture of the Church, we will look at some practical ways we can do ministry. We can spend our time so that it may be said of us, they "sounded out the word of the Lord"</u> (1:8). Life is not about us at all. It is all about Jesus and others. "For ye are dead, and your life is hid with Christ in God" (Col. 3:3). We are dead to sin, and to the influence of the world. We are alive unto God. We need to do all we can, to help as many as we can, to take part in the Rapture. The model church that the Thessalonians were is what we should be.

In addition to studying the first chapter we will also attempt to answer: "Who wrote Hebrews?"
What are some practical ways to share the gospel and right division?
What are some practical ways to do ministry?
What is good and bad that we will be judged on at the Judgment Seat of Christ?
What happened to Paulicians, why don't we hear more about them?

```
1 Thess. 1:3 ----------1 Thess. 1:9, 10
Work of faith --------Turned to God from idols.
Labor of love --------To serve the living and true God.
Patience of hope ----To wait for His Son from heaven.
```

1:1 Paul, and Silvanus, and Timotheus, unto the church of the Thessalonians which is <u>in God the Father</u> and <u>in the Lord Jesus Christ</u>: <u>Grace be unto you, and peace, from God our Father, and the Lord Jesus Christ.</u> [These saints in the local church in Thessalonica clearly understood the mystery. Paul greets them as being "in God the Father and in the Lord Jesus Christ." They were all the way "in" the truth of God. They understood that they were living in the dispensation of grace. They followed what Christ from heaven taught them through Paul. Dispensation means dispersing or distributing. A gas station dispenses gasoline and a pharmacy dispenses medications. In the Bible, it means God is dispensing a set of instruction for people to believe and obey. Today God is dispensing grace and peace. The dispensation of grace is the present Gentile opportunity to believe and be saved apart from having to bless Israel (Gen. 12:1-3; Eph. 2:13). But we should still bless Israel and all people. This is why Paul as the spokesman for God the Father and the Lord Jesus Christ salutes them on their behalf with grace and peace to those who trust the gospel. Christ made peace possible through the blood of His cross (Col. 1:14, 24). God is offering a time of free grace to the world when anyone can believe the gospel (1 Cor. 15:3, 4) and be saved from the consequences of their sin (2 Cor. 5:19, 21). Paul knew he was writing by inspiration of God. Paul had taught these believers well. They knew that they were part of the group to live in the heavenly places (the body of Christ), not in the kingdom on earth. Most of the church members were former pagan idol worshippers and also Gentile proselytes, "devout Greeks." Paul first visited Thessalonica on his second apostolic journey. After Paul and Silas had been beaten, jailed, and released in Philippi, they passed through some cities in Macedonia. Those cities did not have a synagogue until they came to Thessalonica that did have one. Paul went in and "over three sabbath days reasoned with them out of the scriptures. Opening and alleging, that Christ must needs have suffered, and risen again from the dead; and that this Jesus, whom I preach unto you, is Christ. And some of them believed, and consorted with Paul and Silas; and of the devout Greeks a great multitude, and of the chief women not a few" (Acts 17:1-4). Paul opened the word (explained its' meaning) and alleged (laid it out clearly for them as on a table). Paul and Silas were met by strong opposition from the envious unbelieving Jews. "But the Jews which believed not, moved with envy, took unto them certain lewd fellows of the baser sort, and gathered a company, and set all the city on an uproar [riot], and assaulted the house of Jason, and sought to bring them out to the people. And when they found them not [Paul and Silas], they drew Jason and certain brethren unto the rulers of the city, crying, These that have turned the world upside down are come hither also; Whom Jason hath received: and these all do contrary to the decrees of Cæsar, saying that there is another king, one Jesus. And they troubled the people and the rulers of the city, when they heard these things. And when they had taken security of Jason [bail money], and of the other, they let them go" (Acts 17:5-9). They had to sneak Paul and Silas out by night. "And the brethren immediately sent away Paul and Silas by night unto Berea: who coming thither went into the synagogue of the Jews. These were more noble than those in Thessalonica [the unbelieving Jews], in that they received the word with all readiness of mind [this is how we are to receive God's word], and searched the scriptures daily, whether those things were so. Therefore many of them believed; also of honourable women which were Greeks, and of men, not a few" (Acts 17:10-12). Many believed in Berea, but then the same Jews came after them. Paul was forced to flee to Athens. "But when the Jews of Thessalonica had knowledge that the word of God was preached of Paul at Berea, they came thither also, and stirred up the people. And then immediately the brethren sent away Paul to go as it were to the sea: but Silas and Timotheus abode there still. And they that conducted Paul brought him unto Athens: and receiving a commandment unto Silas and Timotheus for to come to him with all speed, they departed" (Acts 17:13-15). Having accompanied Paul safely to Athens, Paul told his Thessalonian brothers to have Silas and Timothy follow him immediately. The rest of Acts 17 tells how Paul was moved with compassion for the people of Athens and preached the gospel of God at Mars Hill (Acts 17:18), in the big amphitheater (Acts 17:16-34). Paul waited in Athens for Silas and Timothy. After they arrived he sent both of them back to Thessalonica to check on the spiritual welfare of the brethren there. How do we know that Silas went with Timothy? Paul's sending of Timothy is recorded in 1 Thess. 3:1, 2 and their return in Acts 18:5. Some mocked Paul at Athens, after that he traveled to Corinth and met Aquila and Priscilla. He lived and worked with them. He knew the tentmaker trade like they did. Silas and Timothy returned to Paul at Corinth. Silas is not mentioned again after that except in reminiscence (2 Cor. 1:19) and may have returned to the little flock in Jerusalem (Acts 18:5; 1 Thess. 3:6; 2 Thess.

2:1). Silas is also called Silvanus (many Hebrews had Greek and Roman names). Acts 18:5 is when Silas and Timothy returned to Paul in Corinth and when Paul writes First Thessalonians. Silas was a member of the little flock (Acts 15:22-40). He had been Peter's secretary for the writing of Peter's first epistle (1 Peter 5:12). Silas was first mentioned in Acts 15:22. But Silas worked with Paul helping Gentiles and Jews become body of Christ members because that was what God was doing now. Other saints of the circumcision (Barnabas, Luke, Justus, Andronicus, Junia, John Mark, and Aristarchus) helped Paul for the same reason (Col. 4:11). Silas will live in the kingdom on earth with Peter; while Paul will be Raptured with the rest of us. Paul was concerned about the spiritual welfare of the believers in Thessalonica because of the persecution of the unbelieving idol worshippers and unbelieving Jews. Satan doesn't bother to persecute those he already has in his pocket. Satan targets those who understand the mystery.

Paul continued preaching in Corinth. He began preaching in the synagogue "to the Jews first, and also to the Greek" (Rom. 1:16). Paul informed the Jews that God had changed His program and was forming another group of believers to live in the heavenly places. If they trusted that Jesus of Nazareth was their King, and that He died for our sins (believers in mystery), was buried and rose again, then the Jews would become members of the body of Christ. They will live in heaven also. But when the Jews didn't accept his message, Paul said for the second time that he would go to the Gentiles (Acts 13:46, 18:6). Paul left the synagogue and went next door and founded the Corinthian church (Acts 18:1-17).

Who wrote the book of Hebrews? God wrote Hebrews, and the name of the human writer is unknown. But we can speculate, there are three good contenders for the human writer (Silas, Mark, and Luke), unless the writer is someone that is unknown to us in scripture. We need to be sleuths like Sherlock Holmes. I will tell you what my theory was and that I have changed my mind, and then I will tell you the theory of Pastor Bryan Ross of Grace Bible Church in Grand Rapids, Illinois. Then make up your own mind, since we may be completely wrong. We can piece together some clues. The human writer was someone who had heard Peter and the little flock preach Christ's earthly kingdom gospel at Pentecost. "How shall we escape, if we neglect so great salvation; which at the first began to be spoken by the Lord, [Jesus in His earthly ministry] and was confirmed unto us [the writer is in this group] by them that heard him [the twelve]; God also bearing *them* witness, both with signs and wonders, and with divers miracles, and gifts of the Holy Ghost, according to his own will?" (Heb. 2:3, 4). Hebrews was written in the "last days" before the wrath and the kingdom (Heb. 1:2). The dispensation of grace had interrupted prophecy the writer writes to those in the "world to come" (Heb. 2:5)

38

after the Rapture (Rom. 11:25). It was clearly not written by Paul because the doctrine is not grace, but law. Furthermore, Paul was saved by Christ on the road to Damascus in Acts 9 not from hearing the apostles preach on Pentecost in Acts 2. In fact, Paul ruthlessly persecuted the kingdom church until he was saved (Acts 8:1, 9:1, 26:11). However, there are some similarities in Hebrews to what Paul preached. One reason for that is because both letters are written after the cross, and I believe another reason is that the writer of Hebrews was familiar with what Paul taught. (Of course, both writers are inspired by God, but God often utilizes the writer's experience.) I used to believe that Silas wrote Hebrews. Paul sent Silas and Timothy to check on the Thessalonians (1 Thess. 3:5). Although a member of the little flock, Silas decided to join Paul on his second apostolic journey and be part of what God was doing through Paul. Perhaps Timothy and Silas had been put in jail on their return from Thessalonica. After they were released Silas and Timothy may have traveled across Macedonia on the famous Roman road, the Egnatian Way, and taken a ship to the heel of the Italian boot and then come to Corinth by sea via Cenchrea. (Notice that he says, "they of Italy salute you," in Hebrews 13:24, not that it is written from Italy.) This is a plausible alternative route to Corinth to meet up with Paul (Acts 18:5). I thought it possible that Silas may have written Hebrews at that time while waiting for Timothy to be released. Silas was a prophet (Acts 15:32). "Know ye that our brother Timothy is set at liberty; with whom, if he come shortly, I will see you. Salute all them that have the rule over you [Peter, James, and John], and all the saints. They of Italy salute you" (Heb. 13:23, 24). If the writer was not Silas, then it was another believer who heard Peter's group and knew a Timothy (possibly another Timothy). Silas knew that God was currently dispensing grace so all people could believe the gospel of Christ and have eternal life in heaven. Silas knew that after the Jerusalem council, Paul had said that only his gospel is to be preached (Gal. 1:6-9). (*Note all of Paul's epistles were written after the Jerusalem Council.) Therefore, Silas knowingly writes of the "world to come" after the Rapture. Israel will be encouraged when they see that God has fulfilled His promise of the Rapture for the body of Christ (2 Thess. 1:10). Mark and Luke are also good candidates. The important thing is not knowing the human writer of Hebrews, but what God said.

Where was Luke? Luke who wrote the Third Gospel and Acts, was known as "the beloved physician" (Col. 4:14). He was Paul's companion and fellow worker on this second Apostolic journey, but there is no indication that he went any further than Philippi at this time. He may have stayed in Philippi or returned temporarily to Troas to write the gospel of Luke. Luke does not mention Paul or the mystery in that Gospel, just like in the book of Hebrews. Of the rest of the Hebrew epistles (Hebrews through Revelation) only (2 Peter 3:15, 16) mentions Paul. The hope of the book of Hebrews is the kingdom of heaven to come to earth. Our hope is to live eternal in the heavens (2 Cor. 5:1).]

2 We give thanks to God always for you all, making mention of you in our prayers; [Paul was thankful that the body of Christ believers were growing and prayed for them before he mentioned anything else.] **3 Remembering without ceasing your work of faith, and labour of love, and patience of hope in our Lord Jesus Christ, in the sight of God and our Father;** [This is the key verse of this letter. Paul remembered without ceasing three things about them: their work of faith, labour of love, and patience of hope. Paul defines and expands on these three phrases in the next several verses. Their "work of faith" was to turn to God from idols to trust "the faith" Paul preached (1:9) in the PAST. (Notice that Paul does not say that they turned from idols to God.) This is not splitting hairs. They turned "to" God and automatically turned "from" idols. Their "labor of love" is "to serve the living God" by sharing their faith and becoming co-laborers in the building of the body of Christ (1:8, 9) in the PRESENT. Their "patience of hope" is to "wait for his Son from heaven" (1:10) to come in the FUTURE. Notice that it is "in our Lord Jesus Christ;" anything of value is done because His Spirit is in us. Paul adds, "in the sight of God and our Father." Notice the trinity in the last sentence. God sees everything we do because He is in us, so we should live to please Him. The Godhead (Trinity) sees all that we do by the power of His Son's life in us (Gal. 2:20). Paul mentions all three in the Godhead in this chapter. Paul first mentioned the Godhead on Mars Hill (Acts 17:29). The three Christian hallmarks of the Christian life are also mentioned in theses phrases: faith, hope, and charity or love (1 Cor. 13:13). Paul again mentions their faith, charity (love) in 3:5, 6, and hope in 4:13-18, all three are in 5:8. The Colossians had faith, hope, and love (Col. 1:6).

God is currently building the Church, the body of Christ. Christ is the foundation of the body of Christ. Paul is the masterbuilder. Paul laid his foundation on top of Christ "according to the revelation of the mystery" (Rom. 16:25; 1 Cor. 3:10, 11). The blueprint for proper construction of the body of Christ is summarized in 2 Tim. 3:16, 17. This is the edification process described in detail in Paul's thirteen epistles, Romans to Philemon. The maturity of the believer will be evaluated at the Judgment seat of Christ. The Thessalonians were a model church that we should be like. Bob Bopper says that "Whenever you see the word labour or work in Paul's epistles, they are always in direct connection to the judgment seat of the Saviour . . . Most people think salvation is the end result, but salvation is the starting point." (Facebook post in October 2019, I have built on his post here.)

At the judgment seat of Christ (2 Cor. 5:10), the issue of good and bad has to do with being useful or useless, worthy or worthless? Did we present our bodies a living sacrifice for Christ to live through, or not (Romans 12:1, 2)?

At the Judgment Seat of Christ, we will be judged, assessed, and evaluated based on three criteria:

(1) Work of Faith: Was our work on earth done according to "the faith" delivered to us through Paul?

(2) Labour of love: Did our love for Christ constrain us to labour to build the body of Christ? Were we lovingly helping others to be saved, and come to the knowledge of the truth (1 Tim. 2:4)? Did we edify each other (Eph. 4:16)?

(3) Patient in hope: Were we patiently looking for the blessed hope of our Saviour's return? Were we patient with others knowing this world is not our home? We are ambassadors for Christ in a foreign land. We are only stationed here temporarily. God wants us to have something of value at the judgment seat. We have a heavenly hope (Col. 1:5; Titus 2:13).] **4 Knowing, brethren beloved, your election of God.** [Their election for service happened by faith at their conversion. Paul calls them "brethren beloved." We are not beloved in ourselves, but because we are "accepted in the beloved" (Eph. 1:6). The Father elected the Son to serve Him (Isa. 42:1). Paul is confident that they know they were called and saved by faith in "our gospel," which they believed and received (1 Thess. 2:12; 2 Thess. 2:13, 14). When a person believes the gospel, they are baptized into the body of Christ by the Spirit (1 Cor. 12:13). This does not mean that each individual member of the body of Christ is elect; what is elect is the "body of Christ." The individual is "elect" in the sense that they are holy, sanctified set apart from the lost, as members in this group, the "one new man" (Eph. 2:15). We are called by the gospel. We are first saved and next sanctified or elect. God had ordained that He would have a group of believing people to serve Him in heaven. "According as he hath chosen us in him before the foundation of the world, that we should be holy and without blame before him in love" (Eph. 1:4). But God has foreknowledge and He knows the end from the beginning (Isa. 46:10). God inhabits eternity (Isa. 57:15). We live for the purpose of glorifying the Holy Lord Jesus Christ and the Holy Father and the Holy Ghost. The universe is theocentric, or God-centered. All things were "created by him, and for him" (Col. 1:16). God is holy. Heaven and earth exist for God, for His glory, and for His purpose. We are mere created creatures, but we are free to choose to believe and or not.] **5 For our gospel came not unto you in word only, but also in power, and in the Holy Ghost, and in much assurance; as ye know what manner of men we were among you for your sake.** [The gospel came to them not only in the power of the word, but also in the power of the Holy Ghost, and with much assurance." Paul assured them frequently that he spoke the truth Christ from heaven had revealed to

him. They did not just tell them about "our gospel" but demonstrated it by their actions (2:10) "in power" and "in the Holy Ghost" for their sakes. We have Christ's glorious POWER in us (Col. 1:11). We also have the Holy Ghost to help us (Rom. 5:5). Believers have Christ's imputed righteousness by faith alone in Christ alone (Rom. 4:3-5, 23-25; 2 Cor. 5:21). Paul taught once saved always saved, secure, and sealed (Eph. 1:13, 14; Rom. 5:1, 8:31-39). Paul will elaborate on what "manner of men" (1:9) they were later in the letter. They were sincere, honest, and humble "for your sake." Paul and his friends loved them and did all they could for their salvation and sanctification. They constantly honored Christ and what He had done, not themselves.] **6 And ye became followers of us, and of the Lord, having received the word in much affliction, with joy of the Holy Ghost: 7 So that ye were ensamples to all that believe in Macedonia and Achaia.** [To follow Paul is to follow Jesus Christ who sent him. The Thessalonians became followers of what Paul taught by "Jesus Christ, according to the revelation of the mystery" (Romans 16:25). They were "followers of us" (2 Thess. 3:6-9). They followed Paul to follow Christ from heaven (1 Cor. 1:11). It is key to follow our apostle Paul (and those who preach and teach what he said), not Peter. In spite of their affliction, they received the word with much joy of the Holy Ghost. They had no false doctrine to unlearn, only pagan superstition. They joined the group that will live in heaven, the body of Christ. They believed the "mystery" Paul preached while undergoing the affliction and persecution of the unbelieving Jews and pagan idolaters. The Jews were angry because of what they heard Paul say. Paul said believing what Moses said and performing the laws of Judaism was unnecessary, just believe in what Christ did for you and be saved (Acts 13:39). They had the joy of the Holy Ghost because they will live "eternal in the heavens" (2 Cor. 5:1). They became "ensamples" or examples to other believers in the body of Christ in Macedonia and Achaia because they not only followed apostle Paul, understood the mystery, but shared it.] **8 For from you SOUNDED OUT THE WORD OF THE LORD not only in Macedonia and Achaia, but also in every place your faith to God-ward is spread abroad; so that we need not to speak any thing.** [The word of the LORD are the sound words Paul preached (2 Tim. 1:13). They were not only examples to these churches, but "every place your faith to God-ward is spread abroad; so that we need not to speak any thing" (1 Thess. 1:8). There was no need for Paul to encourage them to share their faith because this model church was already doing so. What Paul preached was "the word of God" (1 Thess. 2:13). Wherever Paul went the faith of the Thessalonians had gone before him. We are "complete in Christ" (Col. 2:10). We are "accepted in the beloved" (Eph. 1:6). We operate out of a place of total acceptance. We are already "joint-heirs with Christ" (Rom. 8:17). We have all spiritual blessings in heavenly places (Eph. 1:3). We already possess eternal life (Titus 1:2). We are not under the law which says "do," but under grace that says "done." We have a personal relationship with the living God (1 Cor. 6:17). As His workmanship (Eph. 2:10) we serve God motivated by a heart full of love and gratitude. We are energized by His Spirit in us. So how can we practically sound forth the word of truth like the Thessalonians?

Here are some practical ways to do ministry. Paul prayed. We can pray for people to be saved and come to the knowledge of the truth (1 Tim. 2:4) and to grow spiritually (Col. 1:9). We can share right division wherever we go. We can put the gospel (1 Cor. 15:3, 4) on a business card and hand them out. We can hand out grace tracts. (I made one called "How to be Saved in 0 (Zero) Easy Steps." We can have a bumper sticker on our cars with the gospel. We can share the gospel and right division everywhere we go. (I sometimes carry witnessing material in a fanny pack, in my purse, and in my car.) We can share the truth with our family, on social media, Facebook, and YouTube, etc. We can send books, tracts, and Bibles to those who need them. Using LBC we can ship books inexpensively to the Philippines (800-338-5424). Using the postal system, we can mail boxes to Africa and other places around the world. Because many of you have bought our books, your money is helping us send our books and Bibles to places all over the world. From the proceeds of this ministry, we have ordered large font KJV Pew Bibles from Bulkbibles.com and are preparing to ship them out along with *God's Secret*, *Just as God Said* and other books. We recently sent some books to India. We are preparing a box for the Philippines and another for Africa. I found rightly dividing recipients for these packages on Facebook. When you buy our books, you have a part in a ministry that "sounded out the word of the Lord." Another way to contribute is to go to our website, mariannemanley.com, and contribute through Paypal. God loves a cheerful giver. We have a few faithful grace givers who regularly support the ministry financially and we are very grateful for them. Others buy our books and send them to family and friends. Others share, watch, and "Like" our videos on social media and in emails. Our YouTube channel is Salvation, rightly dividing, and the Rapture. We should all give to grace ministries that do God's will (1 Tim. 2:4) and bless us. We need to do all we can for as many as we can before the Rapture.] **9 For they themselves shew of us what manner of entering in we had unto you, and how ye turned to God from idols to SERVE THE LIVING AND TRUE GOD;** [Their enthusiasm for sharing the gospel and the doctrine they learned from Paul reflected on the manner in which Paul and his friends had shared the truth with them. What was Paul's manner? "And Paul, as his manner was, went in unto them, and three sabbath days reasoned with them out of the scriptures" (Acts 17:2). Paul used the word of God because faith comes by hearing it. This is what we are to do. Paul is our pattern, our example, and he was the first one into the body of Christ (1 Tim. 1:16). Paul wrote about idol worship of the lost Gentiles in Romans 1:19-25. Gentiles who knew God rejected Him. "Who changed the truth of God into a lie and worshipped and served the creature more than the Creator" (Rom. 1:25). Paul did not go into Thessalonica and say, "It is not right for you to worship idols. That's a terrible thing to do." He never approached pagans like that. What did Paul do? He preached the cross, Christ crucified and risen again (1 Cor. 1:17, 18, 2:2). What was the result? They were soundly saved, turned to God from idols and were serving the living and true God, not a powerless statue that could not see, hear, or speak. Note that one must turn to God (faith) before turning from sin. They heard Paul preach the good news that Jesus Christ was now saving Gentiles in mystery, apart from having to go through the nation of Israel. Paul told them that the risen, ascended, glorified Lord Jesus Christ had appeared to him on the road to Damascus and chosen him to be "the apostle of the Gentiles" (Rom. 11:13). He told them that believers would live in the heavenly places. God is forming the body of Christ during the dispensation of grace (Eph. 3:1-9). Paul said that anyone who believed who Jesus is and what He had done for them would live in heaven with Him, not in the earthly kingdom which Christ would set up with the nation of Israel. Paul understood the mystery and he understood prophecy. As ambassadors for Christ, we present the gospel (1 Cor. 15:3, 4) and people by faith believe the word of God. A person must first hear the word of God. Faith comes by hearing the word of God (Rom. 10:17). The Spirit of God can use the word of God in the hearts of the believers. God's word has the power to penetrate into our hearts and transform our lives. The Bible is a supernatural book (with the Holy Spirit) it is the "power of God unto salvation" (Rom. 1:16). God's word has the power to save souls and translate them from the "power of darkness, and hath translated us into the kingdom of his dear Son" (Col. 1:13). There is a miraculous "operation of God" (Col. 2:12) that takes place at salvation. The motivation under grace is love and gratitude. Love is the strongest of all motivators (2 Cor. 5:14). We serve our Father out of love for what He and His Son has done for us (Rom. 8:32-39). We love to do what pleases God and edifies His people. A "labor of love" is an expression of obedience as a son or daughter of God (Rom. 12:1, 2). After we are saved we serve God by doing good work (Eph. 2:10).] **10 And to wait for his Son from heaven, whom he RAISED from the dead, even Jesus, which delivered us from the wrath to come.** [Each of the chapters in this letter ends with a reference to the Lord's return for His Church. Paul often praises the Thessalonians and approves of what they have done. He repeats the gospel of their salvation several times in this letter (1:10, 4:14, 5:10). We are waiting for Jesus, the Son of God whom the Father raised from the dead. The Father raising His Son is proof that Christ was who He said He was and did what He said He did. Therefore, the first part of the verse is about our salvation, while the last part of the verse is about our deliverance from having to go through the Tribulation. Paul is careful to say that Jesus "delivered us from the wrath to come." Paul defines "wrath" for us in 1 Thess. 5:9, 10. Paul also confirms the Pre-Tribulation Rapture in Second Thessalonians 2:1 and elsewhere. John the Baptist warned of the wrath to come (Matt. 3:7; Luke 3:7). The Church will not go through the Tribulation. The Rapture, exit, or catching up of the Church is the next event on God's timeline. The body of Christ believers have been delivered from having to go through the Tribulation, Daniel's 70th week, or "Jacob's trouble" (Jer. 30:7). We should be very thankful. The hope of resurrection and ascension to Christ (our Rapture) does and will sustain believers through the most difficult circumstances. Our blessed hope is to be Raptured before we die (Titus 2:13). The dispensation of grace is postponing or delaying the wrath of God. Mankind cannot solve the world's problems and bring peace and prosperity to the earth. The Lord Jesus Christ will be the only one who can do that during His first millennial reign on the earth. Our hope is not in a political party or a manmade institution. However, when the righteous are in power we have more peace. Some rulers make our lives easier than others. Christ is our hope. How do we know Christ is coming to escort us to heaven? Because Christ rising from the dead proved that He was the Son of God (Acts 13:33, 17:31; Eph. 1:20). To wait doesn't mean stop and sit, it means to be busy in our work of service to the Lord. We are to give out the word of God rightly divided while we wait. The coming of Christ to take His Church out of the world is not meant to be an escape mechanism to avoid paying our bills or taking a test. It is an incentive to take as many other believers with us as we can. We also want to help believers to have the greatest reward possible at the Judgment Seat of Christ for service done with Christ working in and through us while on earth. A strong, model church began at Thessalonica (and we want to be like them).] **We wait for His Son from heaven.**

> ~1 Thessalonians 1:9-10 (KJV)~
> For they themselves shew of us what manner of entering in we had unto you, and how ye turned to God from idols to serve the living and true God; And to wait for his Son from heaven, whom he raised from the dead, even Jesus, which delivered us from the wrath to come.

We should live our lives with the idea that the Rapture could happen anytime.

 **Maybe today, Lord!**

The Paulicians an Abbreviated History

Throughout history, many believers have said they believe in Jesus according to what Paul preached. In the past these believers called themselves "true believers," but others called them "Paulicians." The Paulicians were continually persecuted by the Byzantine Emperors. The Roman laws, peace, and roads helped further the gospel of God. The Roman Empire was divided in AD 395. The western Roman Empire fell because of various invaders around AD 450. However, the Eastern Roman Empire continued for about another thousand years. The Koine Greek used to write the New Testament, the Textus Receptus, was preserved in that Empire (possibly by the Pauline Christians). (Greek is perhaps the most versatile language in the world.) After the Ottoman Turks invaded and destroyed the Eastern Roman Empire and sacked Byzantium (Constantinople) in AD 1453, they persecuted the Paulicians. Many Paulicians lived in Bulgaria (Bogolomists). Many fled to the Italian Alps (Waldensians and joined with the Paulicians there), many moved to France (Cathars), and even as far as London.

Many Christians who fled from the Ottoman Turks brought their Greek Bibles with them into Europe. Erasmus collected them and published the best ones. Tyndale, Luther, and others translated the Greek Textus Receptus published by Erasmus. Eventually, the King James Bible was translated and printed in 1611.

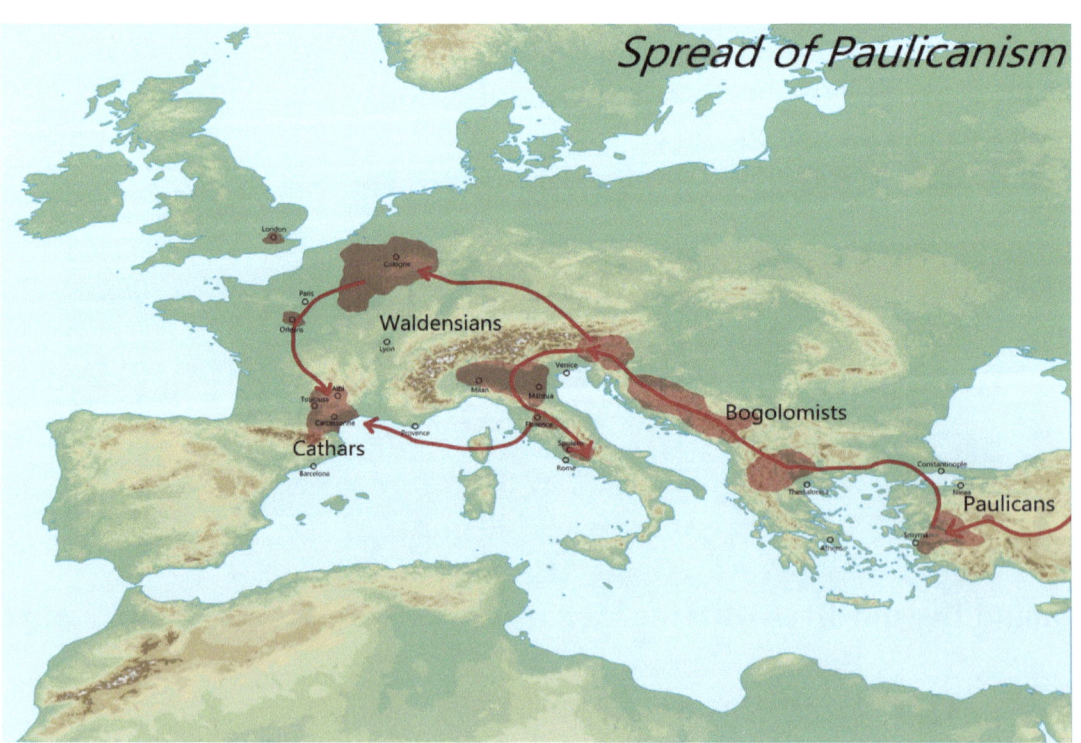

Persecution of Paulicians

There was a large group of Paulicians concentrated in Armenia at the base of Mount Ararat. The Turkish government systematically slaughtered, exterminated, and killed 1.5 million Armenians inside their own borders (genocide). (See the picture from the 1915 genocide found on Wikipedia.org). Some escaped. The Armenians are still alive all over the world and their country is in Georgia of Russia. In comparison, Hitler killed 6 million Jews and 5 million Christians.

Throughout time some have believed what Paul preached: That God is forming a new group, the body of Christ, to live in heaven. Armenians can now be found all over the world, but are they still Pauline? That is the question. "If ye continue in the faith grounded and settled, and be not moved away from the hope of the gospel, which ye have heard, and which was preached to every creature which is under heaven; whereof I Paul am made a minister" (Col. 1:23).

God wants us all to understand the entire Bible from the point of view of what Paul wrote to us in the body of Christ in his thirteen letters (Romans to Philemon). I have only shared a brief overview of their history. Pastor Bryan Ross has an excellent in-depth series about the history of the Pauline believers called the Grace History Project (Grace Life Bible Church) available on the internet.

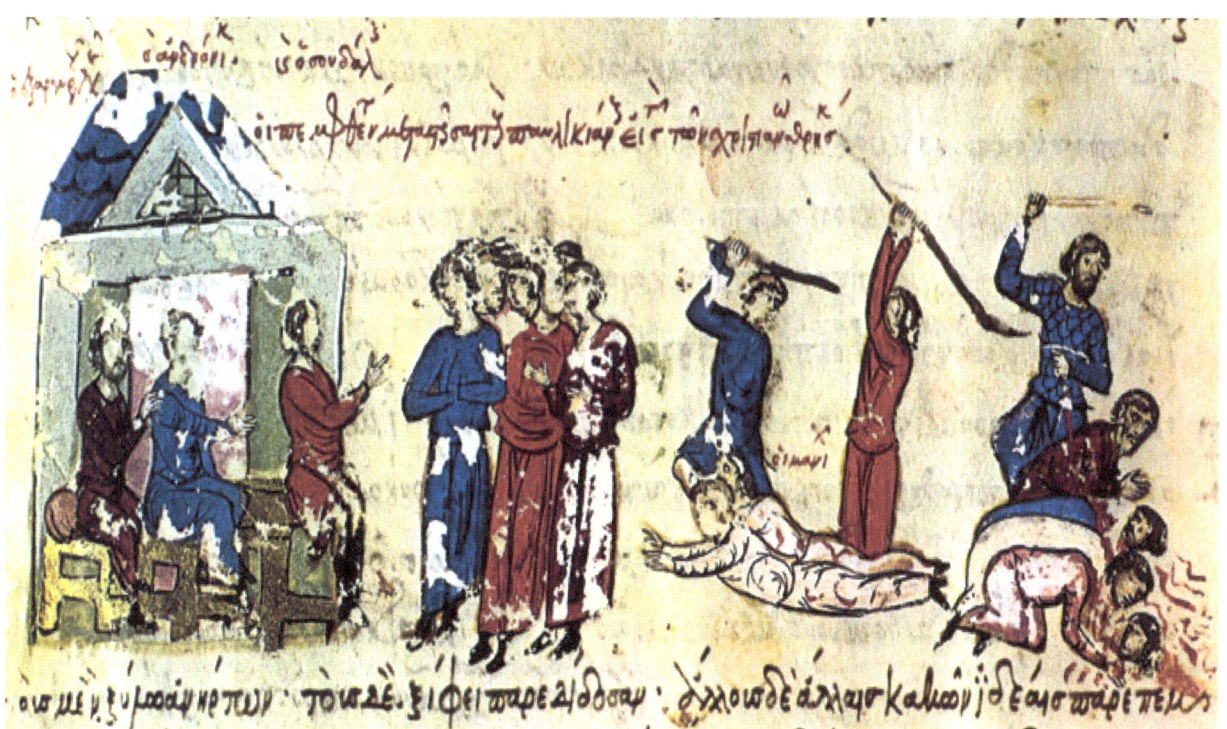

Paulicians were persecuted by the Byzantine emperors.

Christian women captives being taken deep into Turkey.

Satan constantly opposes God.
Ever since Genesis 3:15, when Satan heard that the seed of the woman would bruise his head, Satan had wanted to kill the Seed before He could hurt him.

Satan had been calculating the time the Redeemer would come to Israel according to Daniel's timeline and had gone ahead spreading disease, evil spirits, and false religious teaching (the tradition of men). When Jesus Christ arrived. There may have been more devils possessing people than people in Israel. God knew that Satan's plot was to kill Jesus.

God had a plan that included the "heaven and the earth" (Gen. 1:1). God had also prepared the world for His Son's arrival and the spreading of the gospel. Because of Alexander the Great's Empire, the Greek language, which is perhaps the most versatile, was being spoken in most of the known world.

Greek culture was also widespread.
Next came the Roman Empire with law and order, peace, and great roads.

                                                  Several helpful Maps follow.

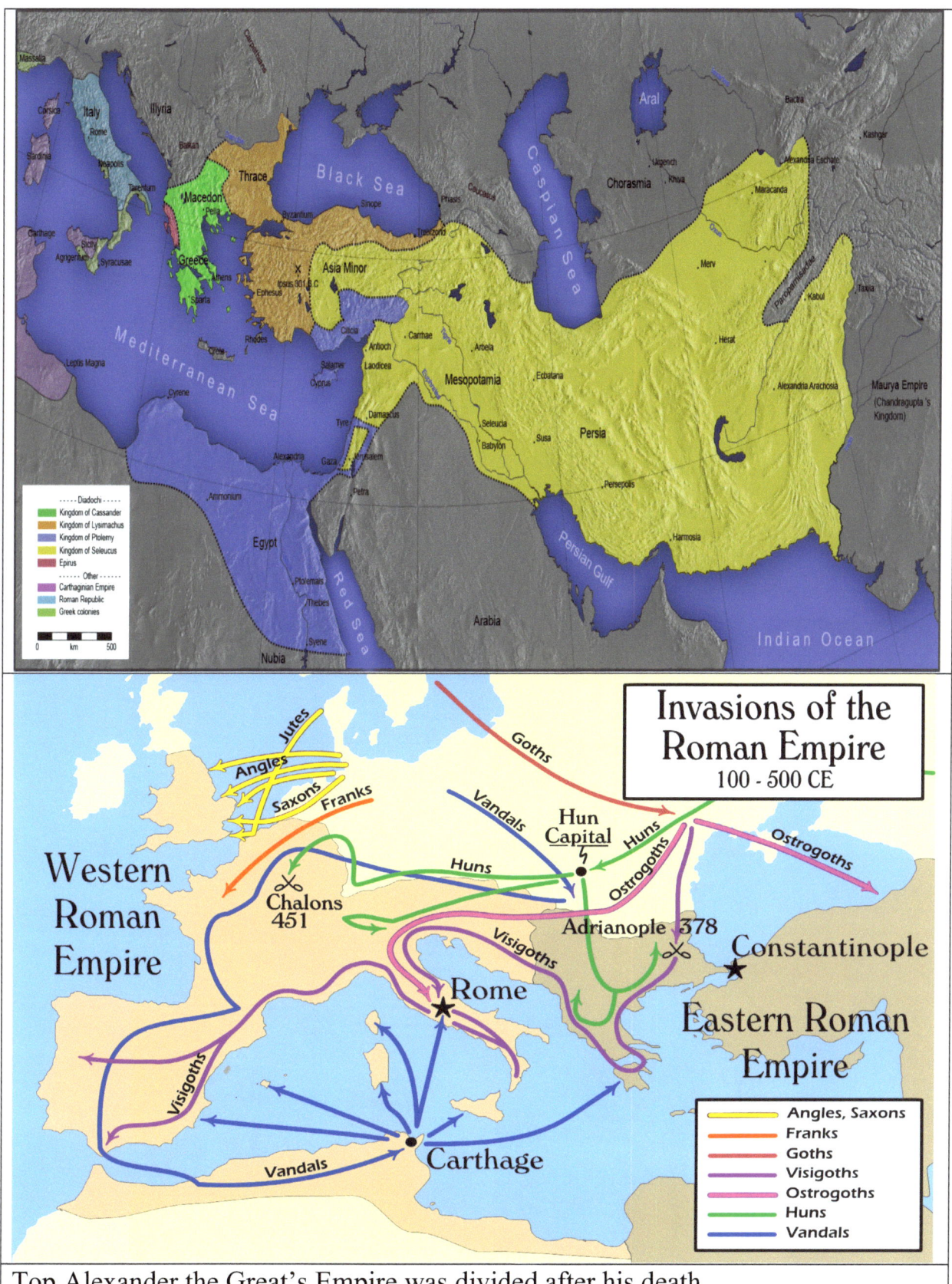

Top Alexander the Great's Empire was divided after his death.
Below the fall of Western Roman Empire c. 450 AD.

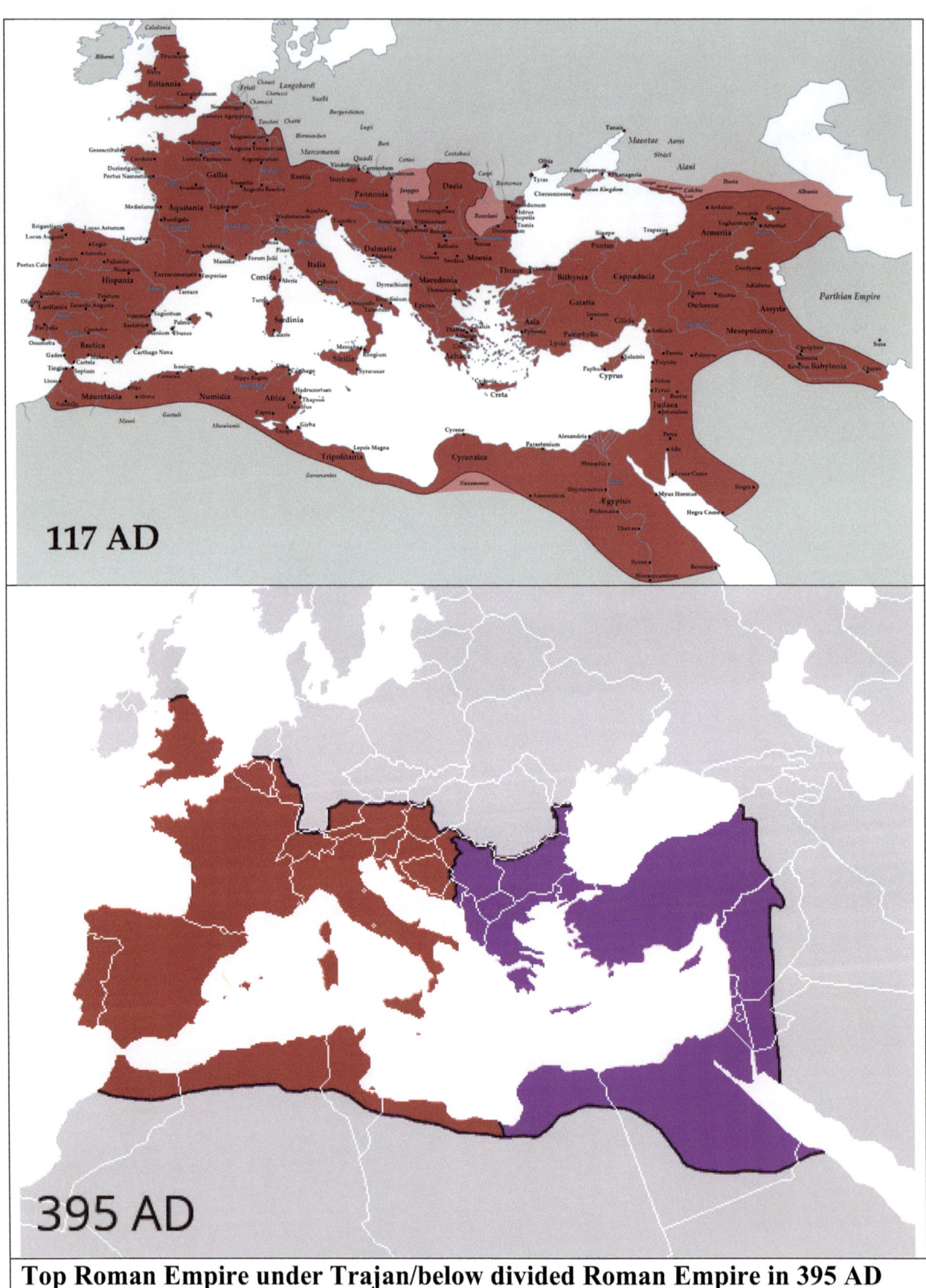

Top Roman Empire under Trajan/below divided Roman Empire in 395 AD

Constantinople fell in 1453, the fall of Eastern Roman (Byzantine) Empire by the Ottoman Turks. The above map of 1606 shows the Empire of the Turks in pink.

Massacre of Armenians by the Turks in 1915, 1.5 million of them (Wikipedia).

Four Roman Districts on a helpful map (circa 300 AD).

***Notice Thessalonica and Armenia.**

1 Thessalonians Chapter 2 The Model Minister (Paul) and his reward.
2:1-6 Faithful preacher with a pure motive.
2:7-10 Cherished them with gentle love as a nursing mother would.
2:11, 12 Concerned for them like a father for his children.
2:13 Receptive hearts result in genuine faith.
2:14-20 They are Paul's reward, his joy, and crown.

The apostles had pure motives (1-6) exemplary conduct with unselfish concern (7-12) and shared the authentic true words of God (2:13). The exemplary evangelism of the ministers resulted in the exemplary conversion of these new believers. They are Paul's reward, his joy, and his crown (2:14-20). There are no apostles today. <u>Paul was a model to the body of Christ; no other individual teacher or preacher is a model apostle. Nevertheless, we should all live right</u>.

Review: In the last lesson we learned that the Thessalonians were a <u>model church</u>. They turned to God from idols. The Thessalonians received the doctrine of the mystery that Paul and his co-workers delivered to them by the power of the Holy Ghost. They became followers of us and of the Lord. After **receiving** <u>by **faith** the</u> <u>**word**</u> with **power** <u>and **joy**</u> <u>of the **Holy Ghost**</u> they **sounded it out** and **shared** the **truth** everywhere. They were serving the true God and waiting for His Son, Jesus, which He raised, to come, who delivers us from having to go through the wrath (Matt. 3:7), the Tribulation. They were an exemplary model church because they had an exemplary model minister. **<u>Paul will now use the way he ministered to them as a model for how they (and we) should minister to others</u>. We are all to be ministers.**

<u>The nation of Israel fell and is on hold, but Jews have hope in the body of Christ.</u> The nation of Israel received a one-year extension of mercy to accept Jesus Christ as their Messiah. Empowered by the Holy Ghost, Peter and the other followers of Christ's earthly ministry, preached a renewed offer of the kingdom (Luke 13:6-9, 23:34). The nation of Israel rejected the offer. <u>They fell in Acts 7 when the Jewish religious leaders denied the ministry of the Holy Ghost through Stephen, a member of the little flock</u>. "Ye stiffnecked and **uncircumcised** in heart and ears, ye do always <u>resist the Holy Ghost</u>: as your fathers did, so do ye" (Acts 7:51). This was the unforgivable **blasphemy of the Holy Ghost** which the Lord Jesus warned the Israelites about (Matt. 12:31, 32). <u>Paul refers to the blasphemy of the Holy Ghost in 1 Thess. 2:16</u>. God considers the nation of Israel as uncircumcised Gentiles and in apostasy. However, a Jew or Gentile <u>can</u> believe Paul's gospel and become a member of the body of Christ. There is no ethnic, racial, social or gender distinctions in the <u>body of Christ</u> (Gal. 3:28). The body of Christ is "one new man"

(Eph. 2:15). Peter and his group continued preaching for another 17 years until the Jerusalem Council. <u>In the future, God will make His nation out of that group</u>. Paul went up to the Jerusalem Council of <u>AD 52</u> (Acts 15:1-35; Gal. 1, 2:1-10). So Peter evangelized for 18 years after Christ ascended. Peter, James, and John agreed to let Paul preach to all unbelievers (Gal. 2:6-9). This letter is probably written in AD 53. Although, Paul began to preach the gospel of grace as soon as he was saved 17 years previously, for the past year it has been the only valid gospel. "But though we, or an angel from heaven, preach <u>any other gospel unto you than that which we have preached unto you, let him be accursed</u>" (Gal. 1:8).

The **Acts** period is a time of **transition from Christ's earthly ministry (through Peter) to Christ's heavenly ministry (through Paul).** When the Father revealed to Peter that Jesus was the Christ, then Jesus knew that the Father wanted Peter to be the leader of the twelve (Matt. 16:16-18). Paul says "even so then at this present time also there is a remnant [Peter and the little flock]" (Rom. 11:5).

Peter knew he would one day be in charge of the twelve apostles as ordained by the Father, even if James temporarily took over the leadership of the little flock before the wrath (Matt. 19:28). The Acts epistles are Romans, the Corinthian letters, Galatians, and the Thessalonian letters.

We can use an analogy of God the Father as a farmer. The Father was growing potatoes in Peter's time (the four gospels and early Acts). When Paul was saved God began to grow beets also. For a while, God was growing both potatoes and beets. But since the little flock closed the door to new converts in Acts 15 at the Jerusalem Council, He is only growing beets. <u>Only Paul's gospel is valid today</u> (Gal. 1:6-9). Another analogy, a father had three sons. The first son grew potatoes. The second son potatoes and beets. The third son grew beets. If the father wants to grow beets now, which one is doing his will? Yes, that is right the one who is growing beets! Likewise, if someone is not preaching and teaching Paul's gospel of the grace of God today, then they are not doing God's will. God is forming the body of Christ to live in heaven, not bringing in the kingdom on earth.

<u>What we do in life has everything to do with what our reward will be in heaven</u>. In this chapter, **Paul will show us how to minister so we can have rewards**.

2:1 For yourselves, brethren, know <u>our entrance in unto you, that it was not in vain</u>: [Paul wants the Thessalonians to remember the brief but effective ministry he and his helpers had in Thessalonica before they were abruptly forced to abandon their work among them. He reminds them how the apostles served God when they entered in among them and preached. Their preaching to them was not "in vain" (useless) but brought results because many souls were saved. Paul wants them to follow his model ministry and preaching. He wants these new believers to notice how they ministered to them for their sake. "What manner of men we were among you for your sake" (1:5). Paul was a model to them and to us; Paul is our "pattern" (1 Tim. 1:16). We are all to be ministers.] **2 But even after that we had suffered before, and were shamefully entreated, as ye know, at Philippi, we were bold in our God to speak unto you the gospel of God with much contention.** [Paul said that they were "bold in our God" and continued to proclaim the gospel to them even after they had been shamefully mistreated at Philippi (Acts 16:19-24). Likewise, they should not let their persecution keep them from loving others by preaching the truth. Paul and Silas didn't let the shameful way they were treated at Philippi slow them down in spreading the gospel. They were "bold in our God" to speak the "gospel of God" to them "with much contention" (from the unbelieving Jews). Likewise, the Thessalonians should continue to be bold (1:6), although the unbelieving Jews argued against the truth of what Paul shared.

Paul shared "the gospel of God." The "gospel of God" occurs six times in Paul's writings and once in Peter's (1 Peter 4:17). It is the basic prophesied information that Jesus Christ, the Redeemer, the Son of God and the Son of David, was raised from the dead with power (Gen. 3:15; Rom. 1:1-4). We should not think that because Peter and Paul both preached the "gospel of God" that they preached the same thing. Because by one cross, Christ saved two groups, those who will live in heaven and those who will live on earth. We can think of the "gospel of God" as a pie shell that can have either cherry or apple filling. Peter put the cherry filling in it which was the "gospel of the kingdom." Paul put the apple filling in it which is the "gospel of Christ." (This information was taken from The Gospel Project written and presented by Pastor Bryan Ross of Grace Life Bible Church in Grand Rapids and by Pastor David Reid from Columbus Bible Church in Columbus, Ohio in October of 2013.) Paul preached that Christ died for "our sins" the sins of Jews and Gentiles living in mystery and was raised for our justification (1 Cor. 15:3, 4; Rom. 4:24, 25). Jesus Christ also died for the sins of Jews and Gentiles living in prophecy (Matt. 1:21; Rom. 5:8, 9). There are many gospels in the Bible, Noah, for example, had to show his faith by building an ark. Everyone must believe the gospel God gave to them in their dispensation in order to be forgiven and have eternal life.] **3 For our exhortation was not of deceit, nor of uncleanness, nor in guile:** [Exhortation is urging or encouraging. Their counsel was not deceitful, nor of unclean, nor in guile (cunning, craftiness or fraud). They spoke the pure true words Christ revealed to Paul (Gal. 1:1, 11, 12). They did not corrupt the word of God which Christ gave them to preach (2 Cor. 2:17). Paul gave out the word of

God exactly how he received it from Christ. He did not alter the word of God in any way.] **4 But as we were <u>allowed of God</u> to be <u>put in trust</u> with the <u>gospel, even so we speak; not as pleasing men, but God, which trieth our hearts.</u>** [Paul and his co-workers were allowed of God to preach the gospel Christ had entrusted to Paul. "According to the glorious gospel of the blessed God, which was committed to <u>my trust</u>" (1 Tim. 1:11). God put the gospel in their trust to guard, keep, and proclaim it. They spoke with the goal of pleasing God, not men. Because God tests <u>our hearts and knows our motives</u> (1 Cor. 4:5; Heb. 4:12). A faithful steward's motive is to live to please God, not men (Heb. 11:6). Our goal is to please God rather than men.] **5 For neither at <u>any time used we flattering words</u>, as ye know, nor a cloke of <u>covetousness</u>; <u>God is witness</u>: 6 Nor of men sought we glory, neither of you, nor yet of others, when we might have been burdensome, as the APOSTLES of Christ.** [They know that Paul and his co-workers did not use flattering words at any time, their motives were pure (Prov. 26:28; Psa. 78:36). They spoke the truth of Christ plainly. The <u>strange woman</u> in Proverbs <u>represents false doctrine</u> which flatters (Prov. 6:24). <u>Antichrist</u> will deceive many leaders in Israel with flattery, but not the Bible believers (Dan. 11:21, 32). <u>The name "antichrist" occurs 4 times in the King James Bible, 3 times in 1 John and once in 2 John.</u> God is the witness that Paul did not have a hidden <u>ulterior</u> dishonest motive of taking anything from them. They did not seek fame, prestige, honor, praise, or monetary reward for themselves. <u>Notice that "Paul, and Silvanus, and Timotheus" (1:1)</u> were apostles of Christ to the body of Christ. Paul was the main (primary) apostle (Rom. 11:13) and the others secondary Holy Ghost sent apostles (Acts 14:14) of the Mystery to the body of Christ. <u>Paul was inspired and sent by Christ to be His spokesman and apostle to the body of Christ.</u> Although, as apostles of Christ, they were entitled to payment, they did everything for free without asking for a penny. They supported themselves and gave out the word of God. Paul was the last apostle.] **7 But we were <u>gentle</u> among you, even as <u>a nurse cherisheth her children</u>:** [They were gentle among them as a nursing mother that cherishes her children. They fed them a little milk of the word here, and a little milk there, and carried them along.] **8 So being <u>affectionately desirous of you, we were willing to have imparted unto you, not the gospel of God only, but also our own souls</u>, because ye were dear unto us.** [They didn't want money or material things to stand in the way of them and the truth because they desired for their souls to be saved. They were as a mother who has affection for her children and desires the best for them as she sacrificially gives of herself to her dear ones. With great affection and desire for them to understand the truth, the apostles were willing not only to share the gospel of God, <u>but all the knowledge that was in their own souls</u> because they were so dear to them. Others should be so precious to us that, as we are allowed of God, we should share the gospel and any illumination that the holy Spirit has revealed to us through His word.] **9 For ye remember, brethren, our labour and travail: for labouring night and day, because we would not be chargeable unto any of you, we preached unto you the gospel of God.** [They labored as women in childbirth for Christ to be formed in them (Acts 20:33-35). "My little children, of whom I travail in birth again until Christ be formed in you" (Gal. 4:19). "A man's work is from sun to sun, but a mother's work is never done." A mother does not receive a formal paycheck. A mother is often an example of sacrificial love. God's love is unparalleled, but a mother's love is also strong and dignified. Paul asks them to remember how he and his friends worked night and day to provide for themselves and preached the gospel of God to them. Paul didn't want any money from any of them. But, Paul received monetary help from Philippi twice at that time because God put it on their hearts to give to him (Phil. 4:15, 16).] **10 Ye are witnesses, and God also, how holily and justly and unblameably we behaved ourselves among you that believe:** [They were witnesses, and so was God, how holy, justly, and without blame they had behaved themselves among them that believe. This is how Paul wants them (and us) to conduct ourselves among others. We are to live worthy.] **11 As ye know how we exhorted and comforted and charged every one of you, as a father doth his children, 12 That ye would walk worthy of God, who hath called you unto his kingdom and glory.** [Like a father they urged them to believe and to live right. A father must watch over his family and make sacrifices as he provides for their welfare. A father is a role model for his children. A loving father encourages, comforts, commands, instructs, guides, and directs his children to be responsible to do their duty (2 Thess. 3:4). Paul was approachable and gave personal encouragement, attention, and counsel to each one individually. This is how Paul was and how he expects them and us to be toward others. As their spiritual father, Paul wants them to "walk worthy of God," who has called them (by the gospel 2 Thess. 2:13, 14) into His kingdom (made up of two groups those who live in heaven and those who live on earth) and glory (to eternally glorify His Son). They are to walk worthy and be "holy, just, and unblameable" (2:10) like the apostle while serving God who has called them into His heavenly kingdom (2 Tim. 4:18).]

13 ¶ For this cause also thank we God without ceasing, because, when ye received the word of God which ye heard of us, ye received it not as the word of men, but as it is in truth, the word of God, which effectually worketh also in you that believe. [Whenever Paul writes "for this cause" we need to know what the "cause" was, in this case it is to "walk worthy of God" (2:12) since they have been called into His kingdom and glory. What is the key to their success in such a short time? They had the right response to the word of God, they trusted exclusively what Christ said to through Paul. This local assembly of believers was a model church because of how they received the word of God given to Paul for them. They were a young church but full of faith. They put their faith in the word Christ gave to Paul, because it was in truth the word of God, not the word of men. The word of God saved them and made them want to serve God. Paul is thrilled and thankful to God continuously because when they received the word of God which works effectually in those who believe. The Thessalonians knew that Paul spoke Christ's words to them. Notice that they heard the words, they were not written down. Paul did not write any inspired scripture until after the Jerusalem council (AD 52). He wrote Galatians (Acts 15:35) and then the Thessalonian letters (Acts 18:5 and 18:11). The Spirit of God uses the word of God to work effectually in us who believe it. How did Paul know the word of God would work effectually in them? Because it did in him. First, we must be saved by believing the gospel (1 Cor. 15:3, 4). Second, we must believe that God has preserved His word (Psa. 12:6, 7), in English, we have His word is in the King James Bible. (God has preserved His word in other languages, too.) Third, we must apply 2 Timothy 2:15 and divide the truth of the mystery (Romans to Philemon) from the truth of prophecy (the rest of the Bible). Then as we read and understand the word of God by His Spirit in us and believe it we have the mind of Christ (1 Cor. 2:9-16). Thinking precedes actions. When we think like Christ in heaven would, then we act in the way we should. This is how the word of God works in us. Christ's Spirit in us (Col. 1:27) functions by using His word. When we know Him (Phil. 3:8), His will (1 Tim. 2:4), which part of the Bible is to us (Paul's writings) and who we are in Him (Rom. 8:17; Col. 2:9, 10). Then we can be His effective sons and daughters (2 Cor. 6:18). Jesus Christ can live His life through us as we present our bodies a living sacrifice (Gal. 2:20; Rom. 12:1, 2).] **14 For ye, brethren, became followers of the churches of God which in Judaea are in Christ Jesus: for ye also have suffered like things of your own countrymen, even as they have of the Jews:** [They followed the "little flock' (Luke 12:32) churches of the circumcision in Judea in suffering, not in doctrine. There are three churches mentioned in the Bible (Matt. 16:18; Acts 7:38; Eph. 1:22, 23). The Thessalonians were suffering because of the unbelieving idolaters and Jews who were their countrymen. The kingdom on earth churches in Judea "in Christ Jesus" suffered at the hands of the unbelieving Jews. All believers on this side of the cross are "in Christ" (John 17:21; Rom. 16:7). Those of the circumcision (Peter and his group) were also "in Christ" by faith (there is no salvation outside of being "in Christ" on this side of the cross, because if a person is not in Christ, then they are in Adam). They believed that Christ who came at His first advent is their Messiah to sit on the throne of David in the kingdom on earth. They had no understanding of the good news of the cross before or after Christ's death (Luke 18:31-34; Acts 2:23). Paul calls them "the

Israel of God" (Gal. 6:16) because the apostate unbelieving Jews were persecuting them, but God will make His nation of Israel over, using the believing remnant (Matt. 19:28; 21:43). The true Israel, the believing remnant, the "no people," "a foolish nation," are of the same lump (Israel). Paul said God will make His nation out of the remnant and the rest were blinded (Rom. 9:6, 21; 10:19, 11:5-7, 25). Paul had been one of their persecutors before he was saved in Acts 9 (Acts 8:1). Paul's first apostolic miracle was to temporarily blind the unbelieving Jewish sorcerer Elymas (a type of Israel) who withstood his preaching to a Gentile (Acts 13:6-13). Israel did not realize that Christ had to suffer as the sacrificial Lamb of God and shed His blood for their sins before He came as their King. They are sons of both Abraham and Adam. By one CROSS, Christ died for Jews and Gentiles in both groups, the heavenly believers (in mystery) and the earthly believers (in prophecy).] **15 Who both killed the Lord Jesus, and their own prophets, and have persecuted us; and they please not God, and are contrary to all men: 16 Forbidding us to speak to the Gentiles that they might be saved, to fill up their sins alway: for the wrath is come upon them to the uttermost.** [The wrath of God has come upon their own unbelieving countrymen who persecuted the Thessalonians, as it has on the unbelieving Jews that persecuted Peter's group in Jerusalem, to the uttermost. The nation of Israel's leaders committed the BLASPHEMY of the HOLY GHOST when they stoned Stephen in Acts 7:51-60. The wrath of God is come upon the Jewish persecutors to the uttermost in that they will suffer eternal damnation, the second death. Unbelievers will not be forgiven as the Lord said. "Wherefore I say unto you, All manner of sin and blasphemy shall be forgiven unto men: but the blasphemy against the Holy Ghost shall not be forgiven unto men. And whosoever speaketh a word against the Son of man, it shall be forgiven him: but whosoever speaketh against the Holy Ghost, it shall not be forgiven him, neither in this world, neither in the world to come" (Matt. 12:31, 32). Israel first rejected the Father, then Christ, and then the Holy Ghost. They ran out of the Godhead, the Holy Ghost is the last Person of the Godhead, so no other prospects existed. When Christ was crucified He pleaded, Father, "forgive them: for the know not what they do" (Luke 23:34a). This fulfilled Christ's words, "whosoever speaketh a word against the Son of man, it shall be forgiven him." Israel was forgiven of killing the Lord Jesus in ignorance and given another bonus year to turn to God and believe that He was their Messiah. But, when the Holy Ghost was poured out on Pentecost, Israel continued to reject the Holy Ghost filled disciples of Christ's earthly ministry culminating in the stoning of Stephen. This resulted in Israel being set aside and God ushering in a new dispensation revealed through Paul.

The same Jews that the Thessalonians are dealing with had persecuted Paul and his helpers. What those Jews are doing is not pleasing to God; they are against all men (the kingdom on earth believers and Paul's group). They try to prevent the Gentiles from hearing the gospel preached to them by Paul, so that they can be saved. They are adding to their sins, always filling up their sins. Because they would not believe God, be saved, and join the body of Christ. They have no hope of an earthly kingdom at this time because it has been postponed and interrupted. God has inserted the dispensation of grace, a period of amnesty when God is offering salvation to all people. Those who believe the gospel of Christ that Paul preached will be saved, forgiven, join the body of Christ, and live in heaven. "For this cause I Paul, the prisoner of Jesus Christ for you Gentiles, If ye have heard of the dispensation of the grace of God which is given me to you-ward: How that by revelation he made known unto me the mystery; (as I wrote afore in few words, Whereby, when ye read, ye may understand my knowledge in the mystery of Christ) Which in other ages was not made known unto the sons of men, as it is now revealed unto his holy apostles and prophets by the Spirit; That the Gentiles should be fellowheirs, and of the same body, and partakers of his promise in Christ by the gospel: Whereof I was made a minister, according to the gift of the grace of God given unto me by the effectual working of his power. Unto me, who am less than the least of all saints, is this grace given, that I should preach among the Gentiles the unsearchable riches of Christ; And to make all men see what is the fellowship of the mystery, which from the beginning of the world hath been hid in God, who created all things by Jesus Christ" (Eph. 3:1-9). "Hid in God" the dispensation of grace was in God's mind all along, although God did not tell anyone about it until Paul. Paul's ministry which has a heavenly hope is in effect now.]

17 ¶ But we, brethren, being taken from you for a short time in presence, not in heart, endeavoured the more abundantly to see your face with great desire. [But Paul was taken from the presence of the Thessalonians for a short time. They are briefly physically separated, but not in heart. Paul and company had a great desire to see their faces.] **18 Wherefore we would have come unto you, even I Paul, once and again; but Satan hindered us.** [Paul tried to come to them twice, "once and again," but Satan hindered them. He probably ran into some Jews blocking his travel plans and way. Those Jews were empowered by "the spirit that now worketh in the children of disobedience" which is the spirit of the "prince of the power of the air [Satan]" (Eph. 2:2). Satan also works in unsaved Gentiles. In fact, the purpose of the "course of this world" (Eph. 2:2) is to keep people from knowing God. Paul did see the Thessalonians again several times a few years later.] **19 For what is our hope, or joy, or crown of rejoicing? Are not even ye in the presence of our Lord Jesus Christ at his coming? 20 For ye are our**

glory and joy. [Having let them know how greatly he longs to see them, Paul asks from the heart, "what is our <u>hope, joy, crown of rejoicing</u>?" They are his crown (reward). Paul speaks of the Lord Jesus Christ coming in relation to the Judgment Seat of Christ. At the Judgment Seat of Christ, these believers will be his reward, glory, and joy. Paul lovingly answers that they are all these things, "ye are our glory and joy." More believing members added to the body of Christ is his reward. More reward means more responsibility at the Judgment Seat of Christ. This is what God's will is. "Who will have <u>all men to be saved</u>, and <u>to come unto the knowledge of the truth</u>" (1 Tim. 2:4). What God is doing today is building the body of Christ during the dispensation of grace to live in the heavenly places (Eph. 1:3, 2:6). We learn by imitation. Often it is not so much what is taught that changes our lives, but what is <u>caught</u>. <u>Paul's life was a sermon</u>. He did not want to make a name for himself, but to proclaim and glorify Him who saved his soul from hell and gave him eternal life. He always gave God all the glory. He came to give them the gospel and to build them up in their faith. <u>Paul wants them to remember what he did among them so they can do the same</u>. They did a work of faith, labour of love, and patience of hope because Paul did. Since it was Christ doing the work in and through Paul (and in us and through us) Christ will have all the glory for what was accomplished.]

Christ gave Paul the privilege to be "put in trust with the gospel" (1 Tim. 1:11). Paul committed the gospel to Timothy and expected him to commit it to faithful men (2 Tim. 2:2). Stewards of the mysteries are to be faithful (1 Cor. 4:1-2). Part of the work of the church is to make sure that accurate copies are made of God's word (1 Tim. 3:15, 5:17). The central theme of the Bible is knowing God, to understand His wisdom in what says and does. Christ, in His earthly ministry, said that whoever has spiritual ears to understand His word will receive more (Luke 8:18). It is on the basis of the quality of our work that we will be evaluated at the Judgment Seat of Christ (2 Cor. 5:10). We show God we love Him by reading and studying His word.

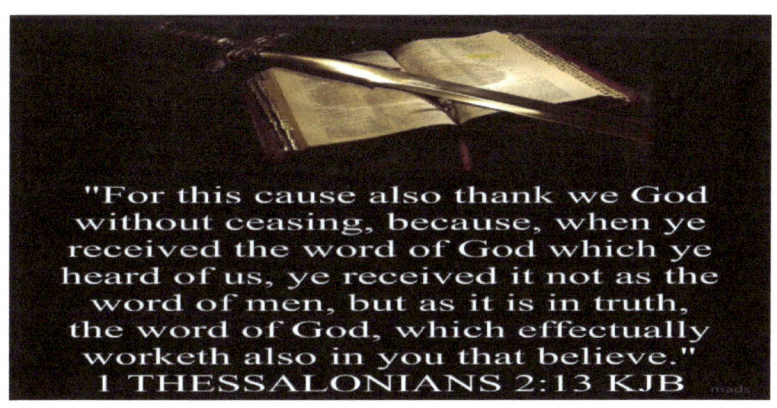

Mother ❤️

Father retires at 60,
But Mother never retires
She works for her Husband
She works for her Children
She looks after her Grand children
She looks after everyone
Everyone retires
But Mother never retires

One Year Extension of Mercy for Israel

Although the prophetic clock according to Daniel's timeline stopped on Palm Sunday, Israel received a bonus year of mercy from God. In addition to asking the Father to forgive them because of their ignorance while on the cross, Jesus had also pleaded with the Father to give His people one more year to repent and receive Him as their Messiah. "A certain *man* [God the Father] had a fig tree planted in his vineyard; and he came and sought fruit [faith] thereon, and found none. Then said he [God the Father] unto the dresser of his vineyard [God the Son], Behold, these three years I come seeking fruit on this fig tree [Israel], and find none: cut it down; why cumbereth it the ground? And he [the Son] answering said unto him, Lord, let it alone this year also [give Israel one more year], till I shall dig about it, and dung [fertilize by the power of the Holy Spirit] *it*: And if it bear fruit, *well*: and if not, *then* after that thou shalt cut it down [cut off Israel for a season]" (Luke 13:6-9).

But Peter and the disciples of Christ, the little remnant (the little flock) did have faith in Him, so the kingdom was taken from the unbelieving nation of Israel and given to the remnant of believing Israel. "Therefore say I [Jesus] unto you [the religious leaders of the nation of Israel], The kingdom of God shall be taken from you, and given to a nation [the little flock] bringing forth the fruits [faith] thereof" (Matthew 21:43).

The little flock (believing remnant) received the kingdom, "Fear not, little flock; for it is your Father's good pleasure to give you the kingdom" (Luke 12:32).

When Peter asked Jesus what he would receive for his faithfulness Jesus answered "Verily I say unto you, That ye which have followed me, in the regeneration [when the Earth is regenerated in the millennium] when the Son of man shall sit in the throne of his glory, ye [the twelve Apostles] also shall sit upon twelve thrones, judging the twelve tribes of Israel" (Matthew 19:28).

Three times a year Israel was to keep a feast to the LORD. These feasts are a picture of God's plan to redeem them. Christ has already fulfilled Passover, Unleavened Bread, and Firstfruits (held in Abib, the first month). The next, Pentecost (50 days later) was fulfilled in Acts 2. The Feast of Trumpets, Day of Atonement, and Feast of Tabernacles (in the 7th month) will be fulfilled when Israel is gathered into their land, the nation is forgiven, and Messiah rules and lives with them. The final feasts, as we will learn, have been postponed.

1 Thessalonians Chapter 3 A Model brother (Timothy).
3:1-5 Why Paul sent Timothy.
3:6-8 Timothy's good report.
3:9-13 Paul's prayer for them.

The Thessalonians were a model church because they had a model minister. In this chapter we will learn about the model brother. But most of all we will learn that believers are to be a channel or vessel of blessing to others. We are to let Christ live through us. But unless we understand the Bible by "rightly dividing the word of truth" (2 Tim. 2:15), we will not be useful sons and daughters of God or channels of blessing. We will also look at the mystery of godliness in 1 Tim. 3:16.

This is why it is really important to understand the "mystery." In order to know (1) the gospel that saves us (1 Cor. 15:3, 4), (2) who our apostle is (Paul, Rom. 11:13), (3) when the body of Christ and the dispensation of grace began (Acts 9), (4) which scriptures are "to" and "about" us (Romans to Philemon), (5) that the rest of the Bible is for our learning (Rom. 15:4), (6) the sound doctrine to the Church, the body of Christ, and (7) how to serve God in accordance to that doctrine. When I was a mixer, mixing Peter and Paul, I had little if any fruit.

In the past (Ex. 19:5, 6) and in the future (Isa 61:6-8) God will use the nation of Israel as a channel of blessing to the world. Today each individual member of the body of Christ is to be a channel of blessing to the world. Sometimes we can get a clog or kink in being a channel of blessing. The sinful flesh is very self-centered. Today we will learn how to unclog and unkink so we can be channels of blessing.

The good thing about Satan's hindrance was that it **forced apostle Paul to write this letter**. It edifies and builds us up in our understanding and faith. These inspired words of Christ from heaven have blessed people for nearly 2,000 years. The phrase "your faith" appears five times in this chapter (3:2, 3:5, 3:6, 3:7, 3:10). Paul was clearly concerned about their faith and wanted them to stand strong in it. Each of the chapters in First Thessalonians ends with a reference to the Rapture. In this chapter, it is in relation to **Christ's presentation of the body of Christ to the Father.** The Rapture was a mystery "behold, I shew you a mystery" (1 Cor. 15:51) which was not revealed anywhere in the Bible until God revealed it to Paul. Notice that whenever Paul writes about the Rapture he doesn't quote Old Testament scripture because the Rapture was not prophesied, but new revelation given by the risen, glorified Lord Jesus Christ to him. **The day of Christ encompasses three events:** (1) the Rapture, (2) the Judgment Seat of Christ, and (3) Christ's presentation of the body of Christ to the Father.

3:1 Wherefore when <u>we could no longer forbear, we thought it good to be left at Athens alone; 2 And sent Timotheus, our brother, and minister of God, and our fellowlabourer in the gospel of Christ, to establish you, and to comfort</u> you concerning <u>your faith</u>: [By "your faith" Paul means is your faith in "the faith" we preach (Christ's doctrine through Paul). Paul uses the phrase "the faith" 30 times in his other letters. It is interesting how he uses the Phrase in 2 Cor. 13:5. When Paul could no longer endure the suspense of how the Thessalonians were doing, the apostles came up with a plan to go around Satan's hindrance of Paul himself seeing the new saints. Paul sent Timotheus, <u>a model brother</u>, <u>a minister of God</u>, and their <u>fellowlabourer in the gospel of Christ</u> to establish and comfort them concerning their faith. Meanwhile, Paul stayed in Athens alone. Paul knew he could trust Timothy to remind them of the doctrine Christ had given him. Timothy would reinforce what Paul had taught them so far. Timothy would be a channel of blessing to them. Timothy was saved on Paul's first apostolic journey (Acts 14:6,7). Timothy was "well reported of the brethren that were at Lystra" (Acts 16:1-3). Paul picked Timothy to minister with him. Paul gave his estimation of Timothy in his letter to the Philippians. "But I trust in the Lord Jesus to send Timotheus shortly unto you, that I also may be of good comfort, when I know your state. For I have no man likeminded, who will naturally care for your state. For all seek their own, not the things which are Jesus Christ's. But ye know the proof of him, that, as a son with the father, he hath served with me in the gospel" (Phil. 2:19-24). <u>Timothy and Silas willingly traveled two hundred miles there and the same distance back to help the Thessalonians</u>. God is working in us (Eph. 2:10) to make us willing servants, channels of blessings. We are to be mature adult sons and daughters who serve God willingly, doing what pleases Him. <u>The phrase "your faith" appears five times in this chapter</u> (3:2, 3:5, 3:6, 3:7, 3:10). Paul was clearly concerned about their faith and wanted them to stand strong in it. How did Paul establish them in the faith? He sent them a brother (3:1, 2); he wrote them a letter (3:3, 4); he prayed for them (3:5-10); and he reminded them of Christ's return (3:11-13). Once we are saved, we can do the same for them, as channels or vessels of blessing of His love. I am blessed that several of my friends have understood the mystery, but many more have been hard-hearted, and unteachable.] **3 That no man should be <u>moved by these afflictions: for yourselves know that we are appointed thereunto.</u>** [Paul had taught them the doctrine of suffering. Satan is against all who are "in Christ." Satan wants to move believers away from Paul's sound doctrine. All believers are appointed to afflictions, but the body of Christ is not appointed to wrath (5:9). Paul had personally suffered at the hands of many of those evil men who were now persecuting the Thessalonians. <u>Their persecution and affliction should NOT move them away from Pauline truth</u>. True believers "are appointed there unto" (3:3). The Galatians had been moved away from the faith

65

that Paul had delivered to them. Paul told the Galatians, "I marvel that ye are so soon removed from him [Christ through Paul] that called you into the grace of Christ unto another gospel: Which is not another; but there be some that trouble you, and would pervert the gospel of Christ" (Gal. 1:6, 7). The Galatians had been seduced into believing that although they were saved by faith they must keep the law in order to live the Christian life. But we are saved by faith and should live the same way, by faith. "For we walk by faith, not by sight" (2 Cor. 5:7). We walk the same way as we were saved, by faith. We live by believing the doctrine that Christ revealed to Paul as recorded in Romans to Philemon. We believe "from the heart that form of doctrine which was delivered you" (Rom. 6:17). Christ's doctrine to us through Paul will work in us when we understand it. When we follow Paul's doctrine we are not under the law. The law makes the dead sinful flesh in us come alive again. "But sin, that it might appear sin, working death in me by that which is good; that sin by the commandment might become exceeding sinful" (Rom. 7:13). The sinful flesh can clog or kink us up so the Spirit of Jesus can't flow through us. Man is naturally self-centered. Paul said, "sin dwelleth in me" (Rom. 7:17, 18). How do we unclog and unkink so we can be a channel of blessing? Although we are dead to sin (Rom. 6:2) and dead to the law (Rom. 7:4), our sinful flesh which is in our mortal bodies will only stay dead if we walk in the Spirit (Rom. 8:1-4; Gal. 5:16-18). Paul discovered that there was a law (a fact, reality, or constant rule) that "evil is present with me" (Rom. 7:21). Not a law like the law of Moses, but a law as in the law of gravity. Paul called it "the body of the sins of the flesh" (Col. 2:11). There is a way to be free of this "law, reality, and fact" and that is to walk in the Spirit by faith. When we understand our identity in Christ we can function correctly. We were baptized into His death (Rom. 6:3, 4) and raised in newness of life, and alive unto God (Rom. 6:11). We can have Christ's life flowing through us; His words are spiritual life. "There is therefore now no condemnation to them which are in Christ Jesus, who walk not after the flesh, but after the Spirit. For the law of the Spirit of life in Christ Jesus hath made me free from the law of sin and death" (Rom. 8:1, 2). Here is the crux: "For what the law could not do, in that it was weak through the flesh, [our flesh was too weak to keep the law] God sending his own Son in the likeness of sinful flesh, and for sin, condemned sin in the flesh" (Rom. 8:3). But Christ succeeded; He was able to keep the law perfectly. Christ condemned our sin nature on the cross. "Sins" are the wrong things we do. "Sin" is our sin nature. Christ was "made sin for us," destroying or crucifying our sin nature in His flesh on the cross, so that we could have His righteousness imputed to us (2 Cor. 5:21). Christ went through with the cross, not because He needed to, but because we needed Him to. Romans is about the righteousness of God, and how God can justify a sinner and make him acceptable and righteous while he continues to sin. Do we continue to sin after salvation? Yes, if people think they are going to be sinless after salvation, they can get discouraged. But we can be sinless if we walk in the Spirit. Christ came through the sacrificial system apart from the law (Rom. 3:21, 22). This is how God solved our sin problem. Every person has sinned. "For *there is* not a just man upon earth, that doeth good, and sinneth not" (Eccl. 7:20). "For all have sinned, and come short of the glory of God" (Rom. 3:23). But we are justified freely by the faith of Christ if we believe the good news that God has said we need to believe (1 Cor. 15:3, 4). After the cross, the Father declared the Old Testament (those saints that died before the cross) righteous because of Christ's sacrifice (Rom. 3:24, 25). The Father can remain just and justify believers in mystery because at salvation the righteousness of Christ was imputed to us (Rom. 3:26, 4:5, 23-25, 5:10; 2 Cor. 5:21). The Father loves His Son, and we are in Him. We become sons of God by having the Spirit of His Son in us. Now with Christ's life working in and through us, we can be effective sons of God. Once we understand the mystery we are not to be moved from that truth. When I was a mixer, mixing Peter and Paul I had little if any fruit. Paul was not moved from preaching and teaching the truth Christ gave him. Paul stayed the course, he stood fast until he was martyred. He told the Ephesian elders that he wanted to reach his kinsmen. "But none of these things move me, neither count I my life dear unto myself, so that I might finish my course with joy, and the ministry, which I have received of the Lord Jesus, to testify the gospel of the grace of God" (Acts 20:24). At the end of his life Paul said, "I have fought a good fight, I have finished my course, I have kept the faith: Henceforth there is laid up for me a crown of righteousness, which the Lord, the righteous judge, shall give me at that day: and not to me only, but unto all them also that love his appearing" (2 Tim. 4:7, 8). In this case, I believe "his appearing" refers to Christ's appearing to Paul on the road to Damascus. Christ's next glorious appearing will be at the Rapture. "Looking for that blessed hope, and the glorious appearing of the great God and our Saviour Jesus Christ" (Titus 2:13). The body of Christ (and the dispensation of grace) began when Christ appeared to Paul and will end when Christ appears in the air to catch us up. "That thou keep *this* commandment without spot, unrebukeable, until the appearing of our Lord Jesus Christ" (1 Tim. 6:14). Christ's "two appearings" are like two book ends with the mystery of the body of Christ being formed in the dispensation of grace in between the two appearings. The adversary will try to move believers from "the faith." Therefore, until the Rapture we are to be "stedfast, unmoveable, always abounding in the work of the Lord" (1 Cor. 15:58).] **4 For verily, when we were with you, we told you before that we should suffer tribulation; even as it came to pass, and ye know.** [Paul had told them when he was with them to expect trouble, suffering, and persecution, which had now come to pass. He had told them that they would suffer tribulation, but not "the Tribulation." Paul and the Thessalonians had both suffered afflictions from the unbelievers. They (and we) are living in the "present evil world" (Gal. 1:4) surrounded by godless men and women. "Yea, and all that will live godly in Christ Jesus shall suffer persecution" (2 Tim. 3:12). Jesus told Ananias, "how great things he must suffer for my name's sake" (Acts 9:16). In Lystra, Paul had healed a man lame in his feet from his mother's womb, and this miracle caused the idol-worshipping Gentiles to want to worship Paul and Barnabas. But when the unbelieving Jews came from Antioch of Pisidia and Iconium they convinced these same people, who wanted to worship them in one moment, to want to stone Paul in the next moment. But God was not finished with Paul, and God revived him from death (Acts 14:19-22).] **5 For this cause, when I could no longer forbear, I sent to know your faith, lest by some means the tempter have tempted you, and our labour be in vain.** [Paul wanted to know "your faith" if they were following Paul's doctrine. When Paul could no longer stand the suspense of how their faith was holding up in the face of strong persecution. Paul got around the tempter's (Satan) hindrance of him by sending brother Timothy and Silas (Acts 18:5) to find out if the tempter had tempted them away from the truth with his lies, so that all their labor to minister to them would be useless.] **6 But now when Timotheus came from you unto us, and brought us good tidings of your faith and charity, and that ye have good remembrance of us always, desiring greatly to see us, as we also to see you:** [Timothy brought (good tidings or glad tidings) or good news. They had NOT been tempted to depart from the truth, so they could avoid persecution. Their faith and love had endured the temptations. Their steadfastness and tender regard for the apostle prompted Paul to write this touching and intimate letter in which he praises them for standing firm in the faith. His heart was overflowing with love and, joy, and pride for how the Thessalonians received the word of God and were holding up under persecution. Paul's heart was warmed and comforted when he heard that the Thessalonians wanted to see him again. He longed to see them, too. It was a young church but they believed that Christ was speaking to them through Paul. In effect they told Timothy, "please tell Paul that as soon as he can to please return and teach us again; for we are hungry for more." They were doing fantastic in what they had taught them. But Paul wants to teach them more since his ministry to them was cut short. They were not deserting or departing from Paul. This was not the response Paul had from the Corinthians or the Galatians. He told the Corinthians, "I will very gladly spend and be spent for you; though the more abundantly I love you, the less I be loved" (2 Cor. 12:15). He said to the Galatians, "I am afraid of you, lest I have bestowed upon you labour in vain" (Gal. 4:11). The Thessalonians proved their faith by their charity toward others. Love is caring about others; while charity is Christ's love in us and through us, among other believers. "And above all these things put on charity, which is the bond of perfectness" (Col. 3:14). Charity is selfless sacrificial benevolence toward others. "Now the end of the commandment is charity out of a pure heart, and of a good conscience, and of faith unfeigned" (1 Tim. 1:5). Christ through Paul loved them. A pure, genuine, true Pauline understanding of the Bible will naturally produce charity and other fruit of the Spirit of Jesus Christ (Gal. 5:22, 23). Charity leads us to value (esteem) other members in the body of Christ.] **7 Therefore, brethren, we were comforted over you in all our affliction and distress by your faith:** [The apostles were comforted that despite their afflictions, they still believed the doctrine they taught them. The apostles' afflictions were worth it and they didn't have to be distressed about their faith because it was still going strong. Their worry was alleviated because the Thessalonians were enduring their afflictions. God wants obedience without compromise. We are not to follow the path of least resistance (that is a worldly idea from the Devil). We are to stand for the truth even in the midst of persecution. Jesus did not take the easy way out. Paul suffered greatly to give us the gospel. "Who now rejoice in my sufferings for you, and fill up that which is behind of the afflictions of Christ in my flesh for his body's sake, which is the church" (Col. 1:24). Paul rejoiced in his sufferings because he was happy to serve Christ for the sake of His people. In Thessalonica, Paul had been smuggled out of Jason's house and brought to Berea. Later on in Ephesus, he had to leave town because the mob wanted to tear him apart in their uproar instigated by the silver and copper idol makers. The ministry Paul had built over three years in Ephesus came to an abrupt end. We are to "endure hardness as a good soldier of Jesus Christ" (2 Tim. 2:3), not to take the easy way out.] **8 For now we live, if ye stand fast in the Lord.** [Paul said in effect, "It would kill us if you didn't stand fast in your faith. But now we can live if you stand fast in the Lord." It gave Paul a surge of life (a giant shot in the arm) to hear that the young church was standing firm in the faith he delivered unto them in the middle of persecution. When we know who we are in Christ, that we are "complete in him" (Col. 2:10), then we can stand fast in the Lord. We are to have faith in what Christ preached to the body of Christ through Paul, not what Christ preached in His earthly ministry to Israel as recorded in Matthew, Mark, Luke, and John (Rom. 15:8). In the past (Ex. 19:5, 6) and in the future (Isa 61:6-8) God will use the nation of Israel as a channel of blessing to the world. The believing remnant of Israel will be a channel of blessing, good news and a kingdom of priests to the Gentiles (Zech. 8:13). The believing remnant will live in dependence of Christ. Today, each individual member of the body of Christ is to be a channel of blessing to the world).] **9 For what thanks can we render to God again for you, for all the joy wherewith we joy for your sakes before our God; 10 Night and day praying exceedingly that we might see your face, and might perfect that which is lacking in your faith? 11 Now God himself and our Father, and our Lord Jesus Christ, direct our way unto you.** [They were so relieved and overjoyed with gratitude to God for how well these believers were doing in the faith. They prayed and thanked God so many times for them they didn't know what else they could thank God for. We talk to God about His people, then we talk to His people about God. They prayed night and day. Paul had taught them many things and may have had to leave them abruptly without having time to finish teaching them all that he wanted them to know. Paul wanted to share more of the progressive revelation he was constantly receiving from the Lord Jesus Christ concerning the mystery. Paul wants to "perfect that which is lacking in your faith" (3:10). Paul longed to return and teach them more. The apostles were praying exceedingly that the God the Father and our Lord Jesus Christ would guide them back to them.] **12 And the Lord make you to increase and abound in love one toward another, and toward all men, even as we do toward you:** [Although their standing is perfect before God, Paul wants their state to match their standing. Their practice is to line up with their position in Christ. He prays that the Lord would make them to increase and abound in love one toward another and to all men, even as Paul and his co-workers have loved them. They (and we) are to be channels or conduits of Christ's love to all men, just as the apostles were to the Thessalonians. "Thou shalt love they neighbor as thyself. Love worketh no ill to his neighbor: therefore love is the fulfilling of the law" (Rom. 13:9, 10). Love seeks the highest good for another, their greatest welfare. Paul has been encouraging them to have faith, love, and hope the hallmarks of the Christian faith (1 Cor. 13:13).] **13 To the end he may stablish your hearts unblameable in holiness before God, even our Father, at the coming of our Lord Jesus Christ with all his saints.** ["Establish" means to start building something solid; while "stablish" means to make what has been established, stable. If they follow Christ's doctrine to them through Paul then they will be able to be stable, unblameable and holy at His coming (2:10). When we understand the mystery by rightly dividing the word of truth then the doctrine will work in us to produce something of value at the Judgment Seat of Christ. "And, having made peace through the blood of his cross, by him to reconcile all things unto himself; by him, I *say*, whether they be things in earth, or things in heaven. And you that were some time alienated and enemies in your mind by wicked works, yet now hath he reconciled in the body of his flesh through death, to present you holy and unblameable and unreproveable in his sight: If ye continue in the faith grounded and settled, and *be* not moved away from the hope of the gospel, which ye have heard, *and* which was preached to every creature which is under heaven; whereof I Paul am made a minister" (Col. 1:21-23). We are still saved if we have believed the gospel, but our service will be shipwreck or "castaway" (1 Cor. 9:27) if we do not continue in Paul's doctrine. The Lord Jesus Christ will bring the body of Christ before God the Father and will present their (and our) "hearts unblameable in holiness before God, even our Father, at the coming of our

Lord Jesus Christ." The day of Christ includes three events: (1) the Rapture, (2) the Judgment Seat of Christ (JSC), and (3) then Christ's presentation of the body of Christ to the Father. <u>This verse is talking about Christ presenting us to the Father</u>. It is also true that "them which sleep in Jesus will God bring with him" (1 Thess. 4:14) when the Lord Jesus Christ comes "in the clouds" (1 Thess. 4:17) at the Rapture. The Judgment Seat of Christ for service (Rom. 14:10; 1 Cor. 3:10-16; 2 Cor. 5:10) <u>is after the Rapture</u>. This life is the only opportunity we have that is going to count for a reward there. Any blemishes or false doctrine will be burnt off of the believers there (1 Cor. 3:12-15). The fire of the eyes of Jesus Christ and the fire of the word of God (Jer. 23:29; Rev. 1:14) will burn off the wood, hay, and stubble (false doctrine and work done with false motives). After we are purified, then Christ will present the "glorious church" to the Father (1 Thess. 3:13; Col. 1:22). It will be "holy and without blemish" (Eph. 5:27).

Upon salvation we receive the holy Spirit. It is the life of Jesus in us (2 Cor. 4:7, 10, 11; Gal. 2:20). His life in us helps us to be sanctified as we nourish our inner man with sound doctrine. The holy Spirit in us needs to be fed the word of God rightly divided. Faith comes by hearing the word of God (Rom. 10:17). We can pray for God to increase our faith, but it isn't going to happen unless we increase our time studying and understanding God's word. There is no substitute for a consistent prayer life and study of God's word. <u>We counter false doctrine with true doctrine. This is how Satan's power is defeated and believers become stable.</u> A believer who is ignorant of the Bible rightly divided is prey to every wind of doctrine and will not be established in the Lord (Eph. 4:11-16). A mind void of God's words will be filled with Satan's lies. Not only do we need to present our bodies a living sacrifice for Christ to live through, but we need to "renew" (Rom. 12:1, 2) or reprogram our minds daily with God's word. God is not working physically in our lives, but spiritually. "For it is God which worketh in you both to will and to do of his good pleasure" (Phil. 2:13). The holy Spirit keeps us and continues His work in us until "the day of Christ" (Phil. 1:10, 2:16). We will rejoice in heaven on that day. Paul will tell believers at the end of this letter that he wants "the very <u>God of peace</u> sanctify you wholly; and *I pray God* your whole <u>spirit and soul and body</u> be <u>preserved blameless</u> unto <u>the coming of our Lord Jesus Christ</u>" (5:23). If we walk in the Spirit, then we will be blameless and useful channels of blessings with Christ living in and through us to others. <u>I believe at the JSOC many of us will be sad that we did not do more for God, that we were not as rich in rewards or in our financial support of God's work as we could have been. We are to do His will</u> (1 Tim. 2:4), share Paul's gospel, and "to make all men see what is the fellowship of the mystery, which from the beginning of the world hath been hid in God, who created all things by Jesus Christ" (Eph.3:9).

What is the mystery of godliness? Godliness is God living His life through the believer. "And without controversy great is the mystery of godliness: God was manifest in the flesh [Jesus Christ is manifest in the believer], justified in the Spirit [the life and righteousness of Jesus in the believer justifies the believer], seen of angels [the angels are watching us (Eph. 3:10)], preached unto the Gentiles [Jesus was preached to the Gentiles in the mystery], believed on in the world [in the world those who believe 1 Cor. 15:3, 4 are saved], received up into glory [at the Rapture the body of Christ will be received up into glory]" (1 Tim. 3:16). Jesus died for us, so He could give His life to us, so He could live His life through us. Jesus plus nothing equals everything. He is our hope.]

How can we be unblameable in holiness before God? We have His imputed righteousness, His Spirit, and His word specifically to us, and all the Bible.

The great war: our dead flesh still in our mortal body is still self-centered. But the word of God will do the work of God by His Spirit in us as we understand and believe His words to us through His (and our) apostle Paul.

What the Old Testament Prophets Saw

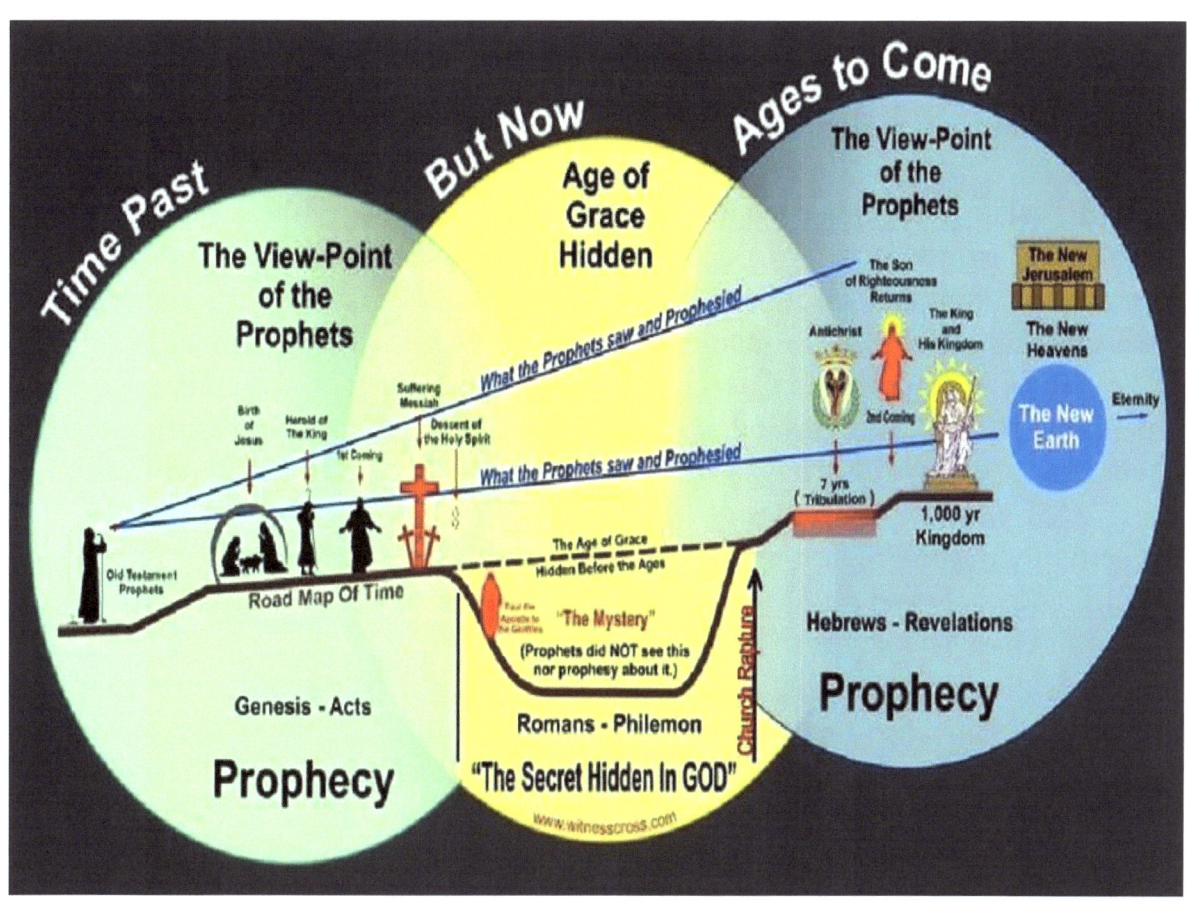

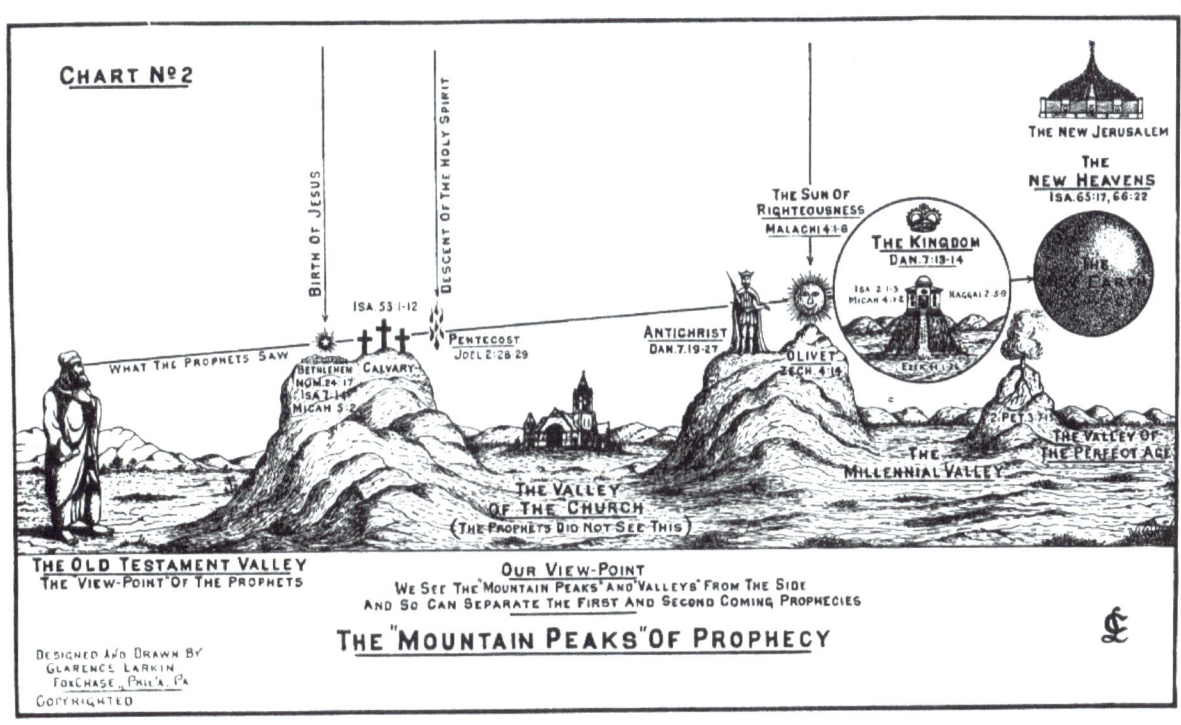

1 Thessalonians Chapter 4 A Model Walk and the Rapture
4:1-8 Walk in holiness.
4:9, 10 Walk in love.
4:11, 12 Walk in honesty.
4:13-18 Walk in hope.

The Old Testament prophets could see events associated with the First and Second Coming of Christ, His sufferings and His glory (1 Peter 1:10, 11). But the prophets did not know anything about the Church, the body of Christ. Christ's sudden return a year or so after the cross to save Saul of Tarsus was un-prophesied and Christ's sudden return to Rapture the Church is un-prophesied. In fact, the entire dispensation of the grace of God, when God is forming the body of Christ to live in heaven was a mystery that has lasted for nearly 2,000 years was un-prophesied.

The certainty of the Pre-Tribulation rapture becomes obvious when we understand the difference between prophecy and mystery. We need to know both, all the counsel of God. The key is to know that the body of Christ began in Acts 9 with Paul's salvation on the road to Damascus, not in Acts 2. The opportunity to live forever as a member of the body of Christ ends with the Rapture. Anyone who has believed the good news that Paul preached will be going up (1 Cor. 15:3, 4).

The word "Rapture" comes from the Latin Vulgate Bible word for "caught up" which is "rapiemur." The Greek word for "caught up" is "harpozo."

Chapters 1-3 are more doctrinal, while chapters 4 and 5 are practical application concerning the believers walk.

Paul disclosed to the Thessalonians the three main tenants of our faith:
Justification = Salvation, having Christ's imputed righteousness and eternal life.
Sanctification = Spiritual growth resulting in reward at Christ's Judgment Seat.
Glorification = Our new bodies at the Rapture. Completely sinless eternal state.

In this chapter, Paul focuses on their sanctification (walk), and their glorification.

4:1 Furthermore then we beseech you, brethren, and exhort you by the Lord Jesus, that as ye have received of us how ye ought to walk and to please God, so ye would abound more and more. [Grace beseeches (begs or implore) and it does not command. They "exhort" or urge them "by the Lord Jesus" how they are to walk, both by word and by example (2:10). Paul had not only told them to "walk worthy of God" (2:12), but the apostles had also demonstrated (modeled) how they should walk (2:4, 10, 3:12). Paul has just said that the Lord will stabilize their hearts unblameable in holiness before God in heaven. By the apostles example they "received of us how you ought to walk" by following "our gospel" (1:5, 3:13, 4:1), Paul's doctrine. Their walk to please God should keep going and growing "abound more and more." The Lord wants our walk, life, or conduct to please God and continue to be copious or overflowing.] **2 For ye know what <u>commandments we gave you by the Lord Jesus</u>. 3 For this is <u>the will of God, even your sanctification, that ye should abstain from fornication</u>:** [These commandments were <u>by the Lord Jesus, not by men</u>. The "will of God, even your sanctification" to grow and mature in the faith and to abstain from fornication. Fornication is two-fold: both spiritual and physical. They are to be pure doctrinally, spiritually, and physically. They are to abstain from spiritual idolatry, the idol worship they came out of (1:9) and the pagan immorality that they had been delivered from, which was then occurring around them. Idolatry and immorality have been prevalent throughout the ages and it still is today. The sanctity of marriage is upheld by abstaining from fornication. Another reason Paul warned the Thessalonians to abstain from fornication was that James had asked him to. "And as they went through the cities, <u>they delivered them the decrees for to keep, that were ordained of the apostles and elders which were at Jerusalem</u>" (Acts 15:20-29, 16:4, 21:25).] **4 That every one of you should know how to possess his vessel in sanctification and honour;** [Sanctification means to be set apart for a purpose. Each individual is responsible to know how to possess his or her vessel so that it is set apart for the purpose of serving God and is used in a way that is <u>honorable</u>. We are to be conduits of the Lord's love (3:12, 13). "Walk in the Spirit, and ye shall not fulfil the lust of the flesh" (Gal. 5:16). How do we walk in the Spirit? We walk in the Spirit when we allow the sound doctrine God gave us through Paul to work effectually in us (2:13). "Holding fast the faithful word as he hath been taught, that he may be able by sound doctrine both to exhort and to convince the gainsayers" (Titus 1:9). We are to depart from false doctrine which is iniquity (2 Tim. 2:19, 20).] **5 <u>NOT in the lust of concupiscence, even as the Gentiles which know not God</u>: 6 That <u>no man go beyond and defraud his brother in any matter</u>: because that <u>the Lord is the avenger of all such</u>, as we also have <u>forewarned you and testified</u>. 7 For God hath <u>NOT called us unto uncleanness, but unto holiness</u>.** [Paul had warned them that the Lord is the Avenger of all such as defraud their brother. The Jews had forbidden Paul to speak to the Gentiles so they might be saved (2:16). The Thessalonians were surrounded by unbelievers that practiced "concupiscence" or sensual, sexual, lustful behaviors. <u>Believers are to lead a life of personal holiness</u>. We call what we do when no one but God is watching, character. Our bodies are the temple of Christ and we should not defile it by sex outside of marriage because then we sin against ourselves and God (1 Cor.

6:15-19). They are not to lust for idols or practice sensual sexual lust <u>like the lost Gentiles who "know not God."</u> Paul kept his body under subjection to his will (1 Cor. 9:26, 27). <u>No one should defraud someone else in "any matter;" their faith, or by stealing their husband or wife.</u> Because the Lord is the avenger of such and will hold everyone accountable for their own actions. God told Israel, "As I live, saith the Lord GOD, I have no pleasure in the death of the <u>wicked</u>; but that the wicked turn from his way and live: turn ye, turn ye from your evil ways; for why will ye die, O house of Israel?" (Ezek. 33:11). Likewise, <u>God has no delight in the death of the wicked in mystery.</u> Paul warned them that God's wrath would come upon them (unbelieving Jews and Gentiles) who hinder God's word from going forth so others can be saved (2:16). The apostles warned them ahead of time saying that God has not called them to <u>spiritual or physical uncleanness, but to walk in holiness.</u> Christ is holy. Our goal is to be like "Christ, according to the revelation of the mystery" (Rom. 16:25), but we will never be Christ (Eph. 4:13, 16, 21-24, 32).] **8 He therefore that despiseth, despiseth not man, but God, who hath also given unto us his holy Spirit.** [Therefore whoever despises to obey the Lord's commandments (4:3) apostle Paul gave them for how to live a holy life despises not man, but God. By an unworthy walk (wrong behavior) they despise God. Paul has mentioned the Holy Ghost (1:5, 6) twice and now the Holy Spirit once. They (and we) received the holy Spirit to help and teach us how to live holy lives. The word "Spirit" does not always refer to the Holy Ghost. Jesus (who was the only Person of the Godhead to put on human flesh) said, "God *is* a Spirit: and they that worship him must worship *him* in spirit and in truth" (John 4:24). The Holy Father is Spirit, the Son is Spirit, and the Holy Ghost is Spirit. When the King James Bible says the Holy Ghost it is referring specifically to the Holy Ghost, but when the Bible says "Spirit" then it could be referring to any one of the three Persons of the Godhead, and the context must help us decide which one. We find that the "Spirit" in the Bible is often the Spirit of Jesus Christ in the believer (Rom. 8:2). Therefore, sometimes the Spirit in us is Christ's, sometimes the Holy Ghost's and sometimes the Father's because all three live in us. <u>We become sons of God by having the Spirit of His Son in us. It is the work of God's holy Spirit that they are hindering.</u>] **9 But as touching <u>brotherly love ye need not that I write unto you: for ye yourselves are taught of God to love one another.</u> 10 And <u>indeed ye do it toward all the brethren which are in all Macedonia</u>: but we beseech you, brethren, <u>that ye increase more and more</u>;** [The Thessalonians were already demonstrating <u>brotherly love</u> (charity) among themselves and to others, so Paul had no need to write to them about that. They (and we) "are taught of God to love one another." Their "labour of love" was evident to all in Macedonia. Paul beseeches them to increase their work of charity more and more. <u>What is the most loving thing we can do for someone?</u> Yes, that is right, to share the gospel with others (1 Cor. 15:3, 4). God's word has the power to save souls and to help people to come to the knowledge of the truth. It is God's will "that all men be saved and to come to the knowledge of the truth" (1 Tim. 2:4). We live holy lives when we let the doctrine make us conduits of God's love and good news to the lost. We willingly present our bodies so the Spirit of Christ can do the work in and through us (Rom. 12:1, 2; Col. 1:27). "Christ liveth in me" (Gal. 2:20).] **11 And that ye study to be quiet, and to do your own business, and to work with your own hands, as we commanded you; 12 That ye may walk honestly toward them that are without, and that ye may have lack of nothing.** [Why does Paul say "study to be quiet"? One way to possess our vessels in sanctification and honor is to learn to tame our tongue. Paul is not saying don't share the gospel. We are to mind our own business and not be overly concerned with what other people are doing. We are not to be gossips. "Speak evil of no man" (Titus 3:2). Paul did not want them to be lazy busybodies. Everyone should provide for themselves, so they don't have to be "parasites" needing to live off of other people, by having others pay for them (2 Thess. 3:10-12). They had already commanded them to quietly mind their own business and to work with their own hands to provide for themselves when they were with them. In order to walk honestly toward those who are without Christ (the lost). This way they would not lack money to buy what they need and would be self-sufficient, taking personal responsibility. They would then be good examples and respectable Christian witnesses to the lost. Our witness would suffer if we had to ask others to pay for us.]

13 ¶ But I would not have you to be ignorant, brethren, concerning them which are asleep, that ye sorrow not, even as others which have no hope. [They are to walk in hope. The Thessalonians had been suffering severe persecution, some may have been killed as martyrs or died for other reasons (1:6, 3:2, 3). There were some at Thessalonica who were apprehensive about if their dead friends and family members in Christ would take part in the Rapture. Paul answers their question regarding their dead loved ones in Christ. The apostle comforts them concerning those believers who had died and instructs them concerning their own hope of the Lord's return. Those who are "asleep" refers to the dead in Christ (4:16). We suffer and are sad when a believer dies. We miss them. But, Paul does not want them to sorrow as those who have no hope of eternal life with God. Their bodies sleep but will awake at the Rapture. Paul did not want them to be ignorant concerning the hope of our Pre-Tribulation Rapture. Paul uses the term "ignorant" nine times in his letters. In each case, they were ignorant on some topic, so Paul helps them. The word Rapture comes from the Latin Vulgate Bible word for "caught up" which is "rapiemur." The Greek word for "caught up" is "harpozo." The Rapture is exclusively found in Paul's epistles. The Rapture was a mystery that Christ only revealed to Paul. This makes sense, since the entire dispensation of grace in which God is forming the body of Christ to live in the heavenly places was a mystery. "Behold, I shew you a mystery; We shall not all sleep, but we shall all be changed, In a moment, in the twinkling of an eye, at the last trump: for the trumpet shall sound, and the dead shall be raised incorruptible, and we shall be changed" (1 Cor. 15:51, 52). Notice that whenever Paul writes about the Rapture he doesn't quote Old Testament scripture because the Rapture was not prophesied, but new revelation given by the risen, glorified Lord Jesus Christ to him. The prophets saw Christ's First and Second Coming, His sufferings and His glory (1 Peter 1:10-12; Isa. 53:3, 60:1-3). But Paul preached what was "not made known to the sons of men" (Eph. 3:5) because it was not searchable in the scriptures. Paul preached the "unsearchable riches of Christ" (Eph. 3:8), "the mystery, which from the beginning of the world hath been hid in God" (Eph. 3:9). Why did God keep the mystery a secret? Because if Satan had known that Christ's death would allow the Father to give His Spirit to two groups of believers, he would not have allowed Christ to be crucified. Satan did not know that he lost both the earth and his place in heaven until he heard what Paul said. Paul said, "Howbeit we speak wisdom among them that are perfect: yet not the wisdom of this world, nor of the princes of this world, that come to nought: But we speak the wisdom of God in a mystery, even the hidden wisdom, which God ordained before the world unto our glory: Which none of the princes of this world knew: for had they known it, they would not have crucified the Lord of glory" (1 Cor. 2:6-8). Christ has two groups of believers: a prophesied group and an un-prophesied group to live in His kingdom consisting of two realms heaven and earth.

What about unbelievers what happens to them? In the past in prophecy, believers were gathered to their people by angels to Abraham's bosom, paradise (Luke 16:22, 23:43). The Bible tells us the horrible truth of what happens to unbelievers. "For what is the hope of the hypocrite, though he hath gained [riches], when God taketh away his soul? . . . This is the portion of a wicked man with God, and the heritage of oppressors, which they shall receive of the Almighty . . . The rich man shall lie down, but he shall not be gathered: he openeth his eyes [he opens the eyes of his soul], and he is not [he realizes he is not in his body]. Terrors take hold on him as waters [he feels like he is drowning], a tempest stealeth him away in the night. The east wind carrieth him away [a spiritual tempest or east wind blows his soul to hell], and he departeth: and as a storm hurleth him out of his place. For God shall cast upon him, and not spare: he would fain flee out of his hand [he would like to escape from God, being taken to hell where there is no exit but he can't]. Men shall clap their hands at him, and shall hiss him out of his place [he will receive cruel treatment by the others in hell]" (Job. 27:8, 13, 19-23). The pit will swallow him up and shut her mouth on him (Psa. 69:15). If someone is in prison they have the possibility of getting out, but no one is getting out of God's prison, which is hell. "Knowing, therefore the terror of the Lord, we persuade men" (2 Cor. 5:11). The justice of God demands that He judge sin. Most people are ignorant of the eternal danger they are in, therefore, in our walk, we try to help as many people as possible to be saved.] **14 For if we believe that Jesus died and rose again, even so them also which sleep in Jesus will God bring with him.** [This is another proof text that Jesus is God. Paul says that if we have believed that Jesus died and rose again, God will likewise (even so) bring with Him those which "sleep in Jesus" (died believing who Jesus was and what He did for them) when He comes for us. Jesus will bring with Him the souls and spirits of the believers when He comes for us. Paul is confident that to be absent from the body is to be present with Christ. "We are confident, *I say*, and willing rather to be absent from the body, and to be present with the Lord" (2 Cor. 5:8). "For to me to live is Christ, and to die is gain" (Phil. 1:21). Our "inner man" (Eph. 3:16) or "inward man" (Rom. 7:22, 2 Cor. 4:16) is composed of our spirit and soul. When we die our spirits and souls go to God and our bodies return to dust and the ground. "Then shall the dust return to the earth as it was: and the spirit shall return unto God who gave it" (Eccl. 12:7). When Rachel died in childbirth her soul separated from her body and departed but continued to exist. "And it came to pass, as her soul was in departing, (for she died)" (Gen. 35:18). We have the blessed assurance to know that we will be raised from the dead (resurrected) and given eternal life because Jesus was (Acts 17:31). It may be that God will use a grain (atom) of our mortal body to fashion our immortal bodies (1 Cor. 15:37). Paul said that "if Christ be not raised, your faith is vain; ye are yet in your sins . . . But now is Christ risen from the dead, and become the firstfruits of them that slept" (1 Cor. 15:17, 20). Since Christ died and rose we will also rise in a glorious body like His (Phil. 3:20, 21).] **15 For this we say unto you by the word of the Lord, that we which are alive and remain unto the coming of the Lord shall not prevent them which are asleep**. [Paul says that he and his coworkers are speaking to them "by the word of the Lord" (for the third time 4:1, 2, 15) not by something they made up or another man made up. The Lord revealed new information to Paul. The Rapture was a mystery given to Paul by the Lord Jesus Christ (1 Cor. 15:51). The Lord said, that those who are alive and remain on earth when He returns shall not "prevent," pre event (go before) or precede those who died believing in Him. Paul is not saying that he believes that he will be alive at the Rapture; his use of "we" refers to the body of Christ. Of course, Christ will bring apostle Paul's soul and spirit with him and he will rise and we will join him in the air, which is amazing to think about that.] **16 For the Lord himself shall descend from heaven with a shout, with the voice of the archangel, and with the trump of God: and the dead in Christ**

shall rise first: [The Lord Himself comes suddenly to rapidly escort us through enemy territory. The "heavens are not clean in his sight" (Job 15:15) or "the stars are not pure in his sight" (Job 25:5). "Stars" is another term for angels. In this case, Satan and his fallen angels (Job 4:18, Rev. 12:7). Michael the archangel is added protection. There are three separate types of sounds at the Rapture. (1) The Lord's shout is our resurrection call. We are waiting to hear our Saviour say, "come on up here!" Christ calls us as He did at the tomb of Lazarus, "he cried with a loud voice, Lazarus, come forth" (John 11:43). Graves will not be opened we will go through the ground or ceiling just like Christ went through doors, stones, and walls. (2) Michael is the archangel to Israel, and his voice will indicate to Israel and also the world, that the Rapture has occurred. It may be Israel's sign that God has restarted His prophetic program with them in which God intervenes physically on earth. The time of "Jacob's trouble" will be looming on the horizon (Jer. 30:7). "And at that time shall Michael stand up, the great prince which standeth for the children of thy people: and there shall be a time of trouble, such as never was since there was a nation even to that same time: and at that time thy people shall be delivered, every one that shall be found written in the book. And many of them that sleep in the dust of the earth shall awake, some to everlasting life, and some to shame and everlasting contempt. And they that be wise shall shine as the brightness of the firmament; and they that turn many to righteousness as the stars for ever and ever. But thou, O Daniel, shut up the words, and seal the book, even to the time of the end: many shall run to and fro, and knowledge shall be increased" (Dan. 12:1-4). But God told John to NOT seal the prophecy (Rev. 22:10). The tribulation is next, but the believing remnant shall be delivered through the Wrath. The resurrection of believing Israel and Gentile kingdom on earth saints whose names are written in the book of life will occur to live in the promised land. Others shall be resurrected to face the judgment of the lost (Acts 24:15). While on earth Jesus told Israel, "Marvel not at this: for the hour is coming, in the which all that are in the graves shall hear his voice, And shall come forth; they that have done good, unto the resurrection of life; and they that have done evil, unto the resurrection of damnation" (John 5:28, 29; Rev. 20:5, 6). The wise who believed what God said, will have eternal bodies in the kingdom on earth. They will turn many to have righteousness by sharing their faith. God wants Daniel to shut up the words until the time of the end when God will implement them. Apostle John was told, "seal not the sayings of the prophecy of this book" (Rev. 22:10). At that time, God will give Israel increased knowledge of what God's words to them mean. (3) The "trump of God." A "trump" is the sound a trumpet makes. In 1 Cor. 15:50, 51 Paul says, "Behold, I shew you a mystery; We shall not all sleep [be dead believers in the body of Christ when the Rapture happens], but we shall all be changed, in a moment in the twinkling of an eye, at the last trump [those alive when the Rapture occurs will be changed "at the last trump"], for the trumpet shall sound, and the dead in Christ shall be raised incorruptible, and we shall be changed." If there is a last trump, it stands to reason that there must have been a first trump. We find the first trump in 1 Thess. 4:16, "with the trump of God: and the dead in Christ shall rise first." There are two blasts, a first trumpet sound (4:16) and a last (1 Cor. 15:52). The trumpet sounds have to do with two events: the resurrection of the dead and living in the body of Christ. Christ's voice was like a trumpet in (Rev. 1:10, 11). We are waiting for a SHOUT of the Lord, the VOICE of the archangel, and the two TRUMP OF GOD.] **17 Then we which are alive and remain shall be caught up together with them in the clouds, to meet the Lord in the air: and so shall we ever be with the Lord. 18 Wherefore comfort one another with these words.** [Only when we understand the Scriptural truth of our Pre-Tribulation Rapture can we be truly comforted at the loss of loved ones and our own blessed hope. There are no signs that precede the Rapture; it is imminent and could occur at any time. We are patiently waiting and looking for the Lord Jesus Christ to appear in the air. "Looking for that blessed hope, and the glorious appearing of the great God and our Saviour Jesus Christ" (1:3; Titus 2:13). Every believer hopes to be alive when Christ returns to Rapture us. We are looking for the upper taker, not the undertaker. Those of us that do not have to experience death should be very grateful. Although Paul has said that for us death is like falling asleep and waking up in the presence of Christ. Regardless of whether we wake or sleep, we will meet Christ in the air. It is comforting to know we will have eternal life with the Lord. "And so shall we ever be with the Lord." Paul never tells us to prepare for the Tribulation, or that Christ's coming for us is anything to fear. We can comfort one another with the Lord's words to us because we have a joyful and "good hope" (2 Thess. 2:16). In the mouth of two or three witnesses that truth is established. Christ told us three times that we should be delivered from the "wrath to come" (Rom. 5:9; 1 Thess. 1:10, 5:9). "By and by, with joy increasing, And with gratitude unceasing, Lifted up with Christ forevermore to be, I will join the hosts there singing, In the anthem ever ringing, To the King of Love who ransomed me" from the hymn *He Ransomed Me* by J. W. Henderson (1916). The certainty of the Pre-Tribulation rapture becomes obvious when we understand the difference between prophecy and mystery. We need to know both, all the counsel of God. The key is to know that the body of Christ began in Acts 9 with Paul's salvation on the road to Damascus, not in Acts 2. Acts 2 is a continuation of Christ's earthly ministry (as recorded in Matthew, Mark, Luke, and John), when mostly Jewish believers are added to the little flock of kingdom on earth believers (Luke 12:33; Acts 2:41, 47, 5:14). The Rapture will be a secret meeting, Christ's coming will not be seen or heard by unbelievers, but some may see a light high in the sky. Just like Paul's companions did not hear the voice or see Jesus, but only saw the light when Christ appeared to Paul on the road to Damascus in Acts 9. "And they that were with me saw indeed the light, and were afraid; but they heard not the voice of him that spake to me . . . God of our fathers hath chosen thee, that thou shouldest know his will, and see that Just One, and shouldest hear the voice of his mouth (Acts 22:9, 14). Only members of the body of Christ will hear His resurrection call. *Notice that Christ does not come all the way down to earth but meets us in the air in the clouds of the first heaven. The clouds in the stratosphere are about 20,000 miles up, but the highest clouds are about 76,000 to 85,000 miles high in the mesosphere. Christ will escort us safely through the second heaven, into the third heaven. The graves will not be disturbed because our glorious bodies will go through the ground and ceilings, just like Christ after His resurrection went through a stone and closed doors (John 20:26).]

1 Thessalonians 4:16 For the Lord himself shall descend from heaven with a shout, with the voice of the archangel, and with the trump of God: and the dead in Christ shall rise first:
1 Thessalonians 4:17 Then we which are alive and remain shall be caught up together with them in the clouds, to meet the Lord in the air: and so shall we ever be with the Lord.
1 Thessalonians 4:18 Wherefore comfort one another with these words.

A first and a last "trump" at the Rapture. The "trump of God." A "trump" is the sound a trumpet makes. In 1 Cor. 15:50, 51 Paul says, "Behold, I shew you a mystery; We shall not all sleep [be dead believers in the body of Christ when the Rapture happens], but we shall all be changed, in a moment in the twinkling of an eye, at the last trump [those alive when the Rapture occurs will be changed "at the last trump"], for the trumpet shall sound, and the dead in Christ shall be raised incorruptible, and we shall be changed." If there is A LAST TRUMP, it stands to reason that there must have been A FIRST TRUMP. We find the first trump in 1 Thess. 4:16, "with the trump of God: and the dead in Christ shall rise first." There are two blasts, a first trumpet sound (4:16) and a last (1 Cor. 15:52). The trumpet sounds have to do with two events: the resurrection of the dead and living in the body of Christ. Christ's voice was like a trumpet in (Rev.1:10, 11).

Detail Drawing of the Three Sounds at the Rapture
(Notice the timing and events of the first and last trumpet blasts.)

The Rapture was a Mystery given to Apostle Paul

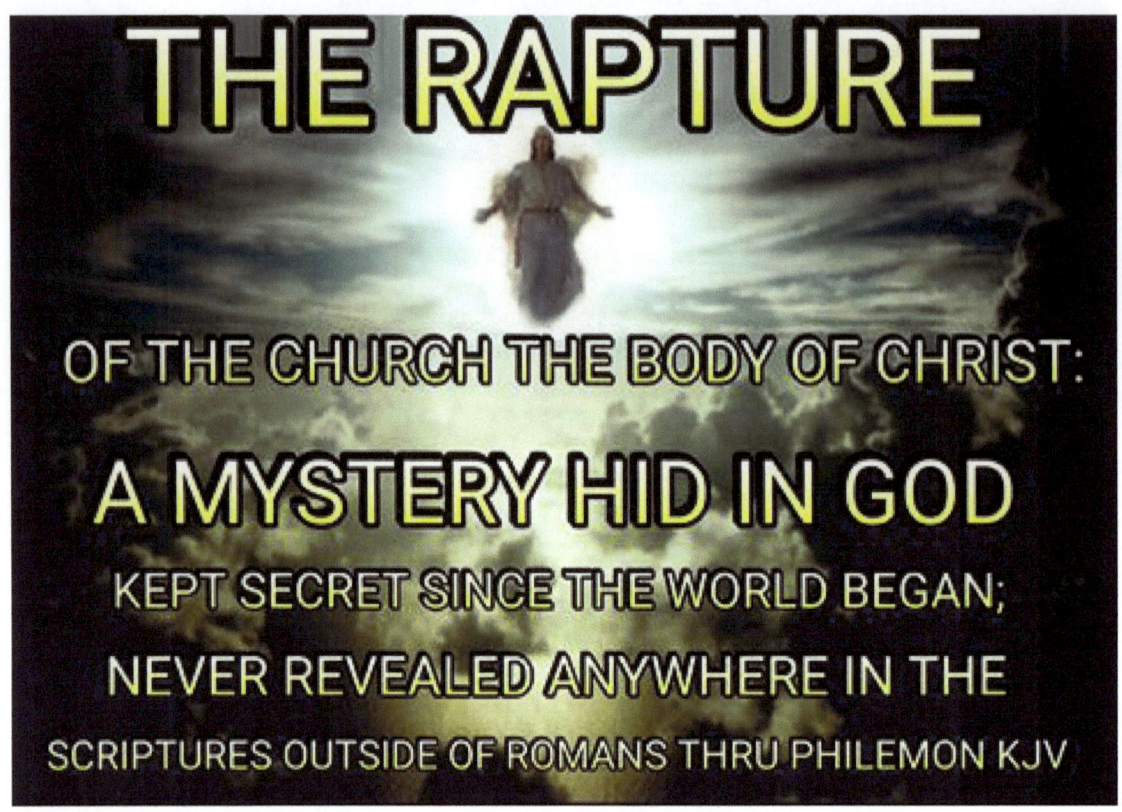

Christ is our hope as He comes to meet us in the air.

Rapture (Mystery)
An un-prophesied mystery only revealed to Paul (1 Cor. 15:51)
Before the Tribulation (Rom. 5:9; 1 Thess. 1:10, 5:9)
Not in conjunction with a battle
Christ comes with "them also which sleep in Jesus" (1 Thess. 4:14)
Christ comes in the air (1 Thess. 4:17)
Imminent not preceded by signs, times or seasons
We wait (Rom. 8:23; 1 Cor. 1:7; Phil. 3:20, 21; 1 Thess. 1:10; 2 Thess. 3:5).
Gathered and accompanied by Christ Himself (1 Thess. 4:16; 2 Thess. 2:1)
An event accompanied by the voice of an archangel (1 Thess. 4:16)
Those taken, or "caught up" are believers (Eph. 1:13, 14; 1 Thess. 4:16, 17).
Quick exit "in the twinkling of an eye" (1 Cor. 15:52)
Christ returns to heaven with the Church (1 Thess. 4:17)
Next is the Judgment Seat of Christ for service (2 Cor. 5:10)
We shall appear with Christ in glory (Col. 3:4; 1 Thess. 3:13)
Paul preached the gospel to every creature and no end came (Col. 1:23)
A joyful blessed hope (2 Thess. 2:16, 3:5; Titus 2:13)

Second Coming of Christ to Earth in Prophecy

Christ comes to judge His enemies and stand on the mount of Olives.

Second Coming (Prophecy)
Prophesied many times (Deut. 30:3; Dan. 2:34, 35; Matt. 24:30, 26:64; John 14:3, 28; Acts 1:10, 11, 2:20; Jude 14, 15; Rev. 19:11-16; 22:20)
After the Tribulation (Matt. 24:29-31)
Christ comes with His mighty angels (Matt. 25:31; 2 Thess. 1:7)
Preceded by signs in the sun, moon, and stars (Joel 2:30-32; Matt. 24:29)
Christ begins His extended return in heaven (Isa. 34:5)
Battle of Armageddon (Rev. 14:20, 16:14-17; Luke 17:37)
Obvious dramatic coming all will see Him (Matt. 24:27, 28; Zech. 12:10)
Christ comes to the earth on the Mount of Olives (Acts 1:11, 12; Zech. 14:4)
Christ returns as King of Kings (Rev. 19:16)
Removes unbelievers, tares (Matt. 13: 24-43, 24:40, 41)
Christ comes to judge the nations (Matt. 25:31-36)
Preached gospel in all the world and then the end comes (Matt. 24:13, 14)
Those taken are unbelievers or tares (Matt. 24:41)
A sad and dreadful day (Zech. 12:10; Mal. 4:5)

Similarities between the Rapture and the Second Coming. The time of coming rapture is unknown and the time of Second Coming is unknown (as a thief to unbelievers Matt. 24:36, 1 Thess. 5:2; 2 Peter 3:10, but the Second coming can be calculated by believers after the signing of the covenant by Antichrist). Christ comes and there are clouds and trumpet sounds and one or more angels).

Christ the Lord is Risen Today (hymn)
by Charles Wesley (1739)

Christ the Lord is ris'n today, Alleluia!
Sons of men and angels say, Alleluia!
Raise your joys and triumphs high, Alleluia!
Sing, ye heav'ns, and earth, reply, Alleluia!

Lives again our glorious King, Alleluia!
Where, O death, is now thy sting? Alleluia!
Once He died our souls to save, Alleluia!
Where thy victory, O grave? Alleluia!

Love's redeeming work is done, Alleluia!
Fought the fight, the battle won, Alleluia!
Death in vain forbids His rise, Alleluia!
Christ hath opened paradise, Alleluia!

Soar we now where Christ hath led, Alleluia!
Foll'wing our exalted Head, Alleluia!
Made like Him, like Him we rise, Alleluia!
Ours the cross, the grave, the skies, Alleluia!

Hail the Lord of earth and heaven, Alleluia!
Praise to Thee by both be given, Alleluia!
Thee we greet triumphant now, Alleluia!
Hail the Resurrection, thou, Alleluia!

King of glory, Soul of bliss, Alleluia!
Everlasting life is this, Alleluia!
Thee to know, Thy pow'r to prove, Alleluia!
Thus to sing, and thus to love, Alleluia!

First Corinthians chapter 15 emphasizes that the <u>living in Christ</u> will be changed, while First Thessalonians chapter 4 emphasizes that the <u>dead in Christ</u> will rise first.

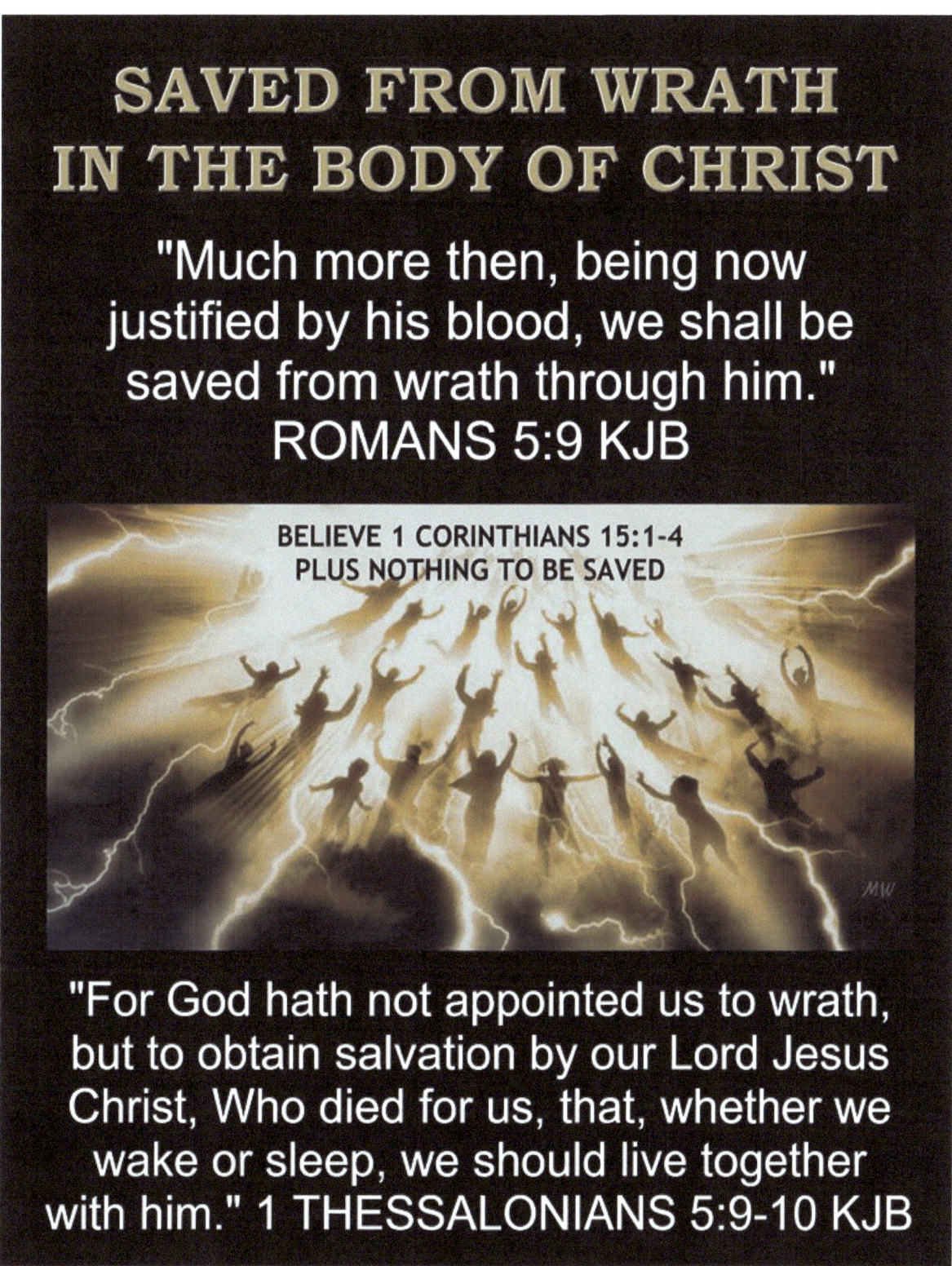

1 Thessalonians Chapter 5 The Model Walk and the Day of the Lord
5:1-11 Walk in light.
5:12, 13 Walk in gratitude.
5:14-28 Walk in obedience to God's will.

To truly understand the mystery of the Rapture (1 Cor. 15:51), it is essential to understand the distinction between mystery and prophecy. We are to study the Bible "rightly dividing the word of truth" (2 Tim. 2:15).

The Greek word for rightly dividing is "orthotomeo" which means to cut straight. <u>Acts 9 is the first straight cut.</u> <u>The last straight cut is the Rapture.</u>

We divide the word of truth where God divides it. God divides between Christ's <u>appearing</u> to Saul (Paul) of Tarsus on the road to Damascus from Christ's <u>appearing</u> to Rapture the body of Christ. We are living in a parenthesis, between these two appearings, in the dispensation of grace.

These appearings are easily seen in Titus. "For the grace of God that bringeth salvation hath <u>appeared</u> to all men [Christ began an all men ministry when He save Paul in Acts 9], Teaching us that, denying ungodliness and worldly lusts, we should live soberly, righteously, and godly, in this present world; Looking for that blessed hope, and the glorious <u>appearing</u> of the great God and our Saviour Jesus Christ [we hope to be Raptured before we die]" (Titus 2:11-13). We live soberly during the dispensation of grace believing true sound doctrine. We separate Paul's instructions to us in Romans to Philemon, from the rest of the Bible. Paul said, "Consider what I say; and the Lord give thee understanding in all things" (2 Tim. 2:7). We study the rest of the Bible from a Pauline point of view.

The mystery the Church will have been "caught up" to meet the Lord in the air (4:17). We are NOT going through the Tribulation. The Church, the body of Christ is saved from having any part in it. Jesus "delivered us from the WRATH to come" (1:10). "God hath not appointed us to wrath, but to obtain salvation by our Lord Jesus Christ" (1 Thess. 5:9).

The Body of Christ believers are of the Day (the dispensation of grace) not the night (the Tribulation), although <u>we live in the night, "this present evil world"</u> (Gal. 1:4; Rom. 13:11). We will be saved out of the world. The evil world will continue into the Tribulation, the darkness of God's wrath, for those not Raptured because "they received not the love of the truth" (2 Thess. 2:10).

5:1 But of the <u>times and the seasons</u>, brethren, <u>ye have no need that I write unto you.</u> [Paul said that there is no need for him to write about the "times and the seasons" concerning the Second Coming of Christ because we are not going to be here. The mystery (the Church that has been cut free) we will have been "caught up" to meet the Lord in the air (4:17). We are NOT going through the Tribulation. The Church, the body of Christ is saved from having any part in it. Notice that Paul declares the sequence of events. Having talked about the Rapture of the Church, he then moves on to the day of the Lord in the <u>prophetic program</u>.

"<u>Times and seasons</u>" do not apply to the body of Christ, they belong to Israel's prophetic program, after the Rapture. God relates to Israel on the basis of signs, "the Jews require a sign" (1 Cor. 1:22). The King James Bible is so wonderful in that the same exact words or phrases are often used. The Bible is no ordinary book and our God is no ordinary God. The beauty of having all of God's word in <u>one</u> language, English for example, and not in two languages, Hebrew and Greek, is that exact words and phrases can be found and cross-referenced in the Old and New Testaments. Using the same phrase, the prophet Daniel, told Nebuchadnezzar what God does. "And he changeth the <u>times and the seasons</u>: he removeth kings, and setteth up kings: he giveth wisdom unto the wise, and knowledge to them that know understanding" (Dan. 2:21). God sets up and takes down kingdoms. <u>After the Tribulation</u> (Matt. 24:29), Christ will come and take down the Gentile rule, destroy Antichrist, set Himself up as the true King, and reign over the whole world for a thousand years. Therefore, there is no need for Paul to write to the Thessalonians about the things that have nothing to do with them. <u>The Church, the body of Christ is looking for a Person, not for times and seasons.</u> The body of Christ will be "caught up" to meet our Head. We will be joined to our Head so we can be "one new man" (Eph. 2:15). When Christ comes for the body of Christ, He does not come all the way to the earth, but meets us in the air (4:17). <u>The Rapture is not in Matthew 24</u>. "Then shall two be in the field; the one shall be TAKEN [in judgment, just as the ones were taken in the flood], and the other LEFT [to enter the kingdom]. Two women shall be grinding at the mill; the one shall be taken, and the other left" (Matt. 24:40, 41).] **2 For <u>yourselves know perfectly</u> that the <u>day of the Lord</u> so cometh as a <u>thief in the night</u>.** [Notice the progression of time, having talked about the Rapture (chapter 4), Paul next discusses the <u>day of the Lord</u>. Paul describes the Tribulation to show that we are not going through it but we will be Raptured before it. We (the body of Christ) will be gone! Israel is appointed to go through the Tribulation because it is the last installment of the fifth course of punishment for their spiritual adultery, as mentioned in Leviticus 26:27-39. But God promises to spare those who at that time, <u>will confess Israel's iniquity and accept their punishment</u> (Lev. 26:40-46). Israel should not be surprised when they are going through the wrath, because it has been prophesied. "Beloved, think it not strange concerning the fiery trial which is to try you, as though some strange thing happened unto you" (1 Peter 4:12). Jesus said, that unless those days were shortened no one would survive that time, but God shortened them for the sake of the believers (Matt. 24:22). The Tribulation will come upon unbelieving Israel and others who do not study the word of God, as a thief in the night. But the wise (those who read the Bible) will not be taken by surprise. The wise will build their life on the Rock, Jesus Christ (Matt. 7:24), not on the sand or clay in the feet and toes of Nebuchadnezzar's statue, Antichrist. (The ten confederate kings or toes are most likely kings of the nations mentioned in Psa. 83:5-8.) The remnant of believers in Israel believe that Jesus of Nazareth, who already came according to Daniel's timeline of 490 years, is their Messiah. Those who agree that Christ has already "come in the flesh" will be the true believers in the Tribulation (1 John 4:2). The Tribulation is the last seven years of Daniel's timeline for when Messiah will come to Israel and set things right. Daniel's timeline began with the order to rebuild the wall around Jerusalem (Neh. 2:6). It is also the last seven years "the times of the Gentiles" (Luke 21:24). <u>God had never let a nation besides Israel rule over Jerusalem "the city of the great King" (Matt. 5:35) until Babylon</u>. The "times of the Gentiles" began with Nebuchadnezzar, "the head of gold" (Dan. 2:38), invasion and rule of Israel. At His Second Coming, Christ comes as the "stone that smote" (Dan. 2:35) and puts down all opposition to His reign over Israel and the earth (Dan. 2:44, 45). Some people include the Tribulation, Jacob's trouble (Jer. 30:7), in the Day of the Lord and others do not. Others teach that day of the Lord begins with the Second coming of Christ. Everyone can agree that after the Rapture, God again resumes intervening physically in the earth. In the dispensation of grace, God is manifesting Himself to the world Spiritually through believers (1 Tim. 3:16) and is not intervening physically. Peter says that the day of the Lord lasts until the first heaven and earth are burnt up. "But the <u>day of the Lord</u> will come as a <u>thief in the night</u>; in the which <u>the heavens shall pass away with a great noise, and the elements shall melt with fervent heat, the earth also and the works that are therein shall be burned up</u>" (2 Peter 3:10). This is the only other exact reference to the phrase "<u>thief in the night</u>." Christ commands the Tribulation saints to watch for Him and says He will come as a "thief" (Matt. 24:42-51). "They" their countrymen who troubled the Thessalonians and the Jews that persecuted the little flock, these unbelievers will <u>not escape God's vengeance</u> (2:14-16). For the unbelievers, the day of the Lord will come upon them suddenly and unexpectedly "as a thief in the night." Christ warns that He comes upon unbelievers as a thief. "Behold, <u>I come as a thief</u>. Blessed *is* he that watcheth, and keepeth his garments, lest he walk naked, and they see his shame" (Rev. 16:15).] **3 For when <u>they</u> shall say, <u>Peace and safety</u>; then <u>sudden destruction cometh</u> upon <u>them</u>, as travail**

upon a woman with child; and they shall not escape. [If the imminent Rapture were to happen then their persecutors would go into the Tribulation. They would believe that the "man of sin" (Antichrist) would bring in "peace and safety." This verse includes the beginning and end of the Tribulation. The seven years of Tribulation are divided into the first 3 ½ years and the last 3 ½ years. Paul has been using the pronouns "you" and "ye" and "yourselves" but now he begins using "they" and "them." The "they" are all the enemies of God who will receive His wrath. The wrath of God has come upon their own unbelieving countrymen who persecuted the Thessalonians, as it has on the unbelieving Jews that persecuted Peter's group in Jerusalem, to the uttermost (eternal torment) as mentioned in 2:16. They despise God and hinder the holy Spirit's work and His word through the saved to the lost (4:6, 8). In the first three and a half years, unbelievers in Israel will say "peace and safety," then in the second three and a half years, sudden destruction will come upon them like labor on a woman having a baby. Labor starts at an unpredictable time. Labor begins slowly and then becomes stronger and harder (God will pour out the seven seals, trumpets, and vials). This is the false peace and safety of the real imposter Antichrist. God promised peace to believers "I create the fruit of the lips; Peace, peace to him that is far off, and to him that is near, saith the LORD; and I will heal him" (Isa. 57:19). The Jews thought Christ was the imposter, but He was the genuine Son of God. Although all seven of the years will be very difficult with so many falling away from the truth, Christ calls the last half of the seven years the "great tribulation" (Matt. 24:21). Speaking of that time, their apostle John wrote, "And we know that we are of God, and the whole world lieth in wickedness" (1 John 5:19). Those who hinder God's word will not escape. His enemies SHALL NOT ESCAPE Christ's judgment of them at His Second Coming.] **4 But ye, brethren, are NOT in darkness, that that day should overtake you as a thief.** [Paul reminds the Thessalonian believers that they are NOT in the darkness of Satan, that the day of the Lord should overtake them as a thief (Col. 1:13). They are NOT going to suddenly find themselves in the Tribulation. Paul will use a series of contrasts to show the difference of where they are on God's timeline: darkness and light, day and night, sober and drunk, and hope and wrath. A thief sneaks in unexpectedly when no one is looking. We are to be confidently, eagerly, and actively looking for our great God and Saviour. "Looking for that blessed hope, and the glorious appearing of the great God and our Saviour Jesus Christ" (Titus 2:13). Even those who are saved and are not looking for Him will be Raptured with us. Even wrong dividers, who wrongly preach and teach the post-tribulation Rapture such as RC Sproul and Steven Anderson will be going up with us in the Rapture. Paul was sent "To open their eyes, *and* to turn *them* from darkness to light, and *from* the power of Satan unto God, that they may receive forgiveness of sins, and inheritance among them which are sanctified by faith that is in me" (Acts 26:18). We have been delivered "from the power of darkness, and hath translated us into the kingdom of his dear Son" (Col. 1:13). The Rapture will be the redemption of the entire body of Christ for His glory, "the redemption of the purchased possession, unto the praise of his glory" (Eph. 1:14). The day of the LORD is first mentioned in Isaiah 2:12. The day of the LORD is often called "that day" in prophecy (Amos 8:9). It will be a day of vengeance on unbelievers, but joy for believers in prophecy.] **5 Ye are all the children of light, and the children of the day: we are not of the night, nor of darkness.** [We are the "children of light" (with Christ's light in us, 1 Cor. 15:40) and the "children of the day) (the dispensation of grace), not of the night (the Tribulation) although we live in this present evil world (Gal. 1:4). We are looking for the day of our redemption, "the adoption, to wit, the redemption of our body" (Rom. 8:23). We are in the day of grace, the dispensation of grace. The lost are Satan's darkness (Acts 26:18). The night is the Tribulation. The evil world continues into the Tribulation, the darkness of God's wrath, for those not Raptured because "they received not the love of the truth" (2 Thess. 2:10).] **6 Therefore let us not sleep, as do others; but let us watch and be sober.** [Sleep here has changed meaning. Paul now uses it to refer to people who are asleep to the truth (not died believing in Christ). We are to be awake to the truth, alert, serving God, and watching for Christ's return. We live soberly believing true sound doctrine, Romans to Philemon, and the rest of the Bible from a Pauline point of view (2 Tim. 2:7).] **7 For they that sleep sleep in the night; and they that be drunken are drunken in the night.** [People sleep at night, and that is usually when they are drunk. Unbelievers are asleep to the things of God, such as the gospel Paul preached and many are drunk on false doctrine. We need to be awake to the truth; it is night for those who do not believe the truth. In order to avoid being hopelessly confused about the Rapture we need to differentiate between Christ's ministry to the body of Christ through Paul, and Christ's ministry to Israel through the twelve. To truly understand the mystery of the Rapture (1 Cor. 15:51), it is essential to understand the distinction between mystery and prophecy. We are to study the Bible "rightly dividing the word of truth" (2 Tim. 2:15). The Greek word for rightly dividing is "orthotomeo" which means to cut straight. Acts 9 is the first straight cut. The last straight cut is the Rapture. We divide the word of truth where God divides it. God divides between Christ's appearing to Saul (Paul) of Tarsus on the road to Damascus from Christ's appearing to Rapture the body of Christ. We are living in a parenthesis, between these two appearings, in the dispensation of grace. These appearings are easily seen in Titus. "For the grace of God that bringeth salvation hath appeared to all men [Christ began an all men ministry when He save Paul in Acts 9], Teaching us that, denying ungodliness and worldly lusts, we should live soberly, righteously, and godly, in this present world; Looking for that blessed hope, and the glorious <u>appearing</u> of the great God and our Saviour Jesus Christ [we hope to be Raptured before we die]" (Titus 2:11-13). We live soberly during the dispensation of grace believing true sound doctrine. We separate Paul's instructions to us in Romans to Philemon, from the rest of the Bible. Paul said, "Consider what I say; and the Lord give thee understanding in all things" (2 Tim. 2:7). We study the rest of the Bible from a Pauline point of view. Today, we follow the instructions Christ gave us through Paul, not His instructions through Peter. To follow Peter when God told us to follow Paul, is to follow false doctrine (1 Cor. 4:16, 11:1; Phil. 3:17; 1 Thess. 1:6. 2:14). The drunken have drunk the <u>wine of false doctrine</u>, which is also associated in the Bible with <u>wine of fornication</u> (Eph. 5:18, Rev. 17:2).] **8 But <u>let us, who are of the day, be sober, putting on the breastplate of faith and love; and for an helmet, the hope of salvation.</u>** [But let us who are awake in the <u>day</u> of the dispensation of grace and reserved for the day of the Raptured, be sober (clear-headed). We have peace in our hearts and minds knowing, that because of Christ, we are not going through the Tribulation. We are to look for the day of our "catching up" at the end of the dispensation of grace, be sober, putting on our armor like good soldiers. <u>Jesus Christ is our armor</u> of light as mentioned in Rom. 13:11-13. The breastplate of faith and love covers our heart (it is the <u>faith of Christ</u> that carries us, and it is His love. These are the fruit of His Spirit in us, Gal. 5:22, 23). It is interesting that Paul calls it the "breastplate of righteousness" in Ephesians 6:14. Like a helmet, our minds are protected by the "hope of salvation" from having to go through the Tribulation. This is a great stabilizing fact that gives us joy and makes us mentally strong. This truth quickly establishes our minds preventing any doubt and despair. <u>Believers can face almost any trouble, difficult circumstances, health issues, or situations if we are certain of our destination with the Lord</u>. The blessed assurance that we will be with Him in heaven without having to go through the Tribulation, has a great stabilizing effect on our mind, heart, and will. We know the truth of what Christ said to us through Paul.] **9 <u>For God hath not appointed us to wrath, but to obtain salvation by our Lord Jesus Christ,</u>** [Again Paul confirms that the body of Christ is not appointed to going through the Tribulation. We are destined to be "caught up" to Christ. He wrote this same thing in Rom. 5:9; 1 Thess. 1:10. We will be saved, from having to endure that horrible time on the earth. We are appointed to obtain deliverance from the wrath by our Lord Jesus Christ. THANK YOU, LORD JESUS!] **10 <u>Who died for us, that, whether we wake or sleep, we should live together with him.</u>** [Jesus is the one who suffered and died for us so we don't have to. Whether we are alive or dead in Christ (sleep), when He comes to meet us, our Rapture is certain. The <u>best part about heaven</u> is that "<u>we should live together with him.</u>" The Lord Jesus Christ is the one who will make heaven <u>such a wonderful place</u>. We will joyfully worship, adore, and give Him all the glory.] **11 Wherefore <u>comfort yourselves together, and edify one another, even as also ye do.</u>** [They (and we) can be comforted because they are not appointed to wrath. God will render rest to them and tribulation to their persecutors. We can <u>comfort</u> each other with the truth of the Rapture (1 Thess. 4:13-18; 1 Cor. 15:51, 52). <u>The certainty of the Pre-Tribulation Rapture is a comfort, going through the Tribulation would NOT be a comfort.</u> Paul tells them to keep comforting and edifying each other, just like they were.]

12 ¶ And we beseech you, brethren, to <u>know them which labour among you, and are over you in the Lord, and admonish you; 13 And to esteem them very highly in love for their work's sake. And be at peace among yourselves.</u> [Know who the true workers are among you, who teach you the true word, that Christ revealed to us through Paul (Col. 1:23-26). <u>Value your teachers</u>. Esteem them in love (hold them in high regard) for their work's sake. When we read or hear the <u>word of God it can admonish or correct us</u>. The water of God's word cleanses us. "That he might sanctify and cleanse it [the Church] with the washing of water by the word" (Eph. 5:26). Jesus told the disciples, "Now ye are clean through the word which I have spoken unto you" (John 15:3). "Be at peace among yourselves" means be in harmony like one team and not to fight or bicker.] **14 Now we exhort you, brethren, <u>warn them that are unruly, comfort the feebleminded, support the weak, be patient toward all men.</u>** [The unruly are those who will not obey the rules. Paul urges them to warn those who are <u>unruly</u> by not working to provide for themselves. Comfort the <u>feebleminded</u> who are unsure about the Rapture and what God's word says. Support the <u>weak</u> in the faith and the <u>weak</u> in their body who may need financial help. "Be patient to all men" means don't lose your temper because it will harm your testimony and God's reputation.] **15 See that <u>none render evil for evil unto any man; but ever follow that which is good, both among yourselves, and to all men.</u>** [<u>We are not to avenge ourselves; that is God's job</u>, "being reviled, we bless; being persecuted, we suffer it" (1 Cor. 4:12). <u>We follow after what is good</u> and let God do the recompense to those who treat us badly. "Recompense to no man evil for evil. Provide things honest in the sight of all men. If it be possible, as much as lieth in you, live peaceably with all men. Dearly beloved, avenge not yourselves, but rather give place unto wrath: for it is written, <u>Vengeance is mine</u>; I will repay, saith the Lord. Therefore if thine enemy hunger, feed him; if he thirst, give him drink: for in so doing thou shalt heap coals of fire on his head. Be not overcome of evil, but overcome evil with good" (Rom. 12:17-21).] **16 <u>Rejoice evermore.</u>** [We can rejoice because we are not going through the wrath and Christ has done everything to save us and to give us the gift of eternal life (Rom. 6:23). We will be with Him in heaven forever (4:17).] **17 <u>Pray without ceasing.</u>** [We can get up in the morning and say a little prayer such as, "please help me to serve You, today" and then add to that prayer throughout the day as things come up, or as you think about them. Pray for others to be saved and to have spiritual knowledge like Paul did in his prison epistles. Then, at the end of the day, thank God that we have "all spiritual blessings in heavenly places in Christ" (Eph. 1:3). We maintain a constant attitude of prayer while exalting our Lord Jesus Christ (when we do this, then everything else falls into its proper place).] **18 In every thing give thanks: for this is the will of God in Christ Jesus concerning you**. [We can give thanks that we are saved from hell and from having to go through the Tribulation. We thank God in everything, not for every circumstance or situation. It is God's will for us to be grateful.] **19 Quench not the Spirit.** [They were to allow the Spirit to move freely among themselves. We are not to grieve the Spirit in us by disobeying, behaving badly, thinking badly, not being gracious, or harboring un-forgiveness (Eph. 5:25-30).] **20 Despise not prophesyings.** [The Thessalonian letters were written during the Acts period when the sign gifts were still in effect. Prophesy was one of the sign gifts. All the sign gifts have ceased (1 Cor. 13:8-13). But at that time, the prophets in mystery spoke by the Spirit, those things that the Lord Jesus Christ had already revealed through apostle Paul. The signs gifts ceased after Paul arrived in Rome having the full revelation of the mystery even if he had not written it down yet (Rom. 15:29). In Acts 28:28 Paul put Israel aside for the third and final time, although Jews can still be saved if they believe the gospel (1 Cor. 15:3, 4). This is when the sign gifts ceased. The Church was in its spiritual infancy and saw "through a glass, darkly" during Acts before Paul understood the mystery which Christ was progressively revealing to him. At that time, sign gifts were needed to get the Church going (1 Cor. 13:8-13).] **21 Prove all things; hold fast that which is good.** [They were to prove, test, or discern if the prophesies were from God or not. If they lined up with the word of God which Paul preached (1 Cor. 5:4, 14:37), or not. They could hold fast to that which is good, true prophesies. Today we prove all teachings by the Scripture, the pure word of God rightly divided. In English the pure word of God is found in the King James Bible.] **22 Abstain from all appearance of evil.** [Abstain from all appearance of evil, both spiritual and physical adultery. No one should have any reason to doubt our integrity as far as our faith or morality.] **23 And the very God of peace sanctify you wholly; and I pray God your whole spirit and soul and body be preserved blameless unto the coming of our Lord Jesus Christ.** [Paul wants the God of peace to sanctify them completely: spirit, soul, and body and to preserve them blameless unto the coming of the Lord Jesus Christ. The God of peace saves us from having to go through "the wrath." We are preserved blameless unto His coming if we follow Christ's doctrine to us through Paul which is able to keep us stable, unblameable, and holy (3:13). We do not accomplish a blameless walk above sin and self by our own effort or rule-keeping. The doctrine does the work in us effectually. Right thinking produces right action. The very God of peace does the sanctifying by His living Spirit in us and His living word to us. God is the one who is able to sanctify us wholly or completely and give us peace in the midst of persecution or difficult circumstances. We have the comfort of the scriptures that give us hope (Rom. 15:4). Paul prays that God will preserve us blameless in our spirit, soul, and body until the Rapture. We can trust the God of peace. This is a very important verse in the Bible because it is the only verse that includes all three parts of our triune nature (three in one), although each part is mentioned separately in other verses. God works in us from the inside out, while Satan attacks us from the outside in. Satan attacks our minds by trying to make us doubt our blessed hope of the Rapture; our goal in mystery is to live in heaven with Christ forever. Psychologists need to know this truth about our makeup if they are seeking to help someone. Man is a triune being. The word of God differentiates between spirit and soul. The spirit in our mind is the part of us that is able to communicate with God. "And be renewed in the spirit of your mind" (Eph. 4:23). "But he that is joined unto the Lord is one spirit" (1 Cor. 6:17). The soul is our true self or heart, the seat of our affections, will, desires, and emotions. Spirit is pneuma in Greek (nephesh in Hebrew), soul is psuche in Greek (ruach in Hebrew), body is soma in Greek.] **24 Faithful is he that calleth you, who also will do it.** [We can trust the God of peace. God called them (and us) by the gospel. He will preserve us as we live by faith in the true sound doctrine He has given us through Paul. God justifies and sanctifies us by faith. Christ will keep us in true doctrine if we care to understand His word to us through Paul. God is faithful not only to save us, but to keep us by His Spirit in us and His word to us (Phil. 1:6, 2:13; 2 Thess. 3:3, 4). God will keep us until He will Rapture us. God will do it!!!]

25 ¶ Brethren, pray for us. [Paul asks them to pray for them, too.]

26 ¶ Greet all the brethren with an holy kiss. 27 I charge you by the Lord that this epistle be read unto all the holy brethren. [Paul asks them to give the other believers a holy kiss from him. In our culture, a handshake or wave will do. Paul charges or commands them by the Lord to have this letter read to all the other believers. Paul said he wrote what Christ revealed directly to him (4:1, 4:2, 4:15; 5:27). As the word of God to the Gentiles grew, making copies of the word of God became one of the primary functions of the local church. God saw to it that the Greek New Testament was preserved just as the Hebrew scribes preserved the Old Testament. The local church is responsible to teach and maintain the Bible; to be "the church of the living God, the pillar and ground of the truth" (1 Tim. 3:15).]

28 ¶ The grace of our Lord Jesus Christ be with you. Amen. [Paul closes the letter simply, by exalting Christ. It is the grace of the Lord Jesus Christ that we all have. Paul wants us kept by His grace, walking by faith in His doctrine to us through Paul.]

1 Thessalonians Chapter Summaries
Chapter 1: How the Thessalonians were saved and their work of faith, labour of love, and patience of hope.
Chapter 2: Paul's ministry in Thessalonica. Satan had hindered Paul twice from coming to Thessalonica. When Paul could no longer stand the suspense of how they were holding up in the face of strong persecution he sent a model brother because he was hindered from going to them himself. Paul got around the tempter (Satan) by sending brother Timothy and Silas to check on them and to establish them in the faith. In other words, they were sent to do "after care." Paul wanted to be sure that these saints were not moved away from "the faith" (the doctrine he taught them), but would thrive and grow. Paul wanted to perfect that which may be lacking in their faith. He longed to teach them more sound doctrine.
Chapter 3: Timothy's visit and good report. Paul is happy that they want to see them again and are standing fast in the faith they delivered to them.
Chapter 4: Living to please God, and the details of our Pre-Tribulation Rapture.
Chapter 5: Following the Rapture comes the day of the Lord, which the Church has no part in because the body of Christ is not appointed to wrath.

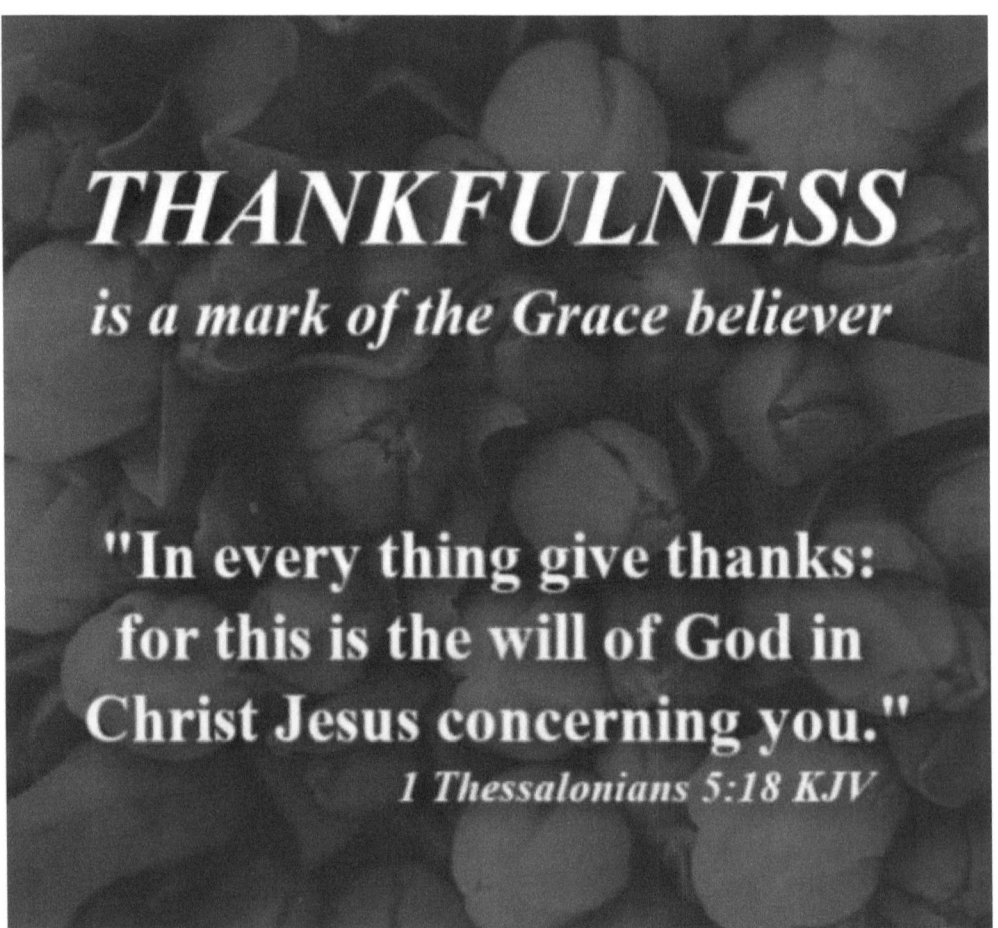

When Will the Rapture Occur?

Paul does not give us a date for the Lord's return for us, but asks us to patiently wait for him (1 Thess. 1:10; 2 Thess. 3:5). No one except God knows when "the fullness of the Gentiles be come in" (Rom. 11:25). The Rapture is imminent; it could occur at any time. I do not pretend to know when the Rapture will actually happen. But I think that we can make an educated guess of the most likely window of time that the Rapture will occur. However, human speculation has often proved to be wrong.

I am going to share when I think the Rapture may occur for the purpose of urging all of us to be busy doing God's will. We know it is God's will that as many people will be saved and to come to the knowledge of the truth as possible (1 Tim. 2:4). We are also to lay up rewards in heaven. God will judge what sort of work we did, the quality, not the quantity. How much work did we allow Christ to do through us? How many souls did we share the gospel with and edify?

To understand when the Rapture will occur, we need to look at prophecy, because there are no signs in mystery. God gave the world the seven-day week (Gen. 2:2, 3). Then in Exodus, He gave Israel the Sabbath day (Ex. 20:8). The Sabbath day is a picture of the millennial reign of Christ. It will be a period of rest for Him and His people. "For we which have believed do enter into rest [kingdom], as he said, As I have sworn in my wrath, if they shall enter into my rest: although the works were finished from the foundation of the world. For he spake in a certain place of the seventh day on this wise, And God did rest the seventh day from all his works" (Heb. 4:3, 4). Could it be that God has a 7,000-year plan for mankind? Christ did not come 2,000 years after His birth, so **perhaps He will come 2,000 years after His death?**

God gave Daniel the timeline for His people in Daniel 9:24-27.
Daniel 9:24 Seventy weeks [490 years] **are determined upon thy people and upon thy holy city**, to finish the transgression, and to make an end of sins, and to make reconciliation for iniquity, and to bring in everlasting righteousness, and to seal up the vision and prophecy, and to anoint the most Holy.

Daniel 9:25 Know therefore and understand, that from the going forth of the commandment to restore and to build Jerusalem **unto the Messiah the Prince shall be seven weeks** [49 years], **and threescore and two weeks** [434 years+49=483. Christ declared Himself to be the King of the Jews when He rode into Jerusalem on Palm Sunday]: the **street shall be built again, and the wall, even in troublous times** [Nehemiah].

Daniel 9:26 And **after threescore and two weeks shall Messiah be cut off** [die on the cross at the same time], but **not for himself**: and the people of the **prince [Antichrist]** that shall come shall **destroy the city and the sanctuary**; and the end thereof shall be with a **flood**, and unto the end of the war desolations are determined.

Daniel 9:27 And **he shall confirm the covenant with many for one week: and in the midst of the week he shall cause the sacrifice and the oblation to cease**, and for the **overspreading of abominations he shall make it desolate** [Antichrist will set himself up to be worshipped], even until the consummation, and that determined shall be poured upon the desolate.

God gave Daniel the timeline for His people (Dan. 9:24-27). Seventy weeks of seven is 70x7 or 490 years. There would be 483 years until Messiah the Prince would come. "Know therefore and understand, that from the going forth of the commandment to restore and to build Jerusalem unto the <u>Messiah the Prince shall be seven weeks, and threescore and two weeks</u>: the street shall be built again, and the wall, even in troublous times" (Dan. 9:25).

Here are the calculations:
(1) After the 7x<u>7 weeks </u>or <u>49 years</u> will be <u>62x7</u> <u>weeks</u> or <u>434 years</u>. There were 49 years from the building of the wall by Nehemiah in which the temple at Jerusalem were rebuilt. The temple took 46 years (John 2:20).
(2) Then there was <u>400 years</u> of silence (Amos 8:11).
(3) Then <u>34 years</u> unto Messiah the Prince (Dan. 9:25), which is Palm Sunday, when Christ declared Himself to be the King of the Jews.
(4) This is <u>69 weeks</u> or <u>a total of 483 years</u>.
<u>God inserted the dispensation of grace between the 69 and 70th week, and interrupted prophecy. The 70th week is the wrath, or Tribulation that will occur after our Rapture.</u>

Notice that <u>Messiah arrived and died in AD 34</u>. I believe Dionysius Exiguus (AD 470-540), who was commissioned by Pope John 1 to work out the date of Christ's death in AD 525 (for the purpose of knowing when Easter occurred for our calendar) did it correctly.

Dionysius was a monk from Scythia (modern day Romania), an astronomer, and a brilliant mathematician. He traveled to Jerusalem and may have had access to documents that no longer exist. Based on his findings, he instituted BC (before Christ) and AD (in the year of our Lord) for our calendar.

Dionysius established that Easter should be celebrated the first Sunday after the full moon that occurs after the spring Equinox (March 21). He set our calendar on firm footing: it coincides with the true date of the death of Jesus. He correctly deduced that Jesus died in AD 34 on Thursday.

Christ said that the only sign He would give for His death was: "For as Jonas was **three days and three nights** in the whale's belly; so shall the Son of man be three days and three nights in the heart of the earth" (Matt. 12:40).

Therefore, in order to fulfill the sign of Jonas (Jonah) and rise on Sunday (Matt. 28:1), Christ would have had to die on Thursday. This means that Passover had to begin at sunset on Wednesday. We must keep in mind that the Jewish days begin in the evening, at sunset.

The date for the Passover changes from year to year. Using the Torah Calendar, I determined that the only year around that time that the Passover began on a Wednesday was in AD 34. I believe Christ was conceived around Dec. 25 in 1 BC (notice there is no year zero) and that Christ was born in AD 1. (Knowing that John the Baptist was born six months earlier helps with this reckoning.) Christ lived 33 ½ years so if we add 1 plus 33 we get AD 34.

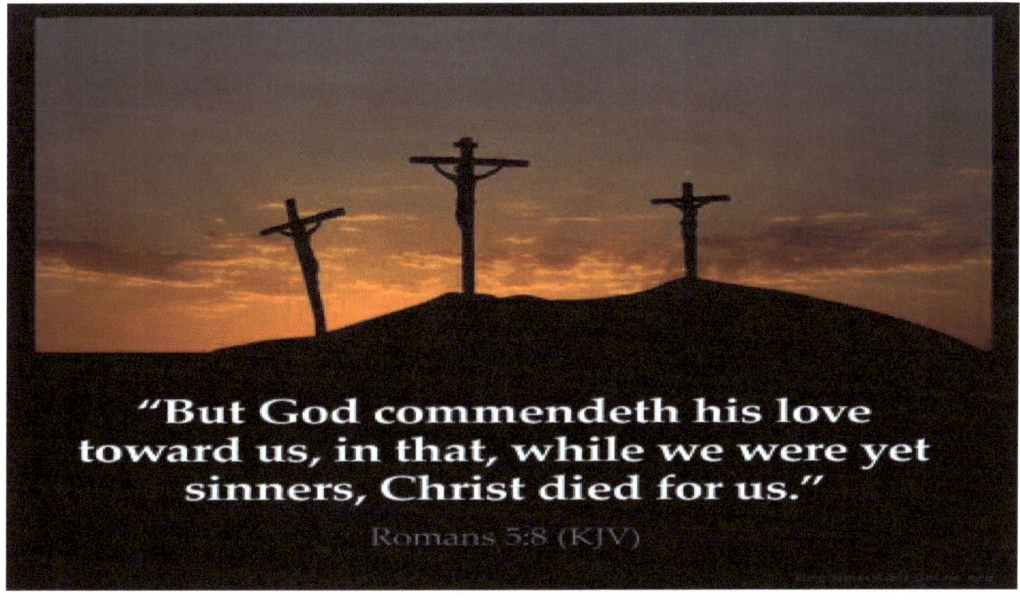

Three Days and Three Nights Timetable

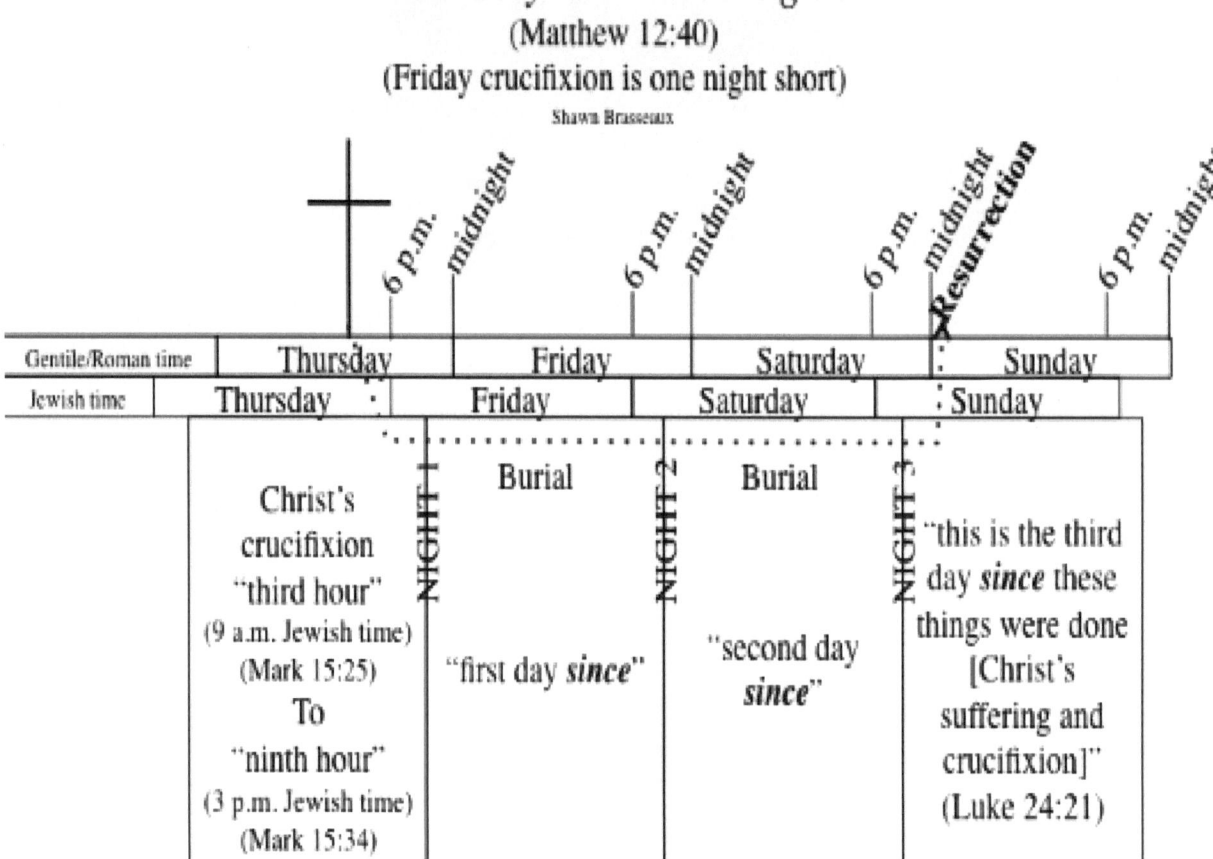

Thursday was the date of Christ's crucifixion

The above timeline was created and shared publically by Shawn Brasseaux.

Keep in mind that the Jewish day goes from evening to evening, so Passover began on Wednesday at sunset (6 pm) and finished on Thursday at sunset (6 pm).

In my book, Could God have a 7,000 Year plan for Mankind? I give these possible dates:
Jesus probably died on Passover Abib (Nisan) 14 at 3 pm, March 24, AD 34.
Jesus rose Abib (Nisan) 17, March 27, AD 34.
Jesus ascended on Omer Day 40, Iyyar or Zif 25, May 3, AD 34.
The Holy Ghost came Omer Day 50, Sivan 6, Shavout (Pentecost) May 13, AD 34.

When Did Jesus Die?

It is not enough for a Christian to believe in God; a Christian must believe God. Believing is taking God at His word. When Jesus gave us the sign for His death. "**For as Jonas was three days and three nights in the whale's belly; so shall the Son of man be three days and three nights in the heart of the earth**" Matt. 12:40, **we must trust that what He said is true.**

Therefore, in order to find out when Jesus died, we simply have to line up the facts with the Hebrew calendar. Jesus must have been in the tomb three days and three nights, and risen on Sunday. Making the match is easy using the website Torahcalendar.com. Nisan (Aramaic) is the same month as Abib (Hebrew).

After comparing all the years from AD 26-34, **we find a match with AD 34**. Jesus died on Passover, Nisan 14 (which began on Wednesday at sunset, and concluded Thursday at sunset.) Jesus died on Thursday, not Friday, to allow for the three days and nights. Because **a Friday crucifixion would only mean two nights.**

This means Jesus would have had to **die on a Thursday before sunset in order to be in the tomb three days and three nights and to rise on Sunday.** The Hebrew days go from sunset to sunset. **So Passover (Nisan14) would need to begin on Wednesday,** at sunset. If we plug several years into the Torah calendar, starting in AD 26 (for example) and continue plugging in the number of years incrementally we discover **the only date that fits is the year AD 34.**

Here are the results anyone can find using the patented calendar on the website Torahcalendar.com. **Comparing the following years: (Remember that Nisan 14 must begin on Wednesday, for Christ to die on Thursday that same day.)**

AD 26 Nisan 14 is on Friday
AD 27 Nisan 14 is on Thursday
AD 28 Nisan 14 is on Tuesday
AD 29 Nisan 14 is on Monday
AD 30 Nisan 14 is on Friday
AD 31 Nisan 14 is on Tuesday
AD 32 Nisan 14 is on Monday
AD 33 Nisan 14 is on Friday
<u>**AD 34 Nisan 14 is on Wednesday**</u>

*****Notice that Passover begins on Wednesday (Nisan 14) and finishes at sunset the following day on the pictured Torah Calendar.**

Torah Calendar for Nisan (Abib) 34 AD

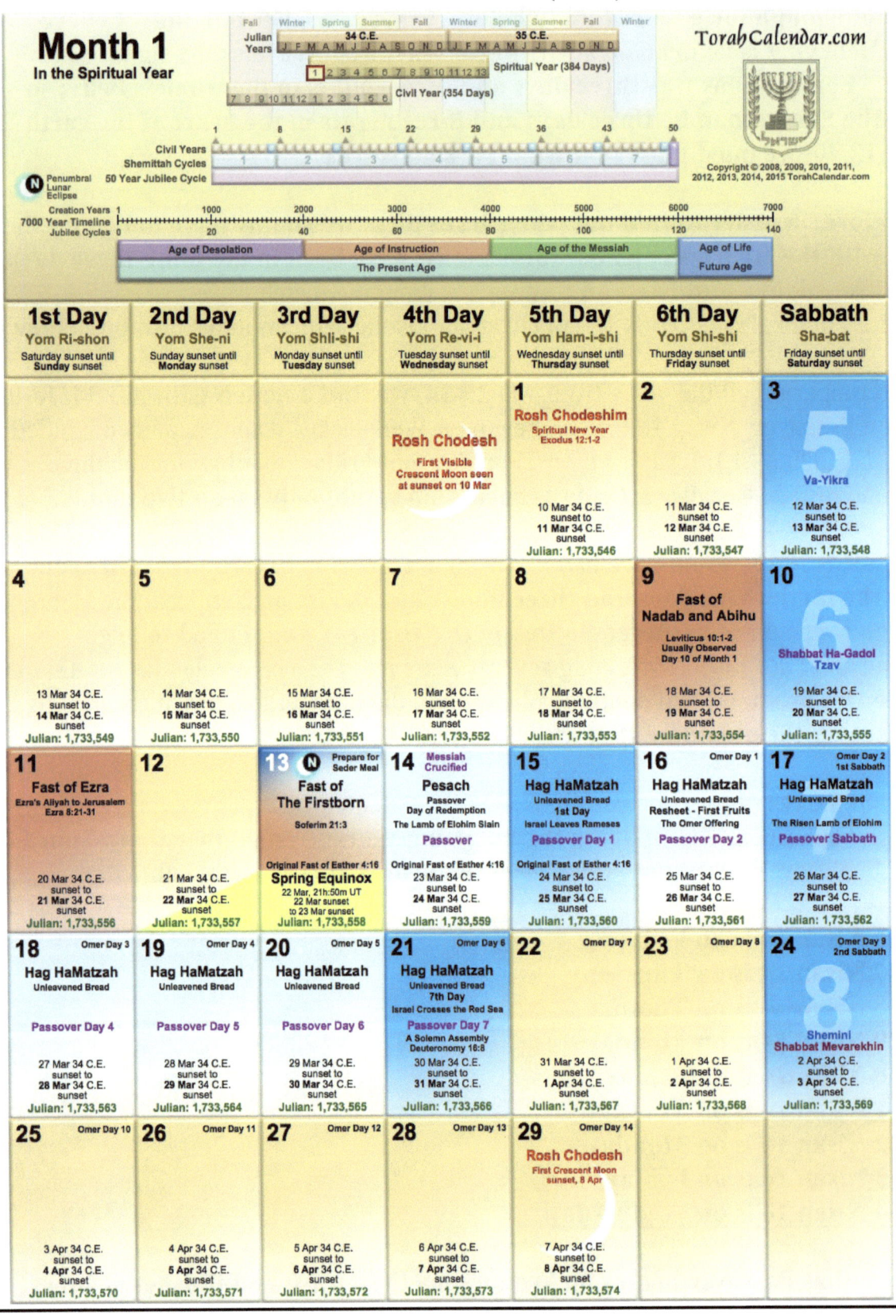

Seven Thousand Years

In a mere 7,000 years, God will have determined who had faith to believe in Him and will live in heaven or on earth. The week in Genesis Chapter 1 and 2 is a pattern for God's plan. "For he spake in a certain place of the seventh *day* on this wise, And God did rest the seventh day from all his works" (Heb. 4:4).

I have all the dates worked out in detail in my book *Could God Have a 7,000 Year Plan for Mankind?* by MC Manley (2016). This book is the same as the one in a smaller format called *AD 34 the Year Jesus Died for All* (2016). These books are available on Amazon on Kindle. (This book is a little rough because I have not been able to update it because the file was not a word document.) Therefore, I am sharing the most important details of that book in this book.

Explanation of Torah Calendar Abib in AD 34

Keep in mind that the Jewish day goes from evening to evening, so Passover began on Wednesday at sunset (6 pm) and finished on Thursday at sunset (6 pm).

In that book, I give these possible dates:
Jesus probably died on Passover Abib (Nisan) 14 at 3 pm, March 24, AD 34.
Jesus rose Abib (Nisan) 17, March 27, AD 34.
Jesus ascended on Omer Day 40, Iyyar or Zif 25, May 3, AD 34.
The Holy Ghost came Omer Day 50, Sivan 6, Shavout (Pentecost) May 13, AD 34.

Therefore, Christ may return for Israel in 2034. We know that the Tribulation is seven years and that the Rapture is before that. So we subtract 7 years: 2034 -7=2027. Therefore, **the latest date for the Rapture is probably 2027**.

However, we know that there is an unspecified time before Antichrist signs the 7-year covenant with Israel. This time period cannot be very long since the little flock sold their belongings as Christ commanded them because the Tribulation loomed on the horizon (Luke 12:33; Acts 2:45, 4:34). They cashed in their property because they would not be able to take the Mark of the beast and buy and sell in the Tribulation (Rev. 13:16-18). In Peter's day, people were getting impatient saying "where is the promise of his coming?" (2 Peter 3:4).

I am guessing that this period may possibly be only about three years. Seven and three is ten. Therefore, if we subtract 10 years from 2034 we have 2024.

We are living in 2019, therefore according to these calculations, the Rapture could happen in 5 to 8 years. However, I remind you that the Rapture could happen at any time. "And that, knowing the time, that now it is "high time" to awake out of sleep: for now is our salvation nearer than when we believed" (Rom. 13:11). The "high time" is when the sand in the hourglass is high. Just a few more grains of sand and time will have run out. The Rapture will happen and we will be saved from the wrath to come (Rom. 5:9; 1 Thess. 1;10, 5:9). Maybe today, Lord!

The prophetic clock stopped on Palm Sunday and was followed by the cross when Messiah was "cut off" (Dan. 9:26). The nation of Israel then received a bonus year to accomplish a renewed offer of the kingdom through the third Person of the Godhead, the Holy Ghost. The one-year extension of mercy was a result of Christ's plea to the Father on their behalf (Luke 13:6-9, 23:34). This extra bonus year is NOT included in Daniel's 490 years.

The Holy Ghost came down to empower the little flock 10 days after Christ ascended to the Father (having ministered to His disciples for 40 days after His death) on Pentecost (Acts 1:3, 2:1-4).

Julius Caesar began the Julian Calendar in 46 BC (365.25 days). Pope Gregory reformed the calendar in 1582 adjusting for the more precise solar year of the Gregorian calendar (365.2425 days).

Some historians, such as Bishop Ussher, believe there is a 4-year discrepancy in the calendar. Furthermore, many believe that Herod the Great died in 3 BC. In that case, our Rapture would occur 4 years earlier, making the window of time for our Rapture between 1 and 4 years. Therefore, in 2019, I think 8 years or less, while others say 4 years or less (because it may be true that the calendar is off by 4 years, since Herod the Great may have died in 4 BC). Many of us like the sound of that thinking because "our gathering together unto him" (2 Thess. 2:1) will be sooner.

Others say that the years in mystery do not apply to God's timeline because it was a mystery. I don't agree because there is not another 2,000 years before the Wrath in God's timeline for mankind. Studying the Thessalonian letters confirm that. In a mere 7,000 years, God will have determined who will have eternal life with Him in heaven and on earth. "For he will finish the work, and cut *it* short in righteousness: because a short work will the Lord make upon the earth" (Rom. 9:28).

While mankind's calendar dates may not be perfect, we can trust that God knows exactly what time it is and precisely when He wants the Rapture to occur. May we be busy working for our glorious God, ready and prepared when He comes! Let us be patient, waiting, watching, listening, and working. Maranatha!!!

Therefore, knowing that the Rapture could occur **in our lifetime** and **at any moment!** Let us be busy helping as many people as possible to believe the gospel: "how that Christ **died for our sins** according to the scriptures; and that he **was buried**, and that he **rose again** the third day according to the scriptures" (1 Corinthians 15:3, 4) and take part in the Rapture.

Second Thessalonians

Paul had used a letter to stabilize the Thessalonians, now the enemy used a letter to destabilize them. The Thessalonians were "shaken in mind" and "troubled" because of the forged letter as from Paul. The counterfeit letter claimed that they were suffering persecution because they were in the Tribulation and had missed the Rapture. Therefore, Paul writes a follow-up letter from Corinth shortly after he wrote the first letter (Acts 18:11).

Someone was sent from Thessalonica to check to see if Paul was still in Corinth. Paul wrote back to give them peace of mind and to comfort their hearts. Although Paul had corrected their thinking about the Rapture in the first letter, they still needed further correction on the important doctrine of our hope (our glorification) and their wrong behavior. Wrong thinking leads to wrong actions. Because false doctrine had crept into the church some were still not behaving correctly and had not gone back to work.

The model church had gotten off track regarding their hope. With very logical arguments Paul sets out to correct the false doctrine and get them back on track. First, Paul praises their faith and love. Despite their problems, the church was growing in faith and love. Paul doesn't say they are growing in their blessed hope.

Next, he instructs the Thessalonians regarding "our gathering together unto him [Christ]" (2 Thess. 2:1) before "the day of the Lord" (1 Thess. 5:2). Then, Paul enumerates events concerning the day of the Lord to show that they (and we) are not in it. Understanding prophecy often helps us to understand mystery more clearly.

Finally, after Paul has cleared up the confusion and given them comforting assurance that our Rapture will precede the day of the Lord, he tells them to get back to work. Paul's letters worked effectually in them that believe.

Second Thessalonians Outline

(1) Persevere despite persecution.
(2) Corrects false doctrine, the day of the Lord explained (we are not in it).
(3) Lazy busy bodies should go back to work and Paul's trademark signature.

Review sentences Second Thessalonians
(1) Rest with us.
(2) Gathered with us.
(3) Follow us in word and work.

<u>Purpose</u>: Paul wrote Second Thessalonians (the main emphasis is doctrine) to:
(1) Encourage the saints to stay strong in their faith and to continue to grow.
(2) To <u>correct false doctrine</u>. We are NOT appointed to be in the Tribulation.
(3) <u>Paul describes the day of the Lord to show that they (and we) are not in it.</u>
(4) <u>To correct the bad behavior of some who were still not working.</u>
(5) To get them back <u>on track about their hope</u> so the <u>Lord of peace could give them peace of mind knowing they will be gathered to Him before the wrath</u>.

Theme: The God loves us and gives us everlasting consolation and by grace good hope to comfort our hearts. This is so we can have stable minds allowing the doctrine to work effectually in us so Christ can do His work through us.

Key verses: "Now our Lord Jesus Christ himself, and God, even our Father, which hath loved us, and hath given *us* everlasting consolation and good hope through grace, <u>comfort your hearts</u>, and <u>stablish you in every good word and work</u>" (2 Thessalonians 2:16, 17).

<u>Satan had attacked their minds concerning their hope</u>. Anyone can get off track and misunderstand some point regarding doctrine if they are not careful. We must study God's word God's way. We need to consider what Paul says first. "Consider what I say; and the Lord give thee understanding in all things" (2 Tim. 2:7). <u>Sound doctrine results in a sound mind</u> (2 Tim. 1:7).

First Thessalonians emphasis	Second Thessalonians emphasis
Coming of Christ in the air	Coming of Christ to the earth
Present age of grace	Future day of the Lord
Spirit's work in the church members	Satan's mystery of iniquity
Reminds them of what he had taught	Corrected false teaching they heard

Second Thessalonians Introduction

When Paul writes about the Rapture he doesn't quote Old Testament scripture because the Rapture was not prophesied. This new revelation was given by the risen, glorified Lord Jesus Christ to him. The Thessalonian church had lost their blessed hope. If we compare 1 Thess. 1:3 with 2 Thess. 1:3, we notice that Paul doesn't praise their hope in the second letter.

Some were telling them that the persecution they were experiencing was the Tribulation. A <u>forged letter</u> claiming to be from Paul contained this wrong doctrine which distressed the members in the church. The Thessalonians most likely sent a messenger to Paul in Corinth to check to see if he was still here. Paul writes to correct the false doctrine and stabilize them in the truth of their Pre-Tribulation Rapture so their hearts can be comforted.

Paul writes to correct wrong thinking regarding our resurrection at the Rapture. <u>Satan frequently attacks this doctrine</u> (2 Tim. 2:18). In chapter 15 of Corinthians, Paul also had to defend the resurrection. He said that anyone who <u>denies our resurrection denies the resurrection of Christ</u>. Paul calls this evil communication. "Be not deceived: <u>evil communications</u> corrupt good manners [good behavior]" (1 Cor. 15:33). At Thessalonica, evil communication had caused the bad behavior for some had stopped working.

In First Thessalonians some were not working because they thought the Rapture was coming at any time. Now some had quit working thinking what is the use of working when the world is coming to an end.

People will come up with any excuse to not work. Work is healthy, honorable, good, responsible, and rewarding. God instituted work before the fall when He told Adam to dress and keep the garden of Eden (Gen. 2:15). Work gives us a satisfying sense of accomplishment.

The Tribulation leads up to the <u>day of the LORD's return which is bad news for His enemies, but good news for His believers</u>. The <u>Day of the Lord extends from the seven Tribulation, then includes the Second Coming of Christ, His Millennial Reign, the Great White Throne Judgment, and ends with fire burning and cleansing the heaven and the earth</u> (2 Peter 3:10). The "day of God" (2 Peter 3:12) comes next with the <u>new heaven and earth</u> (2 Peter 3:13; Isa. 65:17, 66:22; Rev. 21:1). Paul called the day of God the dispensation of the "fulness of times" (Eph. 1:10).

The reason for the day of the Lord has nothing to do with the body of Christ, but is the prophesied punishment of Israel for their spiritual idolatry. The day of the Lord is first mentioned in Isaiah 2:12, but it is referred to all through the Bible. It is part of the fifth course of chastisement (Lev. 26:27-39).

Paul graciously sandwiches his correction of the doctrinal error that had crept into the church between encouragement and the comfort of our hope. This is the sandwich technique that we can use when helping to correct others in the faith. We first point out what they are doing well, then what they need to correct, and then return to bolster them in what they know to be true. Paul had a firm grasp of both prophecy and mystery. We love studying prophecy almost as much as mystery.

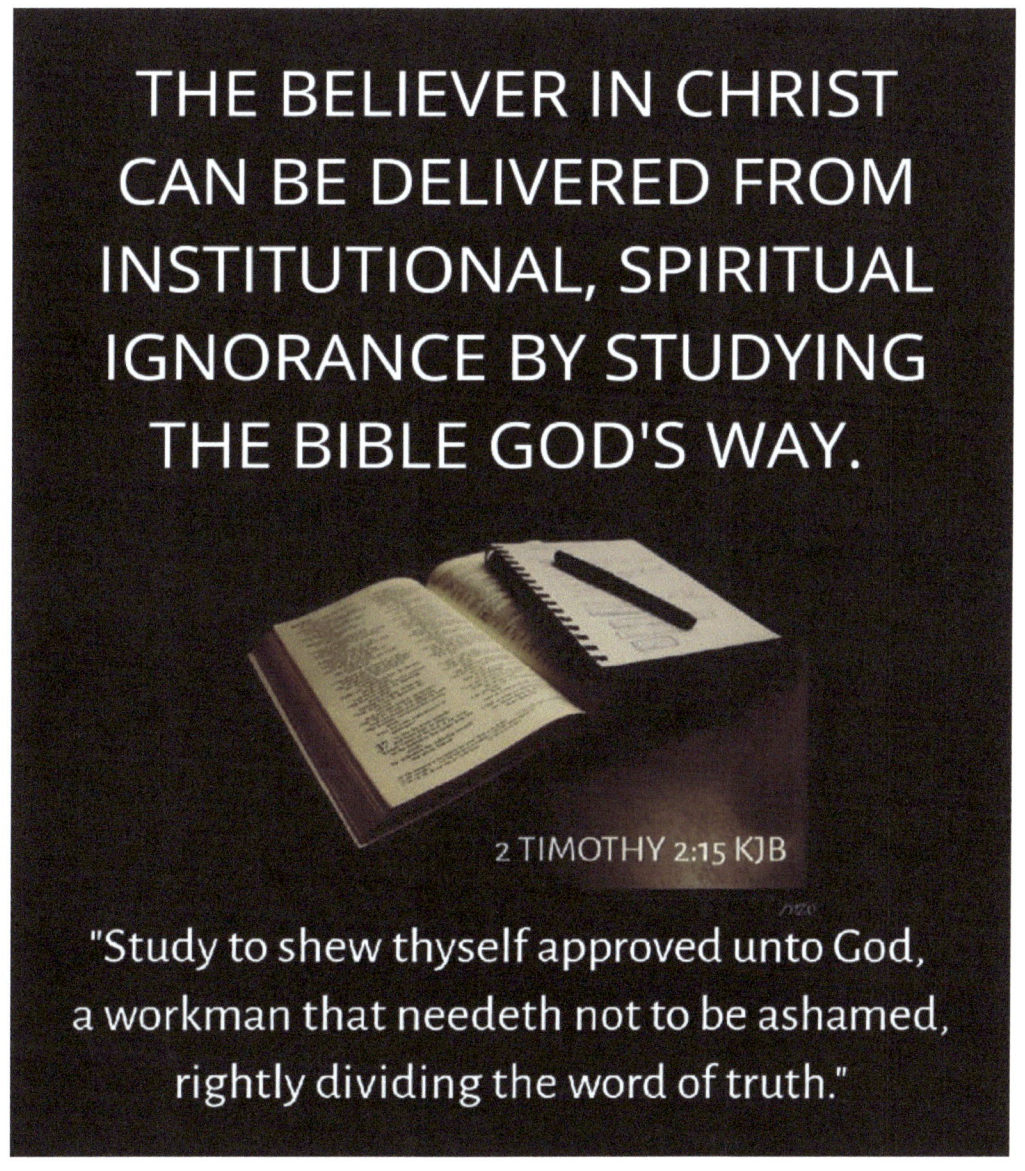

2 Thessalonians Chapter 1 Patience and faith despite persecution
1:1, 2 Greetings.
1:3-8 Praise for spiritual growth despite persecution.
1:9-12 Rest with us, while God recompenses your persecutors.
1:13, 14 His good work of faith with power in them for His and their glory.

Faith, charity, and hope are the hallmarks of the Christian faith. Satan hates the doctrine of our blessed hope and had tried to attack it in Thessalonica, Corinth, and Ephesus. Paul defended the Pre-Tribulation Rapture in 1 Corinthians Chapter 15. He had false teachers regarding the Rapture put out of the church in Ephesus (1 Tim. 1:20; 2 Tim. 2:18). Although Paul had corrected doctrine regarding the Rapture in his first letter to the Thessalonians, Paul had to write Second Thessalonians to correct doctrine regarding the Pre-Tribulation Rapture once again.

Despite its problems, the church had shown great promise and steadfastness. But, the church was being persecuted and wavering in their blessed hope. The church at Thessalonica was growing in faith and in charity (love). But Paul doesn't say they had grown in their hope. He doesn't praise them for their hope because they were wavering in their blessed hope. Some said that their persecution indicated that they were in the Tribulation. A forged letter may have said so. Left unaddressed, that false doctrine could derail the church. We can endure anything if we have hope.

It is not enough to be Biblical we must also be dispensational. In order to fully understand the Rapture, we need to understand the difference between mystery and prophecy. Paul uses the term "dispensation" four times in his letters: 1 Cor. 9:17; Eph. 1:10, 3:2; and Col. 1:25. However, if we try to find the word in 1 Cor. 9:17 in the NIV or in the NKJV it is not there. Therefore, it is essential to use a perfect Bible. In English, it is the King James Bible.

Dispensation means dispersing or distributing. A gas station dispenses gasoline and a pharmacy dispenses medications. In the Bible, it means God is dispensing a set of instructions for people to believe and obey.

1:1 Paul, and Silvanus, and Timotheus, unto the church of the Thessalonians in God our Father and the Lord Jesus Christ: [The fact that Paul still sends the local assembly greetings from Silvanus, Timotheus, and himself is a clue that this letter was written shortly after the first. Silvanus is mentioned in retrospect in (2 Cor. 1:19) and as the scribe for Peter (1 Peter 5:12), but after that, he is not mentioned again. This second letter was probably written shortly after the first. Perhaps a Thessalonian had been sent to see if Paul was still in Corinth or if he had been Raptured. This person brought news concerning the church and the heresy in the assembly. Paul greets them cordially, acknowledging that the members of the church there are "in God our Father" and "in the Lord Jesus Christ."] **2 Grace unto you, and peace, from God our Father and the Lord Jesus Christ.** [Paul greets them as was his custom with grace and peace from God our Father and the Lord Jesus Christ. He is their spokesman, their chosen apostle of the Gentiles (Rom. 11:13). We are living during a period of amnesty when God is freely offering grace and peace by faith in His Son, because of Calvary (2 Cor. 5:19-21). The dispensation of the grace of God is temporarily holding back the WRATH, the Tribulation. There is no preferred nation today. God is inviting all sinners to be reconciled to Him by believing the gospel of Christ (1 Cor. 15:3, 4). Believers can experience true grace and peace knowing that God, who cannot lie, has promised us eternal life (Titus 1:2). Grace always comes before peace in Paul's writings. It is entirely by God's grace that He decided to save those who believe. Salvation is a gift of God, not a work that we did (Eph. 2:8, 9). In fact, if we think that we contributed to our salvation in some way, we nullify it and make it of no effect (Rom. 4:5, 14). We insult God if we say that Christ's death for our sins and resurrection was not enough and that something we did played a part in our salvation such as water baptism, saying a prayer, our good works, and so on. Jesus paid it all. Believers will not be judged for their sins (they were judged on Calvary). Praise and thank You, Lord Jesus! We were spiritually dead, but we received the resurrection life of Jesus Christ in us freely which made us spiritually alive unto God (Rom. 6:11; 2 Cor. 4:7, 10, 11; Gal. 2:20). It is the same for those in prophecy, those of Israel are spiritually dead and life for all is in Christ Jesus (John 1:4). Peter and the eleven were "in Christ" but they are not in the body of Christ. The twelve have a different destiny, they will sit on twelve thrones judging the twelve tribes of Israel (Matt. 19:28). We who are saved, have all been given the ministry of reconciliation. Sinners will go to hell for their sins. "But the scripture hath concluded all under sin, that the promise by faith of Jesus Christ might be given to them that believe" (Gal. 3:22). God can show "mercy upon all" (Rom. 11:32) those who believe in Jesus Christ. Believers have Christ's imputed righteousness (2 Cor. 5:21). We are all to be "ambassadors for Christ" to reconcile others to God (2 Cor. 5:18-20). Christ made peace possible between God and sinners. Helping others to be saved is no easy task because Satan blinds lost people to the "light of the glorious gospel of Christ" (2 Cor. 4:4).]

3 ¶ We are bound to <u>thank God always for you</u>, brethren, as it is meet, because that <u>your faith groweth exceedingly</u>, and the <u>charity of every one of you all toward each other aboundeth</u>; [Paul, Silas, and Timothy were obliged to always be thankful to God for them because their faith was growing exceedingly and their charity (Christ's Spirit in them) was abounding toward each other. Their prayers for the Thessalonians were being answered (1 Thess. 3:12). Despite its problems, the church had shown great promise and steadfastness. Their faith and charity were evidence that Christ's sound doctrine to them through Paul was working. Their problems were that the <u>church was being persecuted and wavering in their blessed hope, which could derail their faith</u>. If we compare 1 Thess. 1:3 with 2 Thess. 1:3, we <u>notice that Paul omits to praise their hope in this second letter</u>. Even after the first letter, the church was still confused about the Rapture. Paul writes to correct their misunderstanding. In the process, he emphasizes the importance of correcting doctrinal error. A long sentence begins at verse 3 and continues until the end of verse 10.] **4 So that we ourselves glory in you in the churches of God for your patience and faith in all your persecutions and tribulations that ye endure:** [Paul gloried in them as he told other churches about how their faith was holding up as they patiently endured persecution. Paul praises them for their great example to the other churches, in Corinth and Cenchrea (Rom. 16:1) and other places. It was to God's glory that they were flourishing despite the persecution and tribulation that they were enduring. We need to remember that the little flock churches were also churches of God, but they preached the gospel of the kingdom, not the gospel of Christ.] **5 Which is a manifest token of the righteous judgment of God, that ye may be counted worthy of the kingdom of God, for which ye also suffer:** [Paul acknowledges that they are suffering. True believers have suffered persecution throughout the ages. God counted them worthy to enter His heavenly kingdom because they trusted the gospel Paul preached. Remember the kingdom of God has two realms, heaven and earth. Their faith, charity, and patience in all their persecutions and tribulations were a manifest token that His Spirit was in them. It will be righteous for God to <u>reward</u> them in the kingdom for which they suffer. They were continuing strong and enduring in Paul's doctrine despite hardships, which will make them worthy of rewards at the Judgment Seat of Christ. They will be more suited for increased responsibility in their job positions in heaven because they were patient to endure persecution which caused their faith to grow. Jesus Christ was the greatest and bravest Hero of all time. We love and admire the Lord Jesus Christ for His great courage in His costly sacrifice on our behalf (Rom. 5:8). We should have the courage to endure our light afflictions. "Yea, and all that will live godly in Christ Jesus shall suffer persecution" (2 Tim. 3:12). Paul called what he endured "light afflictions" (2 Cor. 4:17). He also said, "Who now rejoice in my sufferings for you, and fill up that which is behind of the afflictions of Christ in my flesh for <u>his body's sake, which is the church</u>" (Col. 1:24). Most of us have not suffered much in comparison to our Lord or Paul. Paul suffered much more than most of us. He will probably hold a position similar to God's prime minister in heaven. Some of us have received the cold shoulder from family and friends because of our faith. Our suffering could still get worse on earth. The dispensation of grace will end in apostasy, not in revival (1 Tim. 4:1, 2; 2 Tim. 3:1-5, 3:12, 13, 4:1-4). All suffering will be worth it all when we see Jesus.] **6 Seeing it is <u>a righteous thing with God to recompense tribulation to them that trouble you;</u>** [Just as it is righteous for God to reward them, likewise it is righteous for God to recompense (repay) tribulation on those who trouble them. Their persecutors who cause them tribulation would suffer great tribulation if the imminent Rapture happened. God alone is to judge unbelieving mankind, and will at the Great White Throne Judgment. In his letter to the Romans, Paul wrote, "Dearly beloved, avenge not yourselves, but rather give place unto wrath: for it is written, <u>Vengeance is mine; I will repay, saith the Lord</u>" (Rom. 12:19). We are not to render evil for evil (1 Thess. 5:15). God is love, but He is also just. God's righteousness demands that He judges the unjust (Gen. 18:25). God has laid up treasures of hail that He has reserved for the day of battle and war at His Second Coming (Job 38:22, 23). The Bible says that that hail will weigh as much as a talent of gold. "And there fell upon men a great hail out of heaven, every stone about the <u>weight of a talent</u>: and men blasphemed God because of the plague of the hail; for the plague thereof was exceeding great" (Rev. 16:21). The order of events is the Rapture, the Tribulation, and then the Second Coming of Christ.] **7 And to you who are troubled <u>rest with us</u>, when <u>the Lord Jesus shall be revealed from heaven with his mighty angels,</u>** [*Notice the comma after rest with us. The comma is a pause that separates the first part of the sentence from the second part. In this case, it separates their joy in heaven, from Christ's judgment on the earth. Those believers who are troubled will "<u>rest with us</u>" (in heaven after the Rapture) while the Lord Jesus Christ recompenses the evil unbelievers. The body of Christ will have been "caught up" and will rest with God in the third heaven during the Tribulation when the Lord Jesus comes with His mighty angels at His Second Coming. His Second Coming is the revelation of Jesus Christ (Rev. 1:1-3). There are three sets of "the sons of God:" good angels (Job 38:7), believing Israel (John 1:12; 1 John 3:1, 2), and the body of Christ (Rom. 8:14, 19). At the Rapture (the adoption, "the redemption of our body" (Rom. 8:23) the true believers are the heavenly "sons of God" (Rom. 8:19) who will be the ones that are "caught up" to heaven to meet the Lord in the air in the clouds. The earthly sons of God will be resurrected in the kingdom (John 5:25-29). Understanding the Bible intellectually as historic or as literature is not the same as trusting in Christ's death for our sins and resurrection from the heart. Each person must be sure they are saved so they can lay hold on eternal life (1 Tim. 6:12). Sons of God are set apart saints. They are set apart for God's glory because they trust in Him. Christ gave His heart to His Father, by trusting Him and His word, and Sons of God do the same. "My son, give me thine heart, and let thine eyes observe my ways" (Prov. 23:26). The holy angels are set apart for God or saints (Jude 1:14, 15). Notice that Christ comes with His angels (Isa. 13:3-5; Matt. 25:31; Rev. 19:11-16). The Lord's army is His angels (Joel 2:11). Jesus Christ is the Lord of an "innumerable company of angels" (Heb. 12:22). Angels are very strong and mighty. We know that just one angel killed 185,000 of the Assyrian army in one night (2 Kings 19:35).] **8 In flaming fire taking vengeance on them that know not God, and that OBEY NOT the gospel of our Lord Jesus Christ:** [The vengeance of God will come on those "that know not God." They do not care to know their Creator (Rom. 1:18-21). They knew of God, but they were still spiritually dead because they had not trusted His word and did not have His Spirit in them (Rom. 8:9; Col. 1:27). Paul said, "that I may know him" (Phil. 3:10). God will avenge those "that obey not the gospel of our Lord Jesus Christ." Those who will not believe the good news of our Lord in mystery or prophecy. To obey God in mystery is to believe what Christ says through His apostle Paul (2 Cor. 10:5). Believing the gospel Paul preached is not optional, we are commanded to believe that gospel. "Believe on the Lord Jesus Christ, and thou shalt be saved" (Acts 16:31) is a command. Paul's "my gospel" is to be believed in this dispensation "according to the commandment of the everlasting God, made known to all nations for the obedience of faith" (Rom. 16:26). What exactly is the gospel we must believe to be saved? "For I [Paul] delivered unto you first of all that which I also received, how that [by crucifixion] Christ died for OUR SINS [Jews and Gentiles in mystery] according to the scriptures; And that he was buried, and that he rose again the third day according to the scriptures" (1 Cor. 15:3, 4). Paul said he was the due time testifier who testified that Christ died for all. "Who gave himself a ransom for all, to be testified in due time" (1 Tim. 2:6). Both the dispensation of grace and the body of Christ began in Acts 9 when Paul was saved on the road to Damascus. Paul was the first member of the body of Christ in the dispensation of grace to be saved (1 Tim. 1:16). At His First Coming, Christ came with love, mercy, and grace to seek and to save the lost sheep of Israel (Luke 19:10). But at His Second Coming, Christ comes in judgment with vengeance (Heb. 10:30; Jude 7; Rev. 8:7, 11:19; 14:14-20). There will be blood for 200 miles up to the horse bridles. "And the winepress was trodden without the city, and blood came out of the winepress, even unto the horse bridles, by the space of a thousand and six hundred furlongs" (Rev. 14:20).

The Lord Jesus rightly divided at a comma between His first and second coming in Isaiah 61:2, as stated in Luke 4:19. The Lord will come in "flaming fire" at His Second Advent. "And I saw the beast, and the kings of the earth, and their armies gathered together to make war against him that sat on the horse, and against his army. And the beast was taken, and with him the false prophet that wrought miracles before him, with which he deceived them that had received the mark of the beast (it necessitates a one-world currency), and them that worshipped his image. These both were cast alive into a lake of fire burning with brimstone" (Rev. 19:19, 20). Jesus Christ will execute wrath on unbelieving Jews and Gentiles, the nations, and Antichrist at the battle of Armageddon by the sword of His mouth and rain down fiery hail and brimstone that God has reserved for the day of battle (Job 38:27; Rev. 16:13-16, 21; Rev. 19:11-21). God will send down fire from heaven at the final rebellion after His first millennial reign (Rev. 20:7-9). Satan will be locked up in hell for Christ's first millennial reign. There will be a crowd of evil worm like souls waiting for him that deceived them (Isa. 14:9-11). But Satan will be let loose for the final purging of the rebels. Then Satan will join the beast (Antichrist) and the false prophet who have already been tormented in the Lake of Fire for a thousand years. "And the devil that deceived them was cast into the lake of fire and brimstone, where the beast and the false prophet are, and shall be tormented day and night for ever and ever" (Rev. 20:10).] **9 Who shall be punished with everlasting destruction from the presence of the Lord, and from the glory of his power;** [The evildoers will be punished with everlasting destruction, not everlasting annihilation. Although Paul never mentioned the word "hell," he describes it perfectly. Hell is a place of "everlasting destruction." They are eternally separated "from the presence of the Lord, and from the glory of his power." Christ will judge the lost and decide on the degree of eternal torment at the Great White Throne Judgment before hell is cast into the Lake of Fire (Rom. 2:6; Rev. 20:14). Hell is currently in the heart of the earth (Matt. 12:40), but it will be cast into the Lake of Fire, a gigantic trashcan which may be located at the bottom of the universe. Unbelievers who die in this dispensation will be judged at that time according to Paul's "my gospel" (Rom. 2:16). The Lord's mighty power will be glorious to behold by His believers at His Second Coming. The believers will be waiting for Him (possibly in the mountains of Petra) and they will admire Him.] **10 When he shall come to be glorified in his saints, and to be admired in all them that believe (because our testimony among you was believed) in THAT DAY.** [When Christ comes to earth the second time, the believers who hope to live in His kingdom on earth will glorify and admire Him. Many will believe because the body of Christ believed and was Raptured. Paul's testimony of the Rapture was true. At Christ's Second coming believers in prophecy will be waiting for Jesus to arrive on earth. The mainly Jewish believers in prophecy will look forward to the day of the Lord ("THAT DAY") as a blessing (Zeph. 3:8-20; John 14:3). Many will have believed in Christ because God kept His promise and Raptured the body of Christ (Titus 1:2). They will not believe other lies about why we disappeared such as the aliens stole us. The Day of the Lord will be a day of horror for the unbelievers. They will ask the mountains and rocks to fall on them and cover them from the face of Him (Luke 23:30). "And said to the mountains and rocks, Fall on us, and hide us from the face of him that sitteth on the throne, and from the wrath of the Lamb" (Rev. 6:16). Revelation 6 is an overview of the Tribulation. But the believers in prophecy will be looking for Him (Zech. 12:10). No signs precede the Rapture but many signs precede Christ's Second Coming to earth. It will be dark and the sign of the Son of man will be dramatic. The sun and moon will be dark. He comes in His glory with bright light in the darkness, every eye shall see Him. "Immediately after the tribulation of those days shall the sun be darkened, and the moon shall not give her light, and the stars shall fall from heaven, and the powers of the heavens shall be shaken: And then shall appear the sign of the Son of man in heaven: and then shall all the tribes of the earth mourn, and they shall see the Son of man coming in the clouds of heaven with power and great glory" (Matt. 24:29, 30). Stephen said that Israel did not recognize Joseph the first time they saw him, nor did they know Moses would deliver them until the second time he came, likewise Israel will not recognize their Messiah until the second time He comes (Acts 7:13, 35-37, 51). Hebrews makes it clear that Christ is coming to the Hebrews for the second time. "So Christ was once offered to bear the sins of many; and unto them that look for him shall he appear the second time without sin unto salvation" (Heb. 9:28). All of the Bible is about the Lord Jesus Christ who came to do the Father's will. "Then said I, Lo, I come (in the volume of the book it is written of me,) to do thy will, O God" (Heb. 10:7). "I delight to do thy will, O my God: yea, thy law is within my heart" (Psa. 40:8).] **11 Wherefore also we pray always for you, that our God would count you worthy of this calling, and fulfil all the good pleasure of his goodness, and the work of faith with power: 12 That the name of our Lord Jesus Christ may be glorified in you, and ye in him, according to the grace of our God and the Lord Jesus Christ.** [Paul switches back to talking about the Thessalonians. The Rapture has been at hand since Paul's day. If they had been "caught up" their persecutors would have gone into the Tribulation. "Wherefore" means "for this reason" that they will rest in heaven while their persecutors go into the Tribulation to face Christ at His Second coming; Paul, Silas, and Timothy are praying that they will be worthy to be in His kingdom. They do not pray that they would escape suffering but that God's purpose would be accomplished through them. Paul and his companions always pray for the Thessalonians that God would count them worthy of their calling to be part of the Kingdom of God in the heavenly places (1:5). That they would remain steadfast in "the faith," the "preaching of Jesus Christ, according to the revelation of the mystery" (Rom. 16:25). "There is one body, and one Spirit, even as ye are called in <u>one hope of your calling</u>" (Eph. 4:4). Paul wants them to be useful to God so Christ's name will be glorified in them. Willing for Jesus Christ to live His life through them to fulfill all the good pleasure of His goodness and His work of faith with His power in them (Rom. 12:1, 2; Gal. 2:20). It is all about Jesus Christ, what He has done, and what He is doing through the believers. Before salvation we were spiritually dead, but after salvation we receive the life of Jesus in us (2 Cor. 4:7, 10, 11). The life of Jesus in us will function properly if we understand the mystery Christ gave us through Paul. We bring honor to the name of Jesus Christ when His power in us is doing the work (Eph. 2:10). We walk by faith in what God says in His word to and about us (2 Cor. 5:7). Paul wants Christ to be glorified in them (Christ does the work by His power in us so He receives the credit), and they are to be glorified in Him according to the grace of our God and the Lord Jesus Christ. <u>It is by the grace of God that we have received His Spirit that does the work of God in and through us using the word of God</u>. It is such a joy that by His grace we are allowed to join in His Glory Plan to reconcile heaven and earth and to glorify and exalt His Son. The name of the Lord Jesus is glorified by Him manifesting Himself to the world through us, which is the mystery of godliness (1 Tim. 3:16). "Christ in us the hope of glory" (Col. 1:27), and the body of Christ are to "the praise of his glory" (Eph. 1:12). Martin Luther said, "today counts forever." Our service on earth is adding to His glory and our glory with Him. We will be joint-heirs with Christ (Rom. 8:17). <u>Like Paul we glory in the cross of Christ. The world has lost its luster and pales in comparison to what our blessed Lord Jesus Christ has done for us. "But God forbid that I should glory, save in the cross of our Lord Jesus Christ, by whom the world is crucified unto me, and I unto the world"</u> (Gal. 6:14).]

THAT THE NAME OF OUR LORD JESUS CHRIST MAY BE GLORIFIED IN YOU, AND YE IN HIM, ACCORDING TO THE GRACE OF OUR GOD AND THE LORD JESUS CHRIST.

2 Thessalonians 1:12

And to you who are troubled rest with us, when the Lord Jesus shall be revealed from heaven with his mighty angels, In flaming fire taking vengeance on them that know not God, and that obey not the gospel of our Lord Jesus Christ: Who shall be punished with everlasting destruction from the presence of the Lord, and from the glory of his power; When he shall come to be glorified in his saints, and to be admired in all them that believe (because our testimony among you was believed) in that day.
2 Thessalonians 1:7-10 KJV
Jesus sent Paul

2 Thessalonians Chapter 2 "Shaken in mind" by false doctrine
2:1, 2 Do not be deceived by any means, we will be gathered before the wrath.
2:3-9 Paul explains the day of the Lord to show they are not in it.
2:13-17 Believers can have peace, comfort, good hope, and stable minds.

When we come to this very interesting chapter we may have several questions:
What are the three sources of false doctrine (2:2)?
What does Paul mean by the "day of Christ is at hand" (2:2)?
What "withholdeth" the wrath (2:6)?
What is the mystery of iniquity (2:7)?
Who is the "he" "that now letteth until he be taken out of the way" (2:7)?
What is the "lie" (2:11)?
Can you give us some clues about who Antichrist will be?
Why did Jesus have to die?
I know that Christ died for our sins, but how is He our substitute?

The purpose of this life is to determine where we will spend eternity. Will we have eternal life with God or eternal torment and separation from God? Will we have anything of value at the Judgment Seat of Christ?

2:1 Now we beseech you, brethren, by the coming of our Lord Jesus Christ, and by our gathering together unto him, 2 That ye be not soon shaken in mind, or be troubled, neither by spirit, nor by word, nor by letter as from us, as that the day of Christ is at hand. [Paul implores them on the sure basis of the Lord Jesus Christ coming in the air to gather us together unto Him (1:7, 10; 1 Thess. 4:16, 17). This is when the dead and living body of Christ believers are "caught up" in our glorified bodies and join Christ in the clouds. Paul says that they should not be "shaken in mind" or "troubled" by false doctrine (teaching). False doctrine, especially concerning our blessed hope, will shake our minds and trouble us. The body of Christ will be "caught up" (Raptured) to heaven before prophecy resumes with the Tribulation period and the Second Coming of Christ to earth. Paul names three sources of false doctrine. He does not want them to be troubled: (1) by spirit (the spirit in a man that did not teach what Paul taught, 2 Cor. 11:3; Col. 2:4, 8; 2 Tim. 3:13) (2) nor by word that they hear someone say, (3) nor by letter as from us." There may have been a misunderstanding concerning what Paul said in 1 Thessalonians chapter 5 about the day of the Lord. The implication is that they had received a letter that they thought was from apostle Paul, but wasn't because Paul could verify that he never sent such a letter. It was most likely a forged letter. To avoid counterfeit scripture, Paul now begins to sign all his letters "with mine own hand" (3:17) to authenticate them. The false doctrine had troubled the Thessalonians without and within. They had been told that the "day of Christ is at hand." I agree with Pastor Richard Jordan that the false teachers at Thessalonica had redefined and misused the "day of Christ" from a good to a bad thing; from having to do with "our gathering together" to meaning the "day of the Lord." Paul describes the order of events leading up to THAT DAY (the day of the Lord) to show them that they (and we) are not in the Tribulation. If the "day of Christ is at hand" (His Second Coming to earth) that would mean they had missed the Rapture and were in the Tribulation. "Our gathering together unto him" is the Rapture. In his first letter to them, Paul repeatedly told them that our being "caught up" was a comfort (1 Thess. 4:13-18).

Paul often warns against men who are false ministers of Christ with false spirits (2 Cor. 11:3, 4, 14, 15; Col. 2:4, 8). Paul told the Corinthians that their biggest problem was the false ministers of Christ (2 Cor. 11:23). "For if he that cometh preacheth another Jesus [Christ on earth, not Christ according to the revelation of the mystery], whom we have not preached [not preached by Paul], or if ye receive another spirit [the one from the angel of light, Satan (2 Cor. 11:14)], which ye have not received, or another gospel [the gospel of the kingdom, not the gospel of the grace of God], which ye have not accepted, ye might well bear with him" (2 Cor. 11:4). That we henceforth be no more children, tossed to and fro, and carried about with every wind of doctrine, by the sleight of men, and cunning craftiness, whereby they lie in wait to deceive" (Eph. 4:14). "But evil men and seducers shall wax worse and worse, deceiving, and being deceived" (2 Tim. 3:13). Those who had the gift of discerning the true word of God during Acts when spiritual gifts were in effect in Thessalonica were not doing a good job (1 Cor. 12:10). Corruption of the word of God began during Paul's life time and continues today with corrupt modern Bibles. Paul was always careful to say exactly what Christ revealed through him (2 Cor. 2:17). The NIV is missing 16 verses and a total of 64,000 words which is equivalent (I have heard) to the length of the entire book of Revelation. False teachers had not only said the Rapture was past, but had redefined the usually joyful and comforting day to one of dread. The phrase "day of Christ" in the King James Bible is a perfect translation of the Greek Textus Receptus. The text should not be changed but understood in the context. In every other place in our Bible the day of Christ, His appearing, or the day of Jesus Christ is a day of joy, comfort, and hope (1 Cor. 1:7, 8, 15:23; Phil. 1:6, 1:10, 2:16; 1 Thess. 4:14-17; 1 Tim. 6:14; 2 Tim. 4:1, 8; Titus 2:13). But in this context the "day of Christ" is used to indicate the "day of the Lord" (1 Thess. 5:2), His Second Coming to earth. When Christ who is the Lord will come to earth in Judgment of unbelievers, but as a blessing to the believers in prophecy. Faithless people who are alive when the Rapture occurs, will go into the Tribulation. The day of the Lord is first mentioned in Isaiah 2:12, but is referred to all through the Bible. The reason for the day of the Lord (the wrath) has nothing to do with the body of Christ, but is prophesied punishment of Israel for their spiritual idolatry (Leviticus 26:27-39). If the body of Christ were in the Tribulation we would need to preach the gospel of the kingdom, not the gospel of Christ. The gospel of the kingdom is that Jesus of Nazareth who came the first time was the true Messiah and He will return and reign as the King of the Jews, just as God said. Jesus Christ was born of a traceable line of descendants (Matt. 1; Luke 3). During the Tribulation, true believers will confess that Jesus has already come in the flesh. "Hereby know ye the Spirit of God: Every spirit that confesseth that Jesus Christ is come in the flesh is of God: And every spirit that confesseth NOT that Jesus Christ is come in the flesh is NOT of God: and this is that spirit of antichrist, whereof ye have heard that it should come; and even now already is it in the world" (1 John 4:2, 3).] **3 Let no man deceive you by any means: for THAT DAY** [The day of the Lord, His Second Coming to earth in judgment preceded by the Tribulation (which was preceded by our Rapture).] **shall not come, except there come a falling away** [Israel will believe Antichrist and sign the covenant.] **first, and that man of sin be revealed** [Antichrist is revealed when Israel signs a 7-year covenant with him.], **the son of perdition;** [God warns all people once again through Paul about the evil to come upon the earth. Paul doesn't want them to be deceived by any means (spirit, word, or letter). He contrasts the Rapture with the Tribulation and the Second Coming of Christ. <u>Paul describes the order of events in prophecy until the day of the Lord to show that they and we are not in it</u>. Paul said, "THAT DAY (the Second Coming of Christ to earth, the day of the Lord, Acts 2:20)" shall not come except that Israel first fall away from God and make a 7-year covenant with Antichrist. They will be happy when Antichrist agrees to let them make animal sacrifices in the rebuilt temple. <u>Antichrist is the "man of sin" in the first half of the week, and the "son of perdition" in the second half of the week. He becomes the son of perdition when Satan enters him</u>. Many in Israel will believe, worship, and follow Antichrist. <u>When on earth Jesus Christ said, "I am come in my Father's name, and ye receive me not: if another shall come in his own name, him ye will receive"</u> (John 5:43).

Paul understood both mystery and prophecy and so should we. Paul gives <u>a summary of the Tribulation</u>. Paul doesn't want them to be deceived away from the true order of events. First Israel will fall away from God and be deceived into worshipping Antichrist. (Apostasy in the dispensation of grace, began in Paul's day, and will grow worse and worse and continue until no one will want to trust the gospel of Christ, 2 Tim. 3:1-5.). The prophetic clock stopped on Palm Sunday and was followed by the cross. The one-year extension of mercy, the renewed offer of the kingdom to Israel by the Holy Ghost through Peter and the disciples, was a bonus year for Israel and does not apply to the 490 years (Dan. 9:24-27). The believing remnant will be reading all of the Bible, but the books of Daniel, Isaiah, 2 Thessalonians, and Hebrews through Revelation will be particularly helpful in getting through the Tribulation. When the Lord Jesus Christ opens the first seal, Antichrist will come forth (Rev. 6:1, 2). The Tribulation is an awful and horrible time (Dan. 8:23-27). I believe Antichrist will not acknowledge the New Testament as Scripture and will tell the Jews that they should build the temple just as Cyrus the Great had once commanded and allow them to offer animal sacrifices in the rebuilt temple in Jerusalem (2 Chron. 36:22, 23). This will fit in well with Jews who deny Christ's first Coming. These Jews are in apostasy because Christ has already offered a perfectly satisfying sacrifice to God. (In the millennium, animal sacrifices will be used legitimately to teach the Gentiles about the offerings the Jews should have known when Christ fulfilled them when He came the first time.) Antichrist will come in peacefully with flatteries (Dan. 11:21). He will be the king of the north who is against the king of the south (Egypt). He is most likely an Assyrian who is a Jew on his father's side (Isa. 10:5; Dan. 11:37). However, since Christ returns to put down Gentile rule, Antichrist's mother may be a Gentile (Dan. 2:35; Luke 21:24). The five "I will's" of Antichrist are in Isa. 10:13, 14. The destruction of Antichrist is in Isa. 10:17, 18. Antichrist will come back into the glorious land of Israel and set up a palace in mount Zion of Jerusalem (Dan. 11:41,

45). Satan and his angels are cast down to earth at that time. Satan knows he has only a short time to deceive as many in the whole world (not just Israel) as he can to follow him down to hell (Rev. 12:7-12). Antichrist is revealed as the "man of sin" when he signs the 7-year covenant with Israel. This begins the prophetic clock of Daniel's 70th week, the Tribulation (Dan. 9:27). After Antichrist dies by a stab to the head, "wound by a sword, and did live" he seems to "resurrect." This is when Satan will "ascend out of the bottomless pit" and enter him (Rev. 13:14, 17:8). Antichrist then becomes the "son of perdition." Antichrist being Satan incarnate, coincides with Satan being cast out of heaven in Revelation chapter 12. That is when the "man of sin" becomes the "son of perdition." Then in Revelation chapter 13, readers learn that the nature of Antichrist is as a leopard like BEAST powered by the Dragon. Satan himself speaks great blasphemies against God through him (Dan. 7:8; Rev. 13:1-10). Satan enters him just like he did Judas. Satan has been at war with God since iniquity was found in him (Ezek. 28:15). Satan counterfeits everything God does. The unholy trinity, the dragon (Satan), the beast (Antichrist), and the false prophet (Rev. 16:13) are a perversion of the Holy Trinity, God the Father, God the Son, and God the Holy Ghost. PERDITION is defined as the utter loss of the soul, future misery, and eternal death. The impenitent sinner is condemned to final perdition. Antichrist and Judas became the son of perdition when Satan entered them and took them over (Psa. 55:20-23; Luke 22:3; John 17:12). The mark of the beast in the forehead may be a leopard spot, while the mark in the hand may be a computer chip. God's angel warns them not to take the mark (Deut. 32:5; Rev. 13:16, 14:9). They will need to keep themselves "unspotted from the world" (James 1:27). In verse 8, Paul says that the "man of sin" shall not be revealed until after our gathering together.] **4 Who opposeth and exalteth himself above all that is called God, or that is worshipped; so that he as God sitteth in the temple of God, shewing himself that he** [Antichrist] **is God.** [God is used four times in this verse. The imposter, Antichrist, opposes and exalts himself above all that is called God or that is worshipped. Antichrist insists on only him being worshipped and on a one world religion. He is a false Christ of a false religion and a corrupt leader who wants a one world government. In contrast, Christ humbled Himself and the Father exalted Him and will exalt Him more (Phil. 2:5-11). However, unlike Christ, Antichrist took Satan up on the offer to rule all the kingdoms of the world so he will have to worship Satan (Matt. 4:8, 9). Antichrist will exalt himself and worship a strange military god, Satan (Dan. 11:36-40; Rev. 13:4). The life of Antichrist can be summarized as a peace maker that becomes a peace breaker and then a ruthless persecutor of the believing remnant of Israel. Ten confederate nations are mentioned in Psalm 83:5-8 (Dan. 7:24; Rev. 13:1, 17:3). He will also change times and laws (Dan. 7:25). The seven years of the Tribulation is divided into two sets of 3 ½ years. A period of 3 ½ years is equal to 1260 days, or 42 months or "a time, times, and a half" (Dan. 12:7). The wise believers will be able to count the days until Christ's Second Advent if they study the Bible. Daniel chapter 12 will be especially useful. In the middle of the Tribulation, Antichrist will break the covenant with Israel that allowed them to offer animal sacrifices there, and cause them to cease (Dan. 9:27, 11:30-33; Psa. 55:20-23). Antichrist will declare himself to be "Christ" and worthy of worship. This is what Satan has always wanted (Isa. 14:12-14). Antichrist will sit in the temple, in the holy of holies on the Mercy seat of the ark of the covenant "between the cherubims" and say that he is God. There is no other place to sit in the temple. The abomination that maketh desolate is Antichrist sitting in the temple of God at Jerusalem "shewing himself that he [Antichrist] is God" (Dan. 9:27, 12:11). Antichrist's number is 666 (Rev. 13:18); Six is the number of man, he is a sort of superman. Empowered by Satan after his strange death, burial, and resurrection, Antichrist is the culmination of all that fallen man can accomplish apart from God. The Christ rejecting world will learn what life without God and a world run by a Satan empowered man will be like. As the last days of the dispensation of grace become more perilous the table is being set for Antichrist. When on earth, Jesus Christ warned the believing remnant that this is the time to drop everything and flee out of Judea (Southern Israel) for God will take care of them in a place in the wilderness. But the Jews that are scattered throughout the world will be severely persecuted. Many believing Gentiles will help the like they did in WWII (Matt. 25:31-40). "When ye therefore shall see the abomination of desolation, spoken of by Daniel the prophet, stand in the holy place, (whoso readeth, let him understand:) Then let them which be in Judaea flee into the mountains: Let him which is on the housetop not come down to take any thing out of his house: neither let him which is in the field return back to take his clothes" (Dan. 11:31; Matt. 24:15-18; Mark 13:14). The souls of those who worship Antichrist will be desolate and destitute. They will suffer eternal expulsion from God's presence. Only the believers who go through the Tribulation will understand what they need to know. God has told them when to expect Antichrist to break the covenant. "And from the time that the daily sacrifice shall be taken away, and the abomination that maketh desolate set up, there shall be a thousand two hundred and ninety days" (Dan. 12:11). Under the man of sin apostate Jerusalem "spiritually is called Sodom and Egypt, where also our Lord was crucified" (Rev. 11:8), but now under the son of perdition Jerusalem is spiritually Babylon. He will kill the two witnesses. "And in her was found the blood of prophets, and of saints, and of all that were slain upon the earth" (Rev. 18:24, see also 1 Thess. 2:15). Jesus Christ said, "it cannot be that a prophet perish out of Jerusalem" (Luke 13:33). The believing remnant will need to flee from Antichrist out of Jerusalem because Jerusalem has become the decadent one world apostate religious and political center, the culmination of the Tower of

Babel of old. False religion began with Lucifer who became Satan, and continued through Cain and his seed. The evil seed-line hit a peak with Nimrod and the tower of Babel. However, Jerusalem with the imposter, Antichrist being worshipped, has blossomed into the full climax. Jerusalem, spiritual Babylon, will be the Mother of all false religion and spiritual adultery. (Many believe Catholicism and Islam were Babylon the great, the mother, but they are only among the daughters.) "And upon her forehead was a name written, MYSTERY, BABYLON THE GREAT, THE MOTHER OF HARLOTS AND ABOMINATIONS OF THE EARTH (Rev. 17:5). The city will be destroyed by God in one hour (Matt. 22:7; Rev. 17:18, 18:16-19). "Babylon is fallen, is fallen, that great city, because she made all nations drink of the wine of the wrath of her fornication" (Rev. 14:8). Those who dwell on the earth will lament the destruction of the opulent city (Rev. 18:12, 13). Many will be deceived into believing that apostate Jerusalem is the New Jerusalem (Rev. 18:23, 24). Peter identified Jerusalem as Babylon for the believing remnant (1 Peter 5:13). Many will believe "the lie" that Antichrist is Christ, and that they can be like him and partake of his spirit. Antichrist will want everyone to bow down to his image which the false prophet will make to speak (Rev. 13:11-18). The wise believing remnant who read the Bible, will know the truth, flee and help others (Dan. 11:30-35). The believing remnant will be able to calculate the very day of Christ's return and the resurrection of the kingdom saints (Daniel 12:6-13). But they will not know when in that day Christ will arrive, (morning, noon, or night). But they will not know when in that day Christ will arrive, (morning, noon, or night). Daniel will be resurrected 45 days (subtract 1290 from 1,335 in Dan. 12:11, 12) after Christ comes to earth and stands on the mount of Olives (Zech. 14:4).] **5 Remember ye not, that, when I was yet with you, I told you these things?** [Paul had mentioned all this advanced information to the new believers when he was with them for three weeks.] **6 And now ye know what withholdeth** [the dispensation of grace which ends with our gathering together, the Rapture, (2:1)] **that he** [man of sin] **might be revealed in his time** [the "prince that shall come" (Dan. 9:26)]. [The "what" is the dispensation of grace which ends with our gathering together, the Rapture (2:1) which is delaying the wrath of God. Paul referred to the Rapture as "our gathering together unto him" (2:1). The "he" is "the man of sin," Antichrist. How is "the man of sin" revealed to the people of Israel? Yes, exactly, he will be the one who signs the covenant with Israel for seven years (Dan. 9:27). In other words, when Antichrist signs the seven-year covenant with Israel, the believers who read the Bible will know who he is and what is going on. Believers in prophecy will trust that Jesus of Nazareth who came the first time is the real Messiah, traverse through the Tribulation, endure until the end of it or be martyred, and have eternal life in the kingdom.] **7 For the mystery of iniquity doth already work: only he** [the body of Christ, the one new man (Eph. 2:15)] **who now letteth** [now holds back, hinders] **will let** [hold back, obstruct]**, until he** [the body of Christ, the one new man (Eph. 2:15)] **be taken out of the way** [our gathering together to meet the Lord in the air]**. 8 And then shall that Wicked be revealed, whom the Lord shall consume with the spirit of his mouth, and shall destroy with the brightness of his coming:** [God warns all people concerning "that Wicked one" and God gives the final outcome: Christ destroys Antichrist and then Satan (Heb. 2:14; 1 John 3:8). To "let" is to hold back, hinder, obstruct, or prevent. (Compare Rom. 1:13 with Rom. 15:22 to see that the Bible has its own built in-dictionary.). The "he" here is the body of Christ, also known as the "one new man" (Eph. 2:15) which now holds back the wrath of God. As long as our Church is in the world, the wrath is held back. Until "he" (the one new man, the body of Christ) will be taken out of the way at the Rapture which ends the dispensation of grace. Then Antichrist will be revealed after that. Since the "man of sin" (Antichrist) is not revealed until after the Rapture, there is no reason for us to speculate about who he is. Has any diplomat signed a 7-year covenant with Israel to allow them to offer sacrifices in the temple? No, the temple is not even rebuilt yet, so we are not in the Tribulation. It is that clear and simple. Paul says the "mystery of iniquity doth already work." The mystery of iniquity is false anti-God religion. The mystery of iniquity began with Lucifer (iniquity was found in him, Ezek. 28:15). He became Satan who wanted to be worshipped (Isa. 14:12-14). Satan convinced Adam and Eve to join him. Then he continued his wicked seed-line through Cain. His wicked religious seed-line opposes those who will believe God and God's seed-line to Messiah (Abel, Seth, Noah, Abraham, Isaac, Jacob, David, and so on). Seth means "appointed in place of," a substitute. After Cain slew his brother Abel, who was the godly seed-line, Seth replaced him (Heb. 11:4). Jesus was a better sacrifice than that of Abel because it is the perfect blood of the God-Man, not a lamb for Israel's New Covenant (John 1:29; Acts 20:28; Heb. 12:24). There are two ways (the broad and the narrow): one way leads to eternal life, while the other way leads to eternal death. Jesus said, "I am the way, the truth and the life" (John 14:6). There are two sets of people in the world, the saved and the lost. Christ said there are tares (false believers) among the wheat (true believers) (Matt. 13:24-30). Apostle John differentiates between the children of God and the children of the devil (1 John 3:10). The mystery of iniquity is Satan manifest in the flesh, the opposite of the mystery of godliness, which is "God was manifest in the flesh" (1 Tim. 3:16). Modern Bibles change "God" to "he" in 1 Tim. 3:16. The "prince of the power of the air [Satan is], the spirit that now worketh in the children of disobedience" (Eph. 2:2). We were "the children of disobedience" (Eph. 2:2) but we were translated out of the power of darkness, into the kingdom of His dear Son (Col. 1:13). We have "redemption through his blood, even the forgiveness of sins" (Col. 1:14). Contrary to popular belief, Christ will come when evil reaches its maximum. Christ will put down all opposition by the sword of His mouth. He is the "Word of God" (Rev. 19:11-21). The "spirit of his mouth" is the "sword of my mouth" (Rev. 2:16), "out of his mouth goeth a sharp sword" (Rev. 19:15). The powerful "Word of God" (Rev. 19:13) with a capital "W," is the Creator who will consume and destroy any creature who presume to fight against Him. <u>The Lord's Second Coming begins in heaven</u> (Isa. 34:5). Have no fear, the strong man's house (Satan's) has been plundered by a stronger, the Lord Jesus Christ (Matt. 12:29). At the "<u>brightness of his coming</u>" the Lord destroys His enemies the beast, false prophet, and their armies which is "great and dreadful day of the LORD" (Mal. 4:1). The Sun and the moon will be dark. The world will lie in darkness and see the sign of the Son of man coming (Matt. 24:30). His bright light will warm believers (John 14:3; Zech. 12:10) and scare unbelievers. Every eye shall see Him. "For as the lightning, that lighteneth out of the one part under heaven, shineth unto the other part under heaven; so shall also the Son of man be in his day" (Luke 17:24). "Behold, he cometh with clouds; and <u>every eye shall see him</u>, and they also which pierced him: and all <u>kindreds</u> of the earth shall wail because of him. Even so, Amen" (Rev. 1:7).] **9 Even him, whose coming is after the working of Satan with all power and signs and lying wonders, 10 And with all deceivableness of unrighteousness in them that perish; because they received not the love of the truth, that they might be saved.** [Paul lets everyone know that Satan will work through the "man of sin." The "even him" is Antichrist (2:4) "that Wicked" who is empowered by Satan to do signs and lying wonders. Perhaps Antichrist will have the power to heal, still the wind, and walk on water by Satan's power (Satan sent wind in Job 1:19). Antichrist will make war with the saints (believers) and the unbelievers will worship him (Rev. 13:7, 8). <u>Just like the regathering of Israel is yet future and did not occur in 1948, neither was prophesy fulfilled when the temple was destroyed in AD 70</u>. Christ was referring to the temple <u>that will be destroyed by Antichrist in Matthew 24:1, 2 or Luke 21:6</u>. "And after threescore and two weeks shall Messiah be cut off, but not for himself: and the people of the prince [Antichrist] that shall come shall destroy the city and the <u>sanctuary</u> . . ." (Dan. 9:26). Another beast comes "out of the earth" which appears as a lamb but speaks as a dragon (a wolf in sheep's clothing). This is the false prophet who is also empowered by Satan. He does many of the same signs as the first beast to support the claim of Antichrist. Unbelievers will also believe the signs and wonders of the false prophet does. <u>He makes fire come down from heaven like God did for Elijah</u> and he makes the image of Antichrist (like the one of Nebuchadnezzar) speak (Rev. 13:11-18). Many people go by feelings, sight, miracles, and experience; not by the word of God, "they receive not the love of the truth." Paul said, "in them" that perish, the spirit of Antichrist, Satan's, will be in them. They could have been saved if they read the Bible because "faith cometh by hearing, and hearing by the word of God" (Rom. 10:17). There are people in both mystery and prophecy who could have been saved if they had faith in what God said in His word to them. They are deceived, unrighteous, and will perish because they neglect to trust the real Christ and to read the truth of what God's word says for themselves in the Bible. Always remember that while Bible believing teachers who are both dispensational and Biblical by understanding the word of God rightly divided and Paul's distinctive ministry can help us, all humans are imperfect. Therefore, everyone should check what is being taught by the scriptures. We need to read and study our final absolute authority the King James Bible for ourselves. We show God we love Him by studying His word to us.] **11 And for this cause God shall send them strong delusion, that they should believe a lie: 12 That they all might be damned who believed not the truth, but had pleasure in unrighteousness.** ["For this cause" that they "received not the love of the truth," God shall send strong delusion on the unbelievers. They refused to believe God's word to them. They did not believe what the Son of God did for them, but worshipped Antichrist, the son of perdition. So the unbelievers can all be damned to hell and the lake of fire because they believed not the truth of what the Son of God did, but took pleasure in unrighteousness. God sent Antichrist (Rev. 6:1, 2; Isa. 10:5-19). They did not care to trust God's true provision of Jesus Christ for the remission of their sins and to read the Bible, God's true word, so they could be saved and know God. These people will believe a lie, the original lie (Isa. 14:12), that Antichrist is God and that they could be as gods (Gen. 3:5). Adam and Eve believed Satan's lie. Adam and Eve knew good and evil, but they ate of the tree of the "knowledge of good and evil" because they wanted to be like gods and judge good and evil apart from God. Only God is the rightful judge (Gen. 18:25; 2 Tim. 4:1, 8). They did not want to be in subjection to God; they wanted to overstep their boundary (Rom. 1:21). They wanted to cast off their ties to God, and rule for themselves just like the Jews in Christ's day, under Herod and Pilate (Psa. 2:3). Adam and Eve's dream of deification turned into a nightmare, when they realized the shame of their nakedness and their helpless condition. Adam and Eve should have died immediately, not the innocent animals. God punished the innocent animals instead of Adam and Eve. God was patient and merciful because he knew He was really fighting against Satan, just like we do (Eph. 6:12). God had a plan from the foundation of the world to restore mankind (1 Peter 1:18-20). Likewise, God poured out His punishment for sin on Jesus Christ when He was on the cross, instead of on all mankind. God requires that blood be shed for the remission of sins: "without shedding of blood is no remission" (Heb. 9:22). By the grace of God, Jesus Christ shed His blood and tasted the Second death for all mankind (Heb. 2:9). But death and hell could not hold the sinless Son of God (Acts 2:24). His blood was not tainted with sin because it was God's blood (Acts 28:20). This is why the Son of God had to die for us, death and hell could not hold the perfect Son of God; but death and hell would have held a human born with sin (Rom. 5:12). We deserve death for our sins (Rom. 6:23). But the precious Lamb of God was sacrificed as all believer's substitute (2 Cor. 5:21; Rev. 13:8). God will laugh at any creature who thinks he can be the Creator (Psa. 2:4). The Son of God was raised from the dead to demonstrate that His blood payment was accepted by Father God (Psa. 2:7; Acts 13:33). But, the LORD God has warned the people to trust His Son (Psa. 2:12), not the fake, counterfeit Antichrist that rose from the dead. The mystery of iniquity began with Satan (Isa. 14:12; Ezek. 28:15; 1 John 3:8). Speaking to the serpent God said, "And I will put enmity between thee and the woman, and between thy seed [the serpent's, Satan's] and her seed [the woman's seed-line to Jesus the Messiah]; it shall bruise thy head [a lethal blow], and thou shalt bruise his heel [not a lethal injury. Satan was so excited when he actually killed Jesus the Messiah]" (Gen. 3:15). Since Lucifer's fall and became Satan, there have been those who would believe and those who would not: two seed-lines running through all dispensations. God revealed that the two seed-lines would war against each other, but God's would win. From that moment on Satan wanted to destroy the seed of the woman before it could bruise its head. Adam and Eve had a son that they thought would be the Redeemer. But Cain turned out to be of Satan's seed line. Satan's wicked seed-line opposes God's seed-line to Messiah (and believers in God). Cain was the first to kill the righteous. "Not as Cain, who was of that wicked one, and slew his brother. And wherefore slew he him? Because his own works were evil, and his brother's righteous" (1 John 3:12). After Cain slew his brother Abel, God said, "What hast thou done? the voice of thy brother's blood crieth unto me from the ground" (Gen. 4:10). Adam and Eve didn't know that the younger son, Abel, was the true seed line to the Redeemer. Seth was appointed in his place. Abel was a prophet and he had most likely told Cain that he should bring a lamb as an offering. But Cain "brought of the fruit of the ground an offering unto the LORD" (Gen. 4:3). Cain had put his trust in his own good works. He could not believe that God would refuse a man who was holy and just in his own sight. Cain's sacrifice was open rebellion against God. Cain declared that God must accept what he decided to bring. (Cain was really the first religious Pharisee; he wanted to be accepted by God on his own terms, not God's.) Christ told the scribes and Pharisees, "Wherefore, behold, I send unto you prophets, and wise men, and scribes: and some of them ye shall kill and crucify; and some of them shall ye scourge in your synagogues, and persecute them from city to city: That upon you may come all the righteous blood shed upon the earth, from the blood of righteous Abel unto the blood of Zacharias" (Matt. 23:34, 35a). (It is interesting that Christ uses the Gentile Arabic alphabet, A to Z, not the Hebrew Alpha to Omega, as in Rev. 1:8.). The Pharisees were hypocrites putting on a show; they were empty and without love for God on the inside (Matt. 23:15). <u>Christ was "the Prophet"</u> (Deut. 18:15, 18, 19). The religious Pharisees perpetuated the traditions of men and Jesus Christ said they were the seed of their father the Devil. "Ye are of your father the devil, and the lusts of your father ye will do. He was a <u>murderer from the beginning</u>, and abode not in the truth, because there is no truth in him. When he speaketh <u>a lie</u>, he speaketh of his own: <u>for he is a liar, and the father of it</u>" (John 8:44). Satan wanted Adam and Eve to die, so he lied and said "ye shall not surely die. For God doth know that in the day ye eat thereof, then your eyes shall be opened, and ye shall be <u>as gods [Satan's angels]</u>, knowing good and evil" (Gen. 3:4b, 5). "Who changed the truth of God into <u>a lie</u>, and worshipped and served the <u>creature</u> more than the <u>Creator</u>" (Rom. 1:25). During the Tribulation the dragon is wroth with the woman that gave birth to the "man child" the believing the <u>remnant of her [Israel's] seed</u>, saved by the 144,000 from every tribe of Israel (Rev. 12:17). The mystery of godliness is that Christ is manifesting Himself to the world through the believer (1 Tim. 3:16). <u>The culmination of the mystery of iniquity is that Satan is manifest in the flesh by entering the body of Antichrist and likewise all the unbelievers.</u> In the Tribulation, God gives the rebels one or more chances to believe Him with increased punishments (Ezek. 20:38). The rebels are those that do not want to submit to God. The believers can tell them which plague is coming next, still the rebels refuse to believe God. Jesus said, "<u>And this is the condemnation, that light is come into the world, and men loved darkness rather than light, because their deeds were evil</u>" (John 3:19). There are only two kinds of people, the lost and the saved.]

13 ¶ But we are <u>bound to give thanks alway to God for you</u>, brethren <u>beloved of the Lord, because God hath from the beginning chosen you to salvation through sanctification of the Spirit and belief of the truth:</u> [But we, Paul makes a contrast, saying we thank God that God chose to save the body of Christ believers from the beginning of the dispensation of grace. God chose that all who have the Son's Spirit in them in this dispensation would be saved from the Wrath, by being caught up before the Tribulation (1 Thess. 1:10, 5:9). We were sanctified by receiving His Son's Spirit when we believed <u>the truth</u> of what His Son did (Eph. 1:13, 14). "God hath sent forth the <u>Spirit of his Son into your hearts</u>, crying, Abba, Father" (Gal. 4:6). The body of Christ is made up of believers from all nations (including Jews). Believers in the body of Christ have been redeemed from the iniquity in which we were held when we were "children of disobedience" (Eph. 2:2). "Who gave himself for us, that he might <u>redeem us from all iniquity</u>, and purify unto himself a peculiar people, zealous of good works" (Titus 2:14). Paul says they are compelled to thank God for them, <u>beloved of the Lord</u>. Believers are <u>beloved of God</u> because we are "accepted in the beloved" (Eph. 1:6). God chose the agency, the body of Christ. "According as he hath chosen us in him before the foundation of the world" (Eph. 1:4). The body of Christ was chosen, not the individual believers were chosen "from the beginning," to be in Christ, His elect (Isa. 42:1). But, God knew who would believe by His foreknowledge. Paul refers to the beginning of the dispensation of grace that began with Paul's salvation on the road to Damascus in Acts 9. The body of Christ also began in Acts 9. Pal was the first person saved into the body of Christ (1 Tim. 1:16). People have free will. Believers are not predestined, but the body of Christ was predetermined and chosen, it was in God's mind. The body of Christ was "hid in God" (Eph. 3:9). God already sees us as seated in heaven (Eph. 2:6). Once we believe and study God's word we are able to learn that we are in a chosen agency, the body of Christ (1 Cor. 12:13). Paul's point to the believers in Thessalonica is that they are not seeing these events because they are not in the Tribulation, and will not have any part in it. The Wrath is about Israel (Jer. 30:7) and has nothing to do with the body of Christ. God had already determined that the body of Christ would be Raptured (1 Thess. 1:10, 5:9). Just like Paul, we are to rightly divide and contrast Christ's program to us in mystery, with His program to Israel in prophecy. We need to know all of the Bible. Comparing and contrasting them make both programs clearer. Salvation, in this context, is from having to go through the Tribulation. But this verse also contains our justification, we believed the truth and were set apart by His Spirit in us. Those who do not believe at this time may be alive during the Tribulation.] **14 Whereunto he called you by our gospel, to the obtaining of the glory of our Lord Jesus Christ. 15 Therefore, brethren, stand fast, and hold the traditions which ye have been taught, whether by word, or our epistle**. [The believers are "called" to salvation by faith in "our gospel" the gospel Christ gave through Paul (1 Cor. 15:3, 4) that Silas and Timothy also shared. Upon salvation, we obtain eternal life with our Lord Jesus Christ and have the privilege to serve Him now and share in His glory in heaven. Paul is generous to call it "our gospel" since he and his coworkers preached that to them but Paul alone received the original revelation. He says, "our epistle" although Paul wrote the letter (c. AD 53). Paul uses the phrase "stand fast" six times in his letters. Usually, after he has corrected some false doctrine. Now that Paul has corrected the wrong teaching regarding their blessed hope of the Pre-Tribulation Rapture (our hope) they should stand fast in that truth and not be moved away from it. Once we have taken back ground we had lost we keep that truth and add more truth to it. We are to be rooted and grounded in the truth that is in "Christ according to the revelation of the mystery" (Rom. 16:25; Eph. 3:17; Col. 2:7). Repetition helps the truth to take root. They are to "stand fast" in all "the faith" that they have learned from Paul and his co-workers either by what they spoke or wrote to them. Paul uses the phrase "the faith" 30 times in his letters. We are to examine ourselves to make sure we are in "the faith" (2 Cor. 13:5) that Christ delivered to us through Paul, the mystery. We are set apart as sanctified because we have God's Spirit in us. As we understand and believe the words Christ has given to us through Paul, then we can function as God intends us to. Then we can understand what God is doing and how to work to serve Him. We are "saved" (justification) and have come to the "knowledge of the truth" (1 Tim. 2:4) and grow spiritually (sanctification). We will obtain glorification at the Rapture and will be with the Lord Jesus Christ forever. The Lord Jesus Christ can be glorified in us now and we can glorify Him in the future. We know that Paul is God's special distinctive apostle to reveal the mystery and that we are God's people that will live in heaven, not on earth.] **16 Now our Lord Jesus Christ himself, and God, even our Father, which hath loved us, and hath given us everlasting consolation and good hope through grace, 17 Comfort your hearts, and stablish you in every good word and work.** [Now that Paul has corrected the false doctrine, with sound doctrine ("good word"). They can enjoy "everlasting consolation" (not destruction) because the Godhead has loved them (and us) and given them good hope for all eternity through grace. God will comfort their hearts so they can have stable minds so the doctrine can work effectually in them (and us) and Christ can do His work through us. It is by God's grace that we have a "good hope." Our blessed hope is an important doctrine that stabilizes, comforts, and protects our minds, our thinking like a helmet (1 Thess. 5:8). When our thinking is right, then our actions can be right. Paul trusts the Lord Jesus Christ Himself and God, even our Father, will not only comfort our "hearts but STABLISH us in every good word and work." We can endure anything if we have hope. We function best when we are certain and secure in our hope of eternal life in heaven. Paul has corrected their good hope so now God can make them stable and they can labor in every good word (sound doctrine) and work (service to the Lord God). "Who gave himself for us, that he might redeem us from all iniquity, and purify unto himself a peculiar people, zealous of good works" (Titus 2:14). We are "to be careful to maintain good works" (Titus 3:8). Christ through Paul comforted those who in error thought they had been left behind at the Rapture, with the truth. Our hearts are comforted by the certainty of our Pre-Tribulation Rapture. The Rapture is our "blessed hope" as we look for the "glorious appearing of the great God and our Saviour Jesus Christ" (Titus 2:13). Christ will "change our vile body, that it may be fashioned unto his glorious body" (Phil. 3:21). When our mortal bodies have put on immortal bodies that is our glorification (1 Cor. 15:53, 54). That is when we are removed from the presence of sin: our dead sinful flesh and the "present evil world" (Gal. 1:4). The body of Christ has absolutely no part in the Tribulation; it is for those in prophecy and we are in mystery. God has proved that all mankind needs His Spirit in them. Believers in this dispensation have "Christ in you, the hope of glory" (Col. 1:27).]

The Seven Years of Tribulation was Prophesied

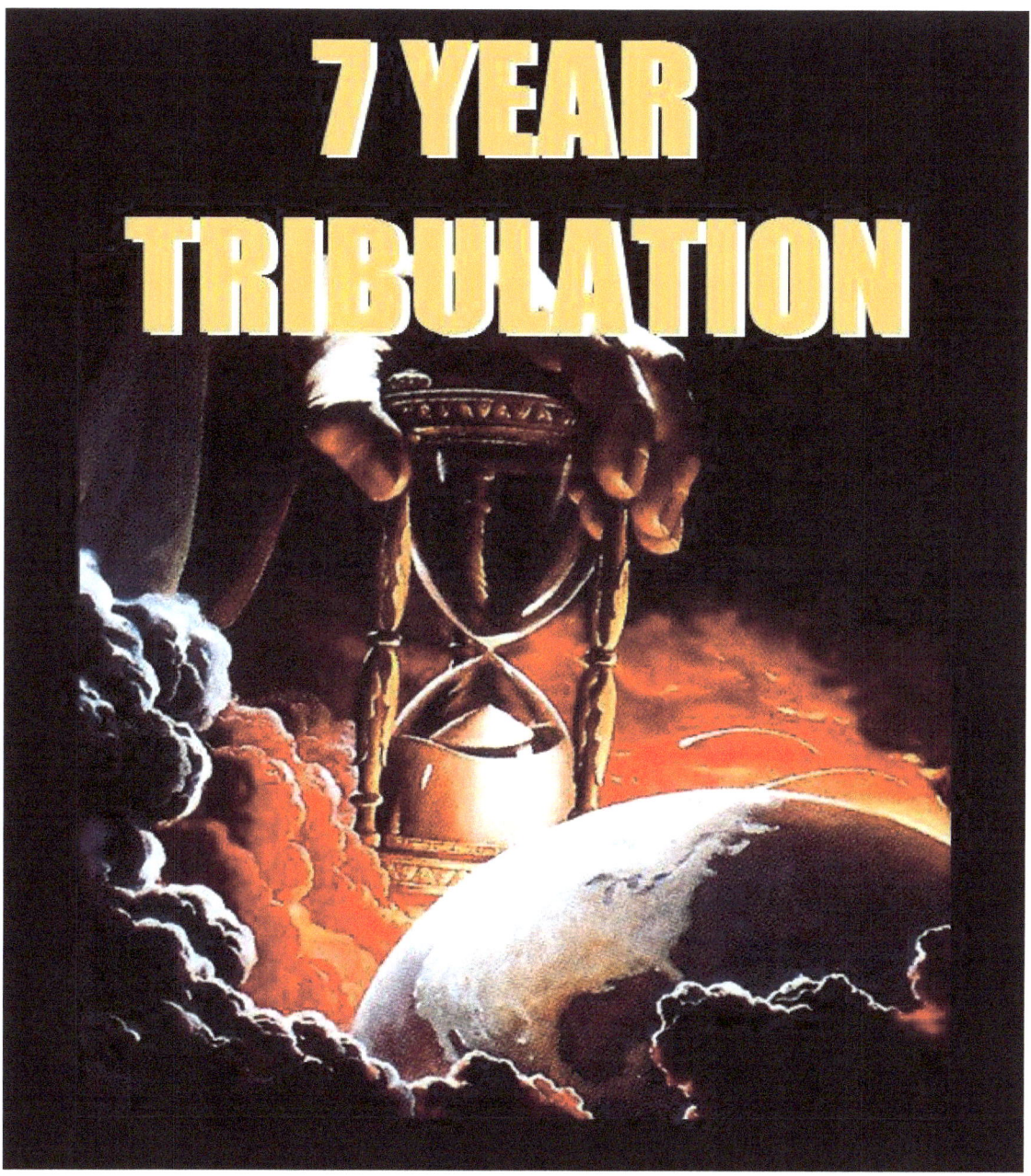

The day of wrath (Daniel's 70th Week, Jacob's trouble, Jer. 30:7) is about Israel (Leviticus 26:27-39). <u>The day of the Lord (Joel 1:15) is prophecy and has nothing to do with the body of Christ.</u> The coming of the Holy Ghost in Acts 2 was also prophesied (Joel 2:28). However, the "times of the Gentiles" (Luke 21:24) or Gentile rule, will also be over at the end of the seven years of Tribulation. This should not be confused with another term Paul uses for the Rapture, the "fulness of the Gentiles" (Rom. 11:25)

The Signs in heaven where all prophesied.

Scary, but true, unbelievers will have a worm-like body as they suffer eternal torment, "for their worm shall not die, neither shall their fire be quenched" (Isa. 66:24). While on earth, Jesus solemnly warned about that place three times "where the worm dieth not and the fire is not quenched" (Mark 9:44, 46, 48). Let's make sure we have an eternal retirement plan in heaven.

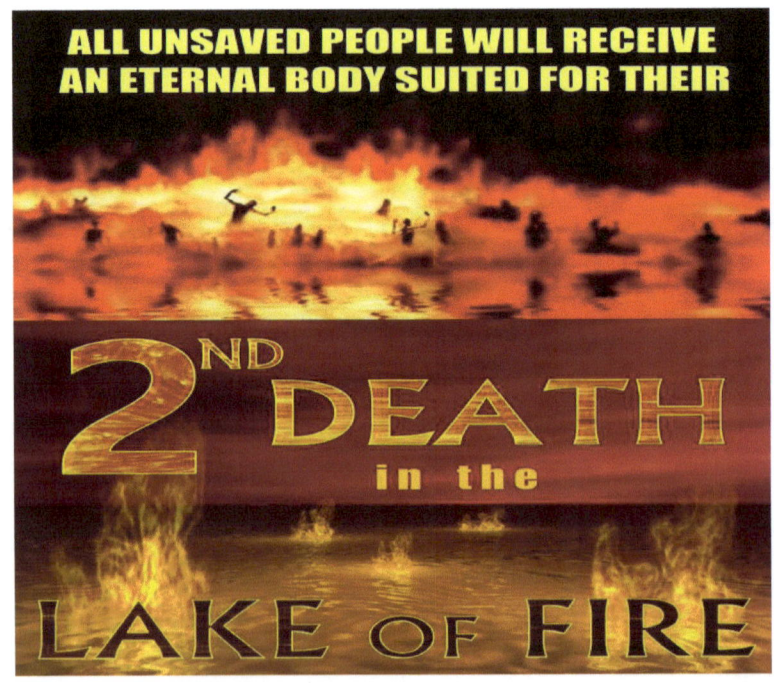

> BUT WE ARE BOUND TO GIVE THANKS ALWAY TO GOD FOR YOU, BRETHREN BELOVED OF THE LORD, BECAUSE GOD HATH FROM THE BEGINNING CHOSEN YOU TO SALVATION THROUGH SANCTIFICATION OF THE SPIRIT AND BELIEF OF THE TRUTH: WHEREUNTO HE CALLED YOU BY OUR GOSPEL, TO THE OBTAINING OF THE GLORY OF OUR LORD JESUS CHRIST. THEREFORE, BRETHREN, STAND FAST, AND HOLD THE TRADITIONS WHICH YE HAVE BEEN TAUGHT, WHETHER BY WORD, OR OUR EPISTLE.
> 2 THESSALONIANS 2:13-15

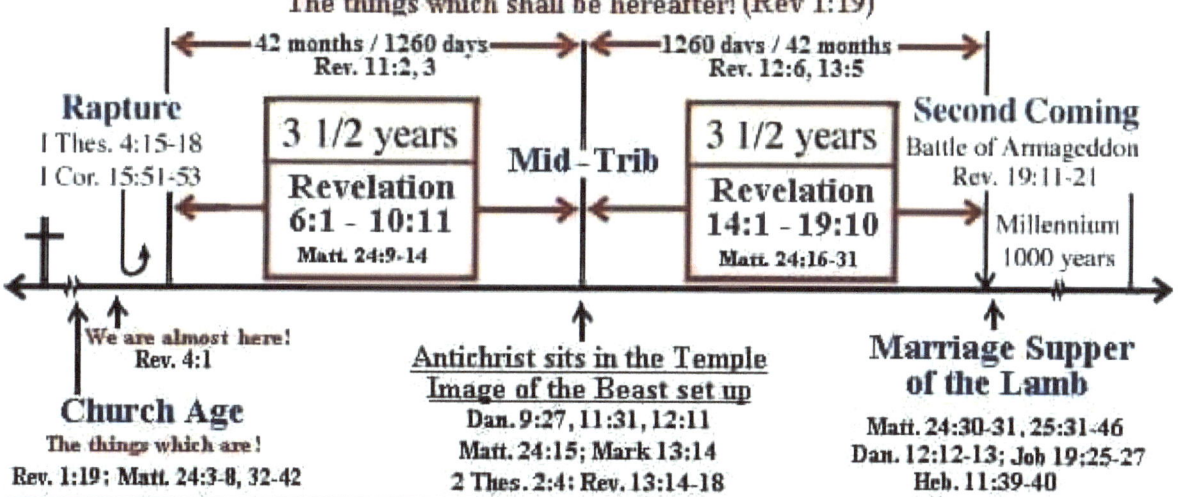

220	1040 (Dan. 8:14)	30	1260 (Dan. 12:11, 12)	45
	2,300 days until Christ's Second Coming (Dan. 8:14, Dan. 9:27)			

The animal sacrifices begin by apostate Jews after the 220 days of building the temple but Christ will return in 2,300 days to cleanse the Temple (seven years or 2,520 minus 2,300 days is 220). So after 1,040 days for Antichrist to set himself up (1,290 days before Christ's return from when the sacrifices ended, add 30 days from coming), then 1,260 days until the Second Coming of Christ. Then 45 days until Daniel is blessed or resurrected (1,335 minus 1,290 days).

A woodcut illustrations of members of the unholy trinity in Revelation 13 from a French Bible in 1530, by the artist Lucas Cranach the elder.

2 Thessalonians Chapter 3 Follow us in word and work
3:1-5 Request for prayer.
3:6-13 If any would not work, neither should he eat.
3:14-16 Do and will do what we command.
3:17, 18 Farewell and Paul's signature of authenticity.

There is so much confusion today about the Rapture and the Tribulation. **In order to truly understand the mystery of the Rapture (1 Cor. 15:51), we need to first consider what Paul said.** Then the Lord will give us understanding of all of His word. "Consider what I say; and **the Lord give thee understanding** in all things" (2 Tim. 2:7).

We are to study Paul's writing in the Bible, not what the church fathers said. Most of them mixed prophecy and mystery. They did not rightly divide the truth for the body of Christ from the rest of the Bible (2 Tim. 2:15). The church fathers catastrophically left Christ's apostle Paul, the formation of the body of Christ, and the dispensation of grace **out of the apostles' creed**.

When we **mix** prophecy and mystery the result is "vain babblings" which we should shun because they lead us to "ungodliness" (2 Tim. 2:16). We are living in the mystery. The Rapture is next; then prophecy will resume. We do not mix prophecy and mystery. Prophecy concerning Israel and the literal kingdom on earth is **not** being fulfilled in the dispensation of grace. 1948 was not the regathering of Israel to her land, that gathering by God is yet future.

Those who do not recognize the authority of apostle Paul will mix the truth. When Christ spoke on earth the Tribulation was at hand, but the mystery interrupted it. We are living in an **un-prophesied dispensation of God**.

In this lesson I will give my own testimony of a time when I was "shaken in mind" and "troubled" concerning our blessed hope.

3:1 Finally, brethren, pray for us, that the word of the Lord may have free course, and be glorified, even as it is with you: 2 And that we may be delivered from unreasonable and wicked men: for all men have not faith. [Paul continues to instruct them in the practical application of the doctrine which he began with the new paragraph in 2:13. The Thessalonians (and us) are to "stand fast" in the truth of our Pre-Tribulation Rapture (2:13-15). Paul is preparing to close the letter and calls them brethren even though they have not been believers for very long. He has just finished talking about our good hope and of the certainty of the Pre-Tribulation

Rapture through the grace of God (2:16, 17). Paul asks them to pray that the word of the Lord would have free course and be received and work effectively in others and be glorified, even as it had in them. Paul also asked the Ephesians for prayer in his letter to them so that he would open his mouth "boldly, to make known the mystery of the gospel" for which he is an ambassador (Eph. 6:18-20). We are all ambassadors and should do the same. Paul wants to get the sound doctrine to the body of Christ everywhere all over the world. It is usually the unreasonable and wicked men who hinder the word of the Lord from having free course. The body of Christ should share and support ministries who teach the word of God rightly divided to reach as many people as possible. We are a team. Paul wants believers to be aware that ministry can be very difficult. Paul often had to contend with those who had no faith and wanted to oppose God's work.] **3 But the Lord is faithful, who shall stablish you, and keep you from evil.** [Paul comforts them by saying that the Lord will help them to be stable in the faith and keep them from evil. The "evil" here is "evil communication" or false doctrine (1 Cor. 15:33). It is the opposite of the "good word" in verse 2:17, which is true doctrine. In this case, it was the evil false teaching that they had missed the Rapture and were in the Tribulation. False doctrine shakes the believers' mind and troubles them. I know because that happened to me. I had listened to a movie on YouTube by Steve Anderson called "After the Tribulation." I had been a pretribulation Rapture believer for 25 years, but I was "shaken in mind" and "troubled." I asked my pastor (at the time) about it. He believed he was "spiritual Israel" and would be resurrected in the kingdom on earth after the Tribulation. Unsatisfied with his answer, I set out to find the truth. I searched YouTube for other messages about the Rapture. Finally, I found Les Feldick, an Oklahoma rancher with a great deal of Bible knowledge. I tried listening to him a few times. In the end, I returned to him, I was desperate so I slowed my mind way down to be in sync with his slow talking. He went on a long journey talking about dispensations, by the time he finally answered my question, he had taught me right division. I finally knew why the legs of the statue in the book of Daniel were so long; they had been cut off or interrupted and are to be resumed after the Rapture. After Les Feldick, I found Pastor Richard Jordan from Chicago, Illinois, and then many other grace pastors. (Wanting to share right division in an easy way I prayerfully wrote God's Secret and had it translated into Spanish. I started over writing that book at least a dozen times until I finally had it right. Editing and perfecting the book took another year.) Meanwhile, I began teaching women's Bible studies in my home twice a week. Another reason why I wanted to teach rightly divided Bible studies was that two of my favorite pastors were not teaching the olive tree in Romans correctly (even after I tried to help them privately). While another of my favorite pastors was wrong about a passage in Ephesians (5:26, 27 to be exact). One day, one of the women in our study asked me to post the Bible lesson for Romans chapter 4, on Facebook because she could not make it to class. I did. (Some women had said they wished they could attend our classes. I was very surprised that the post had more than 500 views. That was the beginning of the Facebook and YouTube ministry we now have.) We decided that the body of Christ could use a commentary on Romans, so I wrote one. While I was writing that, someone on Facebook asked for help with First Corinthians so I said we would write a commentary on that, then Second Corinthians. We have since written commentaries on nearly all of Paul's epistles. After we finish, I plan to write a commentary on Acts depending on if the Lord's coming. The women in the Bible study attend the classes I prepare the notes and they proofread them. Aaron Howay does the final proofreading before publication. All who help receive a book. Many who have watched me teach the Bible say, "if she can do it, I can do it too." I am thrilled that so many faithful teachers all over the world are using our commentaries to teach rightly dividing Bible classes. Paul says the Lord will stabilize them by His word through Paul. In order to understand the difference between prophecy and mystery, we need to be both Biblical and dispensational. The apostle Paul was the steward of the mysteries which have now been revealed in Romans to Philemon. The main mystery is the formation of the body of Christ to live in the heavenly places. However, the Rapture was another mystery exclusively given to us by Christ through Paul (1 Cor. 15:51, 52; 1 Thess. 4:13-18). In chapter 15 of First Corinthians, Paul defended the resurrection saying that anyone who denies our resurrection denies the resurrection of Christ. Paul calls this, "evil communication." "Be not deceived: evil communications corrupt good manners [good behavior]" (1 Cor. 15:33). Paul had to tell the Corinthians that just like Christ was raised from the dead we will also be changed and rise (1 Cor. 15:35-52; 2 Cor. 4:14). Paul speaks of the resurrection of Jesus Christ in all his letters. Having eternal life with Christ is essential doctrine. There were those in Ephesus who also said that the resurrection was past. While Timothy was pastoring in Ephesus, Paul warned him of the men who taught that false doctrine (2 Tim. 2:17, 18). At Thessalonica, evil communication had caused bad behavior for some had even stopped working. False teaching leads to wrong thinking which leads to wrong action. The correct doctrine of our blessed hope stabilizes our minds and protects our thinking like a helmet (1 Thess. 5:8) so we can behave right. Satan attacks our blessed hope of the Rapture; our hope in mystery is to live in heaven with Christ forever. Satan doesn't want believers in the body of Christ to know our hope is eternal life in heaven, not on earth (2 Cor. 5:1). God has two groups of believers and two realms for them to live in (Gen. 1:1). God will "catch up" (Rapture) the body of Christ before the wrath. We combat Satan's false doctrine, with true doctrine from the word of God. What man says is not important; we put no confidence in the flesh (Phil. 3:3). The only thing that really matters is what God says (or for what saith the scriptures). The goal is for Christ and His word to be glorified. Paul's confidence is in the Lord who is in them. The Lord is able to keep us in the truth as we study what Christ said to us through Paul. The Lord will give us understanding of all of His word if we first consider what Paul says. "Consider what I say; and the LORD GIVE THEE UNDERSTANDING in all things" (2 Tim. 2:7). Paul said we are not appointed to wrath, but to obtain being saved from having to go through it by the Lord (1 Thess. 5:8-11). What is the hope in prophecy? That's right, it is to have eternal bodies, Christ's Spirit in them, and to live in Christ's kingdom with Him forever on earth.] **4 And we have confidence in the Lord touching you, that ye both do and will do the things which we command you.** [Paul, Silas, and Timothy have confidence in the Lord concerning them, that they are already doing and will do what they have commanded them. Are there commandments under grace? Yes, there are. But these commandments are not about keeping the law of Moses, but to do what is right out of love for God and His heavenly people. We walk by faith in Christ's word to us through Paul which works effectually in us who believe. Grace changes us, while the law condemns us. Love, not fear, is the strongest motivator of all. We should be pure doctrinally and morally. "Now the end of the commandment is charity out of a pure heart, and of a good conscience, and of faith unfeigned" (1 Tim. 1:5). If we purge ourselves from false doctrine, we will be a vessel fit for the Master's use and prepared for every good work. "If a man therefore purge himself from these, he shall be a vessel unto honour, sanctified, and meet for the master's use, *and* prepared unto every good work" (2 Tim. 2:21). Apostle Paul had the authority from Christ to write His commandments or instructions to the body of Christ.] **5 And the Lord direct your hearts into the love of God, and into the patient waiting for Christ.** [Paul is always careful to point out that the Lord is doing the work in and through them. Everything good is the result of the Lord, His grace, and His love. Paul uses the phrase "love of God" five times in his letters (Rom. 5:5; 8:39; 2 Cor. 13:14; 2 Thess. 3:5; Titus 3:4). When we know our truth, then our hearts are directed by the Lord into the love of God. Then we understand His great love and sacrifice for us and others. The Lord Jesus Christ commended His love on Calvary, and the Father spared not His own Son (Rom. 5:8; 8:32). When we meditate on this truth then we are in awe of the love of God. As we understand God's word of truth to us by His Spirit in us, our love for Him and His people grows. As we commune with Him on our pillow, our hearts overflow with love for God in response to His great love for us (2 Cor. 5:14). We gladly offer our bodies a living sacrifice to God. His love is a fruit of Christ's Spirit in us; love is the fulfillment of the law (Rom. 13:8-10). His Spirit in us uses His word to make us a conduit of His love to others and to produce the fruit of His Spirit in us (Rom.

12:1, 2; Gal. 5:22, 23). Christ is the source of our love. "And the grace of our Lord was exceeding abundant with faith and love which is in Christ Jesus" (1 Tim. 1:14). Remember there are no signs that precede the Rapture. Paul's epistles are silent regarding when the Rapture will occur. They had been waiting in 1 Thess. 1:10, but they got off the right track. Paul tells them (and us) again to patiently wait, knowing Christ will come because God said so in His word to us by inspiration through him. The Rapture is imminent and could occur at any time.]

6 ¶ Now we command you, brethren, in the name of our Lord Jesus Christ, that ye withdraw yourselves from every brother that walketh disorderly, and not after the tradition which he received of us. [Paul gives some commands in the name of the Lord Jesus Christ concerning brothers who walk disorderly. Paul had already dealt with lazy people who refused to work when he was in Thessalonica in his first letter to them (1 Thess. 4:11, 12), however, the problem was still persisting. Therefore, he had to be more forceful in this second letter. Paul commands them in the name of our Lord Jesus Christ to withdraw from anyone who does not follow the traditions they received from us (Pauline teachers in the body of Christ, not denominations). Some are disorderly and unruly because they did not live according to Paul's example to work for their own bread (Acts 20:34). What does it mean to withdraw? To have no company with them (3:14). We are to mark out the able-bodied offenders and to withdraw from them. So then the offenders might be ashamed and correct their foolish ways in the school of hard knocks (real life). We are not to continue to let them eat our food and condone their lazy behavior. If we pay for them they will not learn to take responsibility for themselves. The sooner they learn that there is no free lunch, the better. We are not to put up with their sin. This is not church discipline but rather personal correction and admonition of a member by individual church members. We ought not to encourage laziness. Some are takers, while others are givers. Some are generous while others are disgraceful, embarrassing leeches, or parasites. Of course the church should care for those who have legitimate needs and cannot work (1 Tim. 5). But the church is not obligated to help those who are able to work, but will not. Those who refuse to work become busybodies; they have time on their hands. They interfere with other people's business. They have a bad testimony to the lost (Col. 4:5). The truth of the Rapture should compel us to work harder to be responsible while reaching the reachable and teaching the teachable. We often find people who we can help while going about our daily business in the world. We are not to sit at home and wait for the Rapture. Work is honorable. Our lives should be an encouragement for others to copy. Instead of saying, "what's the use?" We should say, "I will never give up!" Let us be found faithful when Jesus comes and we stand before Him. We will all give an account of how we used our time at the

Judgment Seat of Christ, when our service is evaluated. Only Romans to Philemon, Paul's 13 letters to the body of Christ are directly "to" and "about us." The rest of the Bible is "for us," but mostly about the King and His kingdom on earth and Israel. Acts is a letter of transition from Christ's ministry on earth (to those who will live on earth), to Christ's ministry from heaven (to the body of Christ who will live in heaven.)] **7 For yourselves know how ye ought to follow us: for we behaved not ourselves disorderly among you; 8 Neither did we eat any man's bread for nought; but wrought with labour and travail night and day, that we might not be chargeable to any of you: 9 Not because we have not power, but to make ourselves an ensample unto you to follow us.** [They did not behave disorderly when they were with them but modeled the right behavior. Paul, Silas, and Timothy showed by example how to evangelize while working to provide for their own necessities. They didn't eat anyone's bread without paying for it but worked night and day to pay for themselves (1 Thess. 2:9-12). They did not use their authority as apostles to receive monetary support but supported themselves as their example to do the same. Twice Paul says that believers are to follow us (3:7, 9). He had praised them because they "became followers of us" (1 Thess. 1:6). Paul reproved the Corinthians because they were following him as a man, or Christ's earthly ministry, or other men (1 Cor. 1:12); when they should be following apostle Paul because he preached "Christ, according to the revelation of the mystery" (Rom. 16:25). Members of the body of Christ follow the Lord Jesus Christ's ministry from heaven when we follow apostle Paul (1 Cor. 4:15, 11:1; Phil. 3:17). Paul spoke by direct inspiration from Christ to us (Eph. 3:2).] **10 For even when we were with you, this we commanded you, that if any would not work, neither should he eat.** [They are not only to follow Paul's doctrine, but also Paul's example of working. He had told them when he was with them that believers are to work to pay their own way. He said the same thing in his first letter (1 Thess. 4:11, 12). Now he had to be more forceful. He commands them by the Lord (3:6, 12) that if any would not work, then they should not eat.] **11 For we hear that there are some which walk among you disorderly, working not at all, but are busybodies. 12 Now them that are such we command and exhort by our Lord Jesus Christ, that with quietness they work, and eat their own bread.** [Whoever came to Paul probably told him that some were still not working. Paul doesn't mention that person by name so they will not be blamed and so that the offender will take personal responsibility for their actions. Paul commands the lazy busybodies to work and pay for their own food and eat it quietly. Their disorderly conduct was that they were not working. Paul wants them to eat their own bread, not to eat other people's bread without paying for it. In First Thessalonians some were not working because they thought the Rapture was coming at any time, now some had quit working thinking what is the use of working when the world is coming to an end. People will come up with any excuse not to work when work is healthy, right, good, honorable, and rewarding. God instituted work before the fall when He told Adam to dress and keep the garden of Eden (Gen. 2:15). Work gives us a satisfying sense of accomplishment and money.] **13 But ye, brethren, <u>be not weary in well doing</u>.** [We can have an orderly walk sharing the good word while we work to provide for ourselves. Paul doesn't want the believers (who are working spreading the gospel, and Christ's doctrine to the body of Christ revealed through Paul) to be weary of doing well. Our labor in the Lord is <u>not</u> in vain. The Lord can use it as long as there is one more soul who may be saved and come to the knowledge of the truth (1 Tim. 2:4). "Therefore, my beloved brethren, be ye stedfast, unmoveable, always abounding in the work of the Lord, forasmuch as ye know that <u>your labour is not in vain in the Lord</u>" (1 Cor. 15:58). Those who are heavenly minded, are motivated to do earthly good (Gal. 6:9). We want as many people as possible to take part in the Rapture.] **14 And if any man <u>obey not our word by this epistle, note that man, and have no company with him, that he may be ashamed</u>.** [Paul tells them to take notice of those who do not obey what Paul says and who will not work and have NO company with them. If they are actively seeking a job, then they can probably stay, or they could say come back when you have a job. Paul told the Romans, "Now I beseech you, brethren, mark them which cause divisions and offences contrary to the doctrine which ye have learned; and avoid them" (Rom. 16:17). We are also to mark those who are like-minded and do right (Phil. 3:17; 1 Thess. 5:12, 13). As adult sons and daughters of God, we have been accepted in the beloved and set free. God and Paul expect us to believe and do what God said with love for God and others. Like the apostles, we work hard night and day and share the truth that our group of believers, the body of Christ, will be "caught up" to meet the Lord in the air before God resumes His dealings with Israel, "the times and the seasons" (1 Thess. 5:1). God trusts us to stand in the truth He has given us, and add more of His truth to that truth, and then walk in that truth by faith in God's word. We will receive a reward in heaven for our service to Christ while on earth. Our reward is not only our job in heaven, but also other souls being there and other believers having more responsible jobs because we shared the truth.] **15 Yet <u>count him not as an enemy, but admonish him as a brother</u>.** [How lovingly would we correct our own brother? That lazy man is still saved even if he will not obey, so they can admonish him as a brother in Christ by reminding him what Paul said: <u>if any would not work, then he should not eat</u>. Paul is talking about able-bodied people, he said "<u>would not work</u>," not the handi-capped, elderly, or infirmed who "<u>could not work</u>." The main function of the local church is not to give handouts to lazy people, but to <u>share the gospel with the lost and edify the believers</u>. Of course, we can give a helping hand to those in need, but we should also give them the gospel for their eternal welfare. Paul said that the family should take care of the widows. However, if widows do not have a family, the church can provide for their physical needs. There were certain stipulations on who was a widow (1 Tim. 5:3-10). But younger widows (under sixty) were not to be taken into the number of those who were helped. If they paid for them, the younger women would then learn to "not only be idle, but tattlers also and busybodies" (1 Tim. 5:13). Peter bunches "a busybody in other men's matters" in with other evildoers (1 Peter 4:15). Gossips are called "talebearers" in the Old Testament (Lev. 19:16). A faithful person will not put any more fuel to gossip and stop it in its tracks (Prov. 11:13, 18:8, 20:19, 26:20). Paul said that men and women are not to be "false accusers" (2 Tim. 3:3; Titus 2:3). Paul says that men are to provide financially for themselves and their families, or they deny the faith and are worse than an unbeliever. "But if any provide not for his own, and specially for those of his own house, he hath denied the faith, and is worse than an infidel" (1 Tim. 5:8). In contrast, during Christ's earthly ministry, believers were to sell everything and share among themselves because the Tribulation was looming on the horizon and the believers would not be able to buy and sell since they would not take the mark of the beast (Rev. 13:17). "Sell that ye have, and give alms; provide yourselves bags which wax not old, a treasure in the heavens that faileth not, where no thief approacheth, neither moth corrupteth" (Luke 12:33). "And the multitude of them that believed were of one heart and of one soul: neither said any of them that ought of the things which he possessed was his own; but they had all things common" (Acts 4:32). But God has put prophecy on hold and inserted the mystery.] **16 Now the Lord of peace himself give you peace always by all means. The Lord be with you all.** [The Lord of peace Himself can give them peace by all means (spirit, word, or letter) for their hope is sure. He desires for the Lord to be with them all. They can have real peace and comfort in their minds and hearts because they (and we) have a confident expectation in God's word that the body of Christ will be Raptured. The Rapture is the next event on God's time table: the order of events is the Rapture, the Tribulation, and the His Second Coming.]

17 ¶ The salutation of Paul with mine own hand, which is the token in every epistle: so I write. [Paul begins each letter with his own name to show who it is from, but now, because of the forgery he adds his signature to every letter "in mine own hand."] **18 The grace of our Lord Jesus Christ be with you all. Amen.** [Paul closes his letter with the grace of our Lord Jesus Christ to be with them all.]

Romans 12 RENEW YOUR MIND

Romans 12 KJB

1 " I beseech you therefore, brethren, by the mercies of God, that ye present your bodies a living sacrifice, holy, acceptable unto God, which is your reasonable service."

2 "And be not conformed to this world: but be ye transformed by the renewing of your mind, that ye may prove what is that good, and acceptable, and perfect, will of God."

Above is what we are able to do when we study God's word rightly divided.

We do NOT want to be religious Pharisees, but grace believers of God's truth.

Second Thessalonians Chapter summaries.
(1) Extols (praises) their faith and love in the midst of persecution.
A forged letter had caused them to doubt the pre wrath Rapture, so Paul praises their faith and love but omits praising their hope in the midst of persecution.
(2) Educates them by correcting the false doctrine.
Paul beseeches them based on our gathering unto Christ no to be shaken in mind or troubled (2:1, 2). Paul describes the tribulation and the second coming to show they are not in it (2:3-12). Paul concludes with thankfulness that God had ordained that the body of Christ would be saved from having to go through the Tribulation by being Raptured before it begins. Believers can be consoled by this truth in the midst of persecution. Now that their hearts are comforted and they are stable concerning their hope, they can get back to every good word and work (2:13-17).
(3) Encourages them to live and work by the truth they received from Paul.
Paul asks for prayer so the word of the Lord can have free course and be glorified in others as it was in them. He reminds them that there are unreasonable and wicked men who do not believe that are against God's work. But the Lord is faithful who will keep them stable in the word. Paul commands that if any will not work neither should they eat. These are those who do not follow Paul and should be admonished and not companied with.

Paul wrote two letters to correct the Thessalonians regarding false teaching concerning our Rapture. Why were the Thessalonians a model church? Because they believed the pure doctrine Christ taught them through Paul. They understood that God was saving Gentiles to form another group of people to live in heaven. This group would be removed from the earth before God resumed His prophetic dealings with Israel. Israel had one more week (7 years) to endure God's chastisement of His special people for their spiritual adultery (Lev. 26:27-39). They were receiving a curse, not a blessing, as God had said they would. But God would use the week to purge out the rebel from Israel and purify the believing remnant. This last week is also the last week of the "times of the Gentiles" (Luke 21:24). Antichrist is the last earthly Monarch; he may be part Gentile. Christ will return and put down the Gentile rule. The King will rule the world with His Bride (Israel). Adam and his bride Eve were supposed to have ruled earth under God.

We need to turn off all distractions and study God's word first thing in the morning when our minds are fresh. After Paul sent Timothy and Silas to check on how their faith was holding up under persecution Paul was comforted by their good report (3:6,7).

Cain and Abel

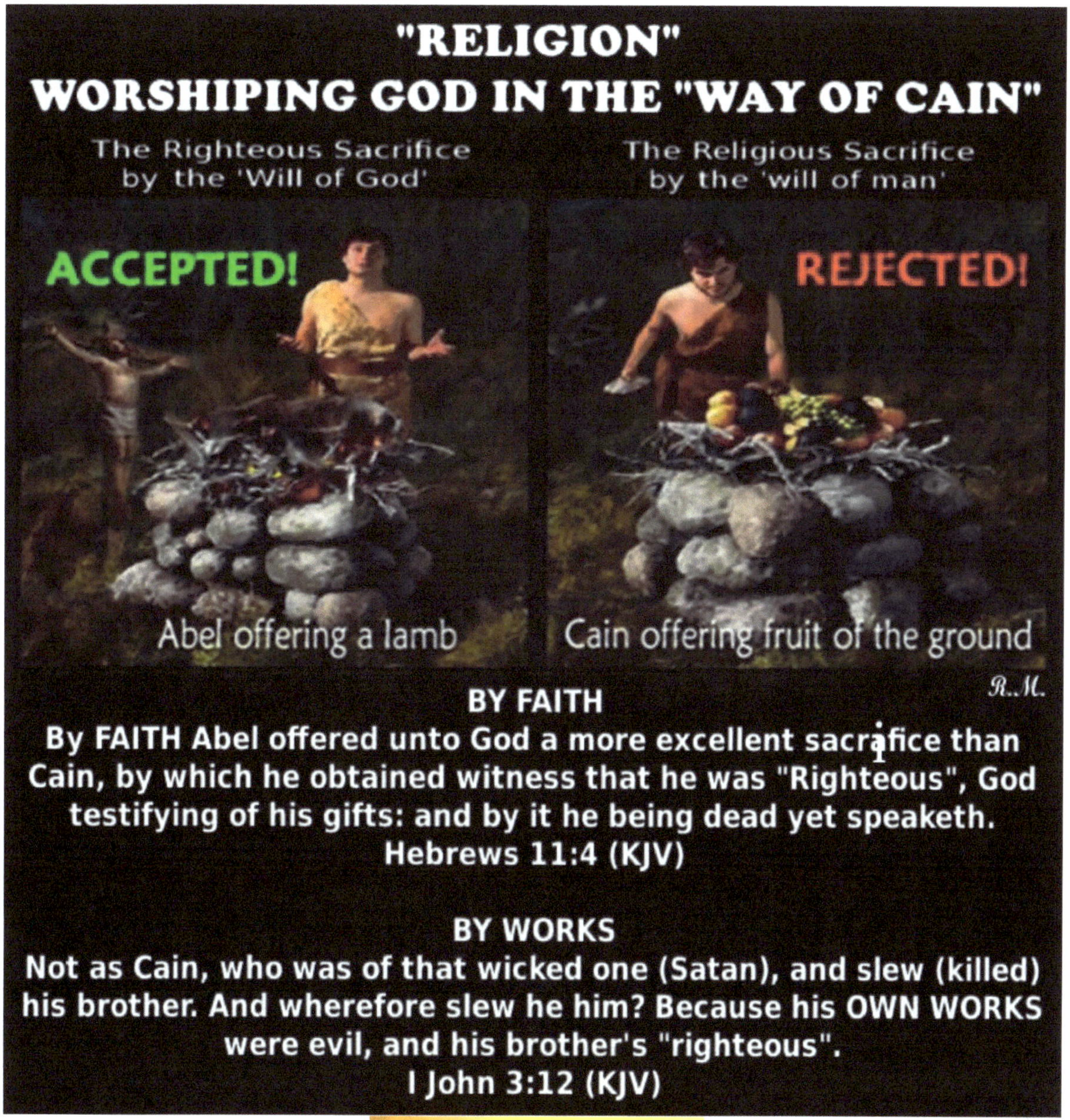

"RELIGION"
WORSHIPING GOD IN THE "WAY OF CAIN"

The Righteous Sacrifice by the 'Will of God' — **ACCEPTED!** — Abel offering a lamb

The Religious Sacrifice by the 'will of man' — **REJECTED!** — Cain offering fruit of the ground

R..M.

BY FAITH
By FAITH Abel offered unto God a more excellent sacrifice than Cain, by which he obtained witness that he was "Righteous", God testifying of his gifts: and by it he being dead yet speaketh.
Hebrews 11:4 (KJV)

BY WORKS
Not as Cain, who was of that wicked one (Satan), and slew (killed) his brother. And wherefore slew he him? Because his OWN WORKS were evil, and his brother's "righteous".
I John 3:12 (KJV)

Two Seed-Lines

I was blessed to recently read, *The Way of Cain the Creation of Man's Religion* by Gary Paul Miller, published in 2009 by Grace Harbor Church www.grace-harbor-church. The following is a condensation of this great book (which I highly recommend). He is a very good writer. By permission, I share some small snippets from his book, with only minor modifications on my part.

Satan had wanted to usurp God's throne (Isa. 14:12-14). The conflict that began then would ultimately result in the destruction of Satan (Heb. 2:14).

Speaking to the serpent God said, "And I will put enmity between thee and the woman, and between thy seed [Satan's seed-line] and her seed [the woman's seed-line to Jesus the Messiah]; it shall bruise thy head [a lethal blow], and thou shalt bruise his heel [not a lethal injury. Satan was so excited when he actually killed Jesus the Messiah]" (Gen. 3:15). Two seed-lines would war against each other. God's Seed would win. Satan's plot throughout history was to kill the woman's seed before it could bruise his head. Christ still triumphed on the cross (Col. 2:15).

Satan planted the seeds of discontent in Eve's heart and she gave them fertile ground in her heart. She believed the lie of the serpent, "Ye shall not surely die" (Gen. 3:4). Seeking to be a god, she took of the fruit and ate of it, and she gave some to Adam who ate of it.

Eve ate first and then she gave the fruit to Adam. Adam saw that the covering of light which God had provided was removed from Eve as she spiritually died before his eyes. And in spite of what he saw, he ate anyway. He could not claim that he was deceived for he saw the result that that fruit had on Eve.

Adam made up his mind that he was going to be a god, ruler, and judge no matter what the cost. Eve was tricked, but Adam was fully aware; he saw the consequences before he ate.

Some have claimed that Adam bit the forbidden fruit because he loved Eve and therefore he ate in order to be with her. But this is not true.

If Adam truly loved Eve, then he would have sought her best interest; for that is what love does. First, he would have attempted to prevent her from biting the fruit; Secondly, he should have cast the fruit to the ground and taken her to God for help, to forgive her. Thirdly, Adam could then have asked God what to do, maybe to undo or fix what she had done. There is provision in the Old Testament for a husband to make a vow his wife has made of no effect, void (Num. 30:6-8, 12, 13).

Adam did not protest Eve's action; he did not seek to undo what she had done by bringing her to the Lord. Instead he concurred and confirmed what she had done by eating the fruit himself. Therefore, <u>God holds Adam responsible for the fall of mankind, not Eve</u>. Adam had no excuse; he saw the outcome and still rebelled. Thus Adam brought sin into the world and he is the one responsible. Adam was responsible for the fall of mankind and entrance of sin and death (Rom. 5:12, 18).

Their dream of deification turned into a nightmare. When they realized the shame of their nakedness and their hopeless and helpless condition. Adam knew it was good to obey God and evil to disobey God so what did the tree mean?

The tree represented who had authority to decide what is good and what is evil. This knowledge belonged to God, not to Adam or any man to usurp.

Adam wanted to be like God, he wanted to exercise his own judgments as to what is good and evil, therefore he ate of the tree.

He rebelled against God's command not to eat of it and also against God's authority to be the judge of all the earth (Gen. 18:25). Like a teen who says "I do not need to be told what to do!" Man wants to be God. The Bible says, "but every man did that which was right in his own mind" (Judges 17:6b).

Adam and Eve <u>should have died immediately</u>, not the innocent animals. God punished the innocent animals instead of Adam and Eve. God was patient and merciful because God knew He was really fighting against Satan, just like we do (Eph. 6:12). God poured out His punishment for sin on Jesus Christ when He was on the cross, instead of on all mankind. God requires blood for the remission of sins, "without shedding of blood is no remission" (Heb. 9:22).

By the grace of God, Jesus Christ shed His blood and tasted the Second death for all mankind (Heb. 2:9). But death and hell could not hold the sinless Son of God (Acts 2:24). His blood was not tainted with sin because it was God's blood (Acts 20:28). <u>This is why the Son of God had to die for us, death and hell could not hold the perfect Son of God</u>; but death and hell would have held a human that was born with sin (Rom. 5:12). We deserve death for our sins (Rom. 6:23). But the precious Lamb of God was sacrificed as all believer's substitute (2 Cor. 5:21; Rev. 13:8).

God's seed line should have gone through Abel, but his brother killed him (1 John 3:10-12). Seth means "to set something in place" or in the place of, a substitute.

Cain put much effort into the preparation of his gift; he picked the best seeds, prepared the soil in the best place, pulled the weeds and thistles, and pruned the plants.

Cain was a hard worker determined in his zeal to bring a beautiful offering to the Lord. But he didn't want to stoop to the level of trading for one of his brother's sheep or being a lowly shepherd, he was a farmer like his father. Adam was his physical father, but Satan was his spiritual father (John 8:44).

Cain was the first to kill the righteous. Cain was a Pharisee, the first religious man. Jesus Christ was born of a traceable line of descendants (Matt. 1, Luke 3). Cain had a generation (Prov. 30:11-14) but it was the wrong way. Jesus Christ is the right way (John 14:6). The generation of the righteous believe God (Psa. 112:2). One line rebels, one line obeys.

The good seed-line began with Abel, but after his death it continued with Seth. Then Noah, Abraham, Isaac, Jacob, David and eventually ending with "the Seed" which is Jesus Christ (Gal. 3:16).

Cain had human wisdom. Those who follow Cain, believe they will not surely die. This is the center thought behind every religion. Be good and live. It is a lie. "And as it is appointed unto men once to die, but after this the judgment" (Heb. 9:27).

Cain's generation continues to this day (Jude 4, 11). The men that place Christ in a position beneath the Father are Cain followers. They want to replace the Creator with themselves.

What Cain started has lasted for thousands of years. They use religion as a cloak (Jude 12, 13). Some want to sing, "I did it my way," all the way to hell! We must believe the word of God and commit our own imaginations to the dung heap. Man's fleshly sin nature is totally corrupt. Cain's way of law-keeping to be righteous on his own, became law-breaking.

We need Christ's righteousness (Rom. 3:21, 22; Phil 3:9). Jesus came into the world and took our sins upon Himself. He bore our sins on the cross and offered Himself as a sacrifice. His sacrifice on Calvary was a result of His love for His creatures and His creation. After He paid for our sins with His own blood, He rose again. Christ is now at the Father's right hand. He has won the victory, but has not yet taken possession of what is rightfully His.

Christ offers His righteousness as a free gift for anyone who will believe the gospel (1 Cor. 15:3,4). God desires to give us what we could never achieve on our own. All we have to do is believe.

By faith Abel obeyed what God said and brought an unblemished firstling from his flock, and offered him with his fat. Then he burned the offering with fire. Abel obeyed (Heb. 11:4; Lev. 1:2, 12; Num. 18:7). The fire consumed the sacrifice and caused it to become a sweet smelling savour. In answer, God sent His fire from heaven to the altar meaning the sacrifice was accepted by His righteous judgment.

Man is not God; man is not the one to judge. God's judgment against sin fell on Jesus Christ. Christ willingly laid himself on the cruel wooden cross, in our place. He paid the price for our sin. Christ's resurrection was proof that His sacrifice was accepted by God. His blood spoke of better things than Abel (Heb. 12:24); because it was the blood of God (Acts 20:28; Phil. 2:5-8).

Cain had put his trust in his own good works. He could not believe that God would refuse a man who was holy and just in his own sight. Cain's sacrifice was open rebellion against God. Cain declared that God must accept what he decided to bring.

Cain was wroth because Abel's offering was accepted by God and his was not (Gen. 4:4, 5). God warned Cain and gave him a chance to change his mind (Gen. 4:6, 7). It came to pass that Cain premeditated the murder of his brother Abel (Gen. 4:8). Adam and Eve must have been broken hearted to find out that Cain not only killed his brother, but was a hypocrite, an ungodly unsaved man.

Cain's goodness would not kill an animal for a sacrifice, but he would shed his brother's blood. Both mankind's good and evil are bad. Today we hear people who want to save the whales, but want to be able to have the right to abort their babies.

God meant for Cain to wander the earth and be childless (Gen. 4:9-15). But, Cain married and had children. Cain was the first to build a city. He named it after his son Enoch (Gen. 4:16, 17). He is a type of antichrist. His seed-line opposed God's. They are Satan's seed, the line of self-righteous religious men. God will avenge Abel's blood.

After Cain slew Abel, the godly seed-line continued through Seth.

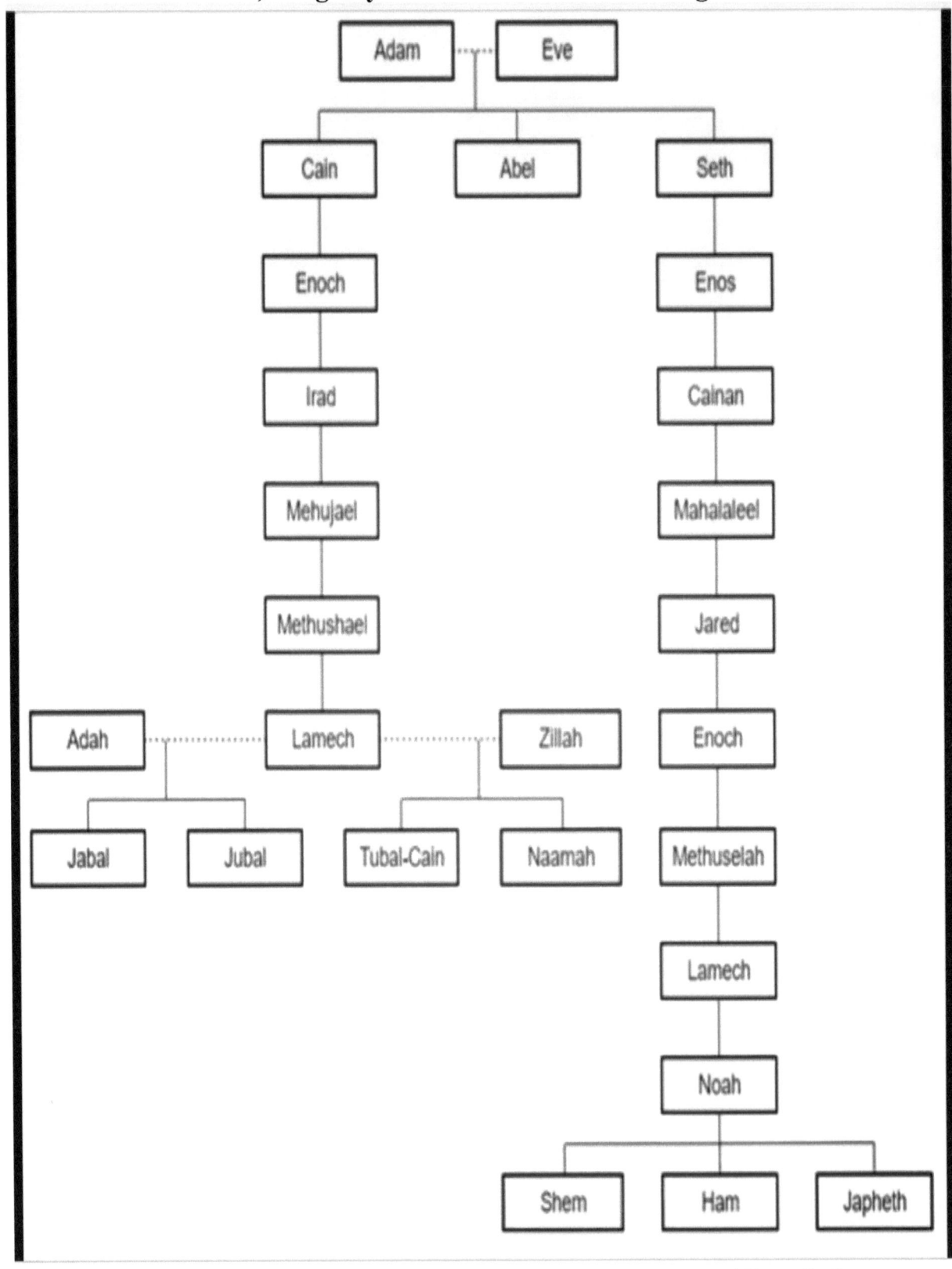

Not shown: Adam and Eve begat other sons and daughters (Gen. 5:4).

The Order of Events After the Rapture

(1) The Tribulation begins after Antichrist signs the 7-year covenant (Dan. 9:27) is also equal to two 3 ½ years (1260 days) or two 42 months or two "a time, times, and a half" (Dan. 7:25, 12:7; Matt. 24:21, 22, 29, 30; Rev. 7:14, 11:2, 12:14).

(2) The Second Coming of the Lord in glory to destroy His enemies the beast, false prophet, and their armies which is "great and awesome" (Rev. 19:11-21)

(3) The judgment of the individuals of the Gentile nations according to how they treated the Jewish believing remnant (Zech. 14:1-9; Matt. 25:31-46) and the judgment of Israel (Ezek. 20:34-38).

(4) Satan bound for 1,000 years (Rev. 20:1-3).

(5) Christ's millennial reign (Rev. 20:4-6).

(6) Satan loosed and final revolt of unbelieving Gentiles (Rev. 20:7-10).

(7) Great White Throne judgement of the wicked (Rev. 20:11-15).

(8) The destruction of the present heaven and earth (2 Peter 3:10-12).

(9) The creation of the new heaven and the new earth (Isa. 65:17-19, 66:22; 2 Peter 3:13; Rev. 21:1).

(10) The New Jerusalem descends to the earth (Rev. 21:9, 10).

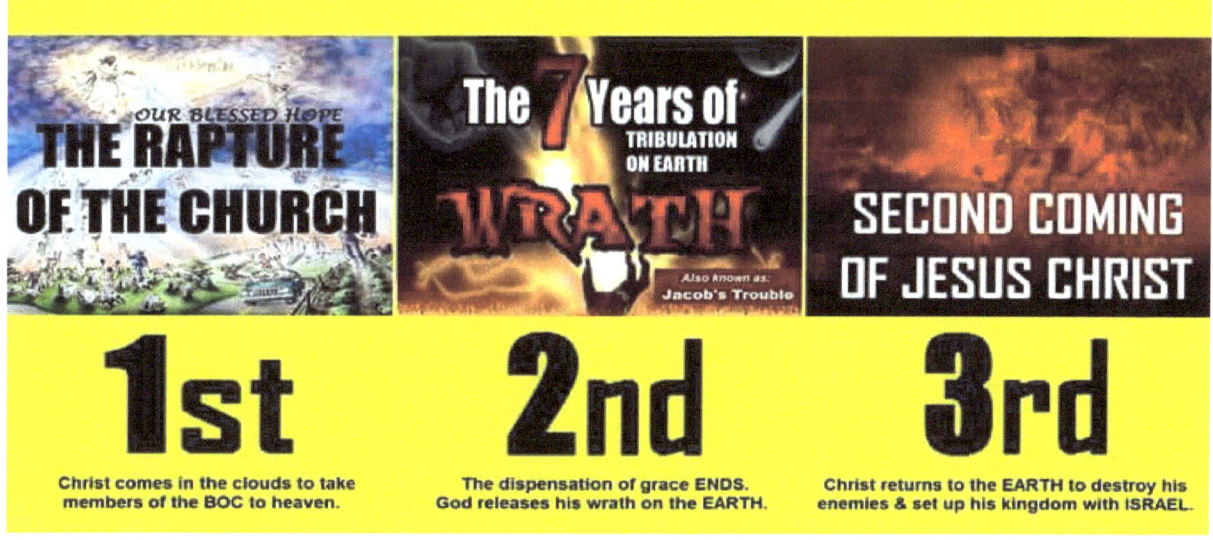

Be Still, My Soul (hymn)
Lyrics by Katharina von Schlegel (1752) Music by Jean Sibelius.

Be still, my soul: the Lord is on thy side.
Bear patiently the cross of grief or pain.
Leave to thy God to order and provide;
In every change, He faithful will remain.
Be still, my soul: thy best, thy heavenly Friend
Through thorny ways leads to a joyful end.

Be still, my soul: thy God doth undertake
To guide the future, as He has the past.
Thy hope, thy confidence let nothing shake;
All now mysterious shall be bright at last.
Be still, my soul: the waves and winds still know
His voice Who ruled them while He dwelt below.

Be still, my soul: when dearest friends depart,
And all is darkened in the vale of tears,
Then shalt thou better know His love, His heart,
Who comes to soothe thy sorrow and thy fears.
Be still, my soul: thy Jesus can repay
From His own fullness all He takes away.

Be still, my soul: the hour is hastening on
When we shall be forever with the Lord.
When disappointment, grief and fear are gone,
Sorrow forgot, love's purest joys restored.
Be still, my soul: when change and tears are past
All safe and blessèd we shall meet at last.

Be still, my soul: begin the song of praise
On earth, be leaving, to Thy Lord on high;
Acknowledge Him in all thy words and ways,
So shall He view thee with a well pleased eye.
Be still, my soul: the Sun of life divine
Through passing clouds shall but more brightly shine.

28 DAYS WITH PAUL

1. Romans 1-3
2. Romans 4-6
3. Romans 7-9
4. Romans 10-12
5. Romans 13-16
6. 1st Corinthians 1-3
7. 1st Corinthians 4-6
8. 1st Corinthians 7-9
9. 1st Corinthians 10-12
10. 1st Corinthians 13-16
11. 2nd Corinthians 1-3
12. 2nd Corinthians 4-6
13. 2nd Corinthians 7-9
14. 2nd Corinthians 10-13
15. Galatians 1-3
16. Galatians 4-6
17. Ephesians 1-3
18. Ephesians 4-6
19. Philippians 1-4
20. Colossians 1-4
21. 1st Thessalonians 1-3
22. 1st Thessalonians 4-5
23. 2nd Thessalonians 1-3
24. 1st Timothy 1-3
25. 1st Timothy 4-6
26. 2nd Timothy 1-4
27. Titus
28. Philemon

KJV

Rapture Verses

1 Corinthians 1:7 So that ye come behind in no gift; waiting for the <u>coming of our Lord Jesus Christ</u>:

1 Corinthians 1:8 Who shall also confirm you unto the end, *that ye may be* blameless in the <u>day of our Lord Jesus Christ</u>.

1 Corinthians 5:5 To deliver such an one unto Satan for the destruction of the flesh, that the spirit <u>may be saved in the day of the Lord Jesus</u>.

1 Corinthians 15:51 In a moment, in the twinkling of an eye, at the last trump: for the trumpet shall sound, and the <u>dead shall be raised incorruptible, and we shall be changed</u>.

2 Corinthians 1:14 As also ye have acknowledged us in part, that we are your rejoicing, even as ye also *are* ours in the <u>day of the Lord Jesus</u>.

2 Corinthians 4:14 Knowing that <u>he which raised up the Lord Jesus shall raise up us also by Jesus</u>, and shall present us with you.

Philippians 1:6 Being confident of this very thing, that he which hath begun a good work in you will perform *it* until the <u>day of Jesus Christ</u>:

Colossians 1:5 For the <u>hope which is laid up for you in heaven</u>, whereof ye heard before in the word of the truth of the gospel;

Colossians 1:23 If ye continue in the faith grounded and settled, and *be* not moved away from the <u>hope of the gospel</u>, which ye have heard, *and* which was preached to every creature which is under heaven; whereof I Paul am made a minister;

Titus 2:13 Looking for that <u>blessed hope, and the glorious appearing</u> of the great God and our Saviour Jesus Christ;

Romans 8:23 And not only *they*, but ourselves also, which have the firstfruits of the Spirit, even we ourselves groan within ourselves, waiting for the adoption, *to wit*, the <u>redemption of our body</u>.

Ephesians 1:14 Which is the earnest of our inheritance until the <u>redemption of the purchased possession</u>, unto the praise of his glory.

Ephesians 4:30 And grieve not the holy Spirit of God, whereby ye are sealed unto the <u>day of redemption</u>.

1 Thessalonians 3:13 To the end he may stablish your hearts unblameable in holiness before God, even our Father, at the coming of our Lord Jesus Christ with all his saints.

1 Thessalonians 4:15 For this we say unto you by the word of the Lord, that we which are alive *and* remain unto the coming of the Lord shall not prevent them which are asleep.

1 Thessalonians 4:16, 17 For the Lord himself shall descend from heaven with a shout, with the voice of the archangel, and with the trump of God: and the dead in Christ shall rise first: Then we which are alive and remain shall be caught up together with them in the clouds, to meet the Lord in the air: and so shall we ever be with the Lord.

1 Thessalonians 5:23 And the very God of peace sanctify you wholly; and *I pray God* your whole spirit and soul and body be preserved blameless unto the coming of our Lord Jesus Christ.

2 Thessalonians 2:1 Now we beseech you, brethren, by the coming of our Lord Jesus Christ, and *by* our gathering together unto him,

1 Timothy 6:14 That thou keep *this* commandment without spot, unrebukeable, until the appearing of our Lord Jesus Christ:

2 Timothy 4:1 I charge *thee* therefore before God, and the Lord Jesus Christ, who shall judge the quick and the dead at his appearing and his kingdom;

2 Timothy 4:8 Henceforth there is laid up for me a crown of righteousness, which the Lord, the righteous judge, shall give me at that day: and not to me only, but unto all them also that love his appearing.

Titus 2:13 Looking for that blessed hope, and the glorious appearing of the great God and our Saviour Jesus Christ;

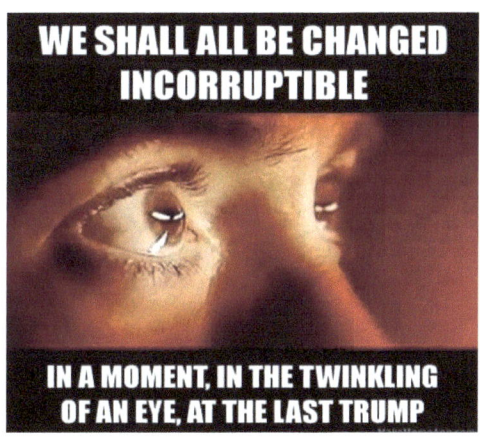

The Second Coming Verses

Deuteronomy 30:3 That then the LORD thy God will turn thy captivity, and have compassion upon thee, and will return and gather thee from all the nations, whither the LORD thy God hath scattered thee.

1 Thessalonians 5:2 For yourselves know perfectly that the day of the Lord so cometh as a thief in the night.

2 Thessalonians 2:2 That ye be not soon shaken in mind, or be troubled, neither by spirit, nor by word, nor by letter as from us, as that the day of Christ is at hand.

2 Thessalonians 2:8 And then shall that Wicked be revealed, whom the Lord shall consume with the spirit of his mouth, and shall destroy with the brightness of his coming:

Hebrews 9:28 So Christ was once offered to bear the sins of many; and unto them that look for him shall he appear the second time without sin unto salvation.

James 5:7 Be patient therefore, brethren, unto the coming of the Lord. Behold, the husbandman waiteth for the precious fruit of the earth, and hath long patience for it, until he receive the early and latter rain.

James 5:8 Be ye also patient; stablish your hearts: for the coming of the Lord draweth nigh.

1 Peter 1:7 That the trial of your faith, being much more precious than of gold that perisheth, though it be tried with fire, might be found unto praise and honour and glory at the appearing of Jesus Christ:

2 Peter 3:4 And saying, Where is the promise of his coming? for since the fathers fell asleep, all things continue as *they were* from the beginning of the creation.

1 John 2:28 And now, little children, abide in him; that, when he shall appear, we may have confidence, and not be ashamed before him at his coming.

Isaiah 2:12 For the day of the LORD of hosts *shall be* upon every *one that is* proud and lofty, and upon every *one that is* lifted up; and he shall be brought low:

Isaiah 13:6 Howl ye; for the day of the LORD *is* at hand; it shall come as a destruction from the Almighty.

Isaiah 13:9 Behold, the day of the LORD cometh, cruel both with wrath and fierce anger, to lay the land desolate: and he shall destroy the sinners thereof out of it.

Jeremiah 46:10 For this *is* the day of the Lord GOD of hosts, a day of vengeance, that he may avenge him of his adversaries: and the sword shall devour, and it shall be satiate and made drunk with their blood: for the Lord GOD of hosts hath a sacrifice in the north country by the river Euphrates.

Ezekiel 13:5 Ye have not gone up into the gaps, neither made up the hedge for the house of Israel to stand in the battle in the day of the LORD.

Ezekiel 30:3 For the day *is* near, even the day of the LORD *is* near, a cloudy day; it shall be the time of the heathen.

Joel 1:15 Alas for the day! for the day of the LORD *is* at hand, and as a destruction from the Almighty shall it come.

Joel 2:1 Blow ye the trumpet in Zion, and sound an alarm in my holy mountain: let all the inhabitants of the land tremble: for the day of the LORD cometh, for *it is* nigh at hand;

Joel 2:11 And the LORD shall utter his voice before his army: for his camp *is* very great: for *he is* strong that executeth his word: for the day of the LORD *is* great and very terrible; and who can abide it?

Joel 2:31 The sun shall be turned into darkness, and the moon into blood, before the great and the terrible day of the LORD come.

Joel 3:14 Multitudes, multitudes in the valley of decision: for the day of the LORD *is* near in the valley of decision.

Amos 5:18 Woe unto you that desire the day of the LORD! to what end *is* it for you? the day of the LORD *is* darkness, and not light.

Amos 5:20 *Shall* not the day of the LORD *be* darkness, and not light? even very dark, and no brightness in it?

Obadiah 1:15 For the day of the LORD *is* near upon all the heathen: as thou hast done, it shall be done unto thee: thy reward shall return upon thine own head.

Zephaniah 1:7 Hold thy peace at the presence of the Lord GOD: for the day of the LORD *is* at hand: for the LORD hath prepared a sacrifice, he hath bid his guests.

Zephaniah 1:14 The great day of the LORD *is* near, *it is* near, and hasteth greatly, *even* the voice of the day of the LORD: the mighty man shall cry there bitterly.

Zechariah 14:1 Behold, the day of the LORD cometh, and thy spoil shall be divided in the midst of thee.

Malachi 4:5 ¶ Behold, I will send you Elijah the prophet before the coming of the great and dreadful day of the LORD:

Acts 2:20 The sun shall be turned into darkness, and the moon into blood, before that great and notable day of the Lord come:

1 Thessalonians 5:2 For yourselves know perfectly that the day of the Lord so cometh as a thief in the night.

2 Peter 3:10 But the day of the Lord will come as a thief in the night; in the which the heavens shall pass away with a great noise, and the elements shall melt with fervent heat, the earth also and the works that are therein shall be burned up.

Revelation 16:15 Behold, I come as a thief. Blessed *is* he that watcheth, and keepeth his garments, lest he walk naked, and they see his shame.

One Day (hymn)

One day when heaven was filled with His praises,
One day when sin was as black as could be,
Jesus came forth to be born of a virgin-
Dwelt among men, my example is He!

Living, He loved me; dying, He saved me;
Buried, He carried my sins far away;
Rising, He justified freely forever:
One day He's coming-O glorious day!

One day they led Him up Calvary's mountain,
One day they nailed Him to die on the tree;
Suffering anguish, despised and rejected;
Bearing our sins, my Redeemer is He.

Living, He loved me; dying, He saved me;
Buried, He carried my sins far away;
Rising, He justified freely forever:
One day He's coming—O glorious day!

One day they left Him alone in the garden,
One day He rested, from suffering free;
Angels came down o'er His tomb to keep vigil;
Hope of the hopeless, my Savior is He.

Living, He loved me; dying, He saved me;
Buried, He carried my sins far away;
Rising, He justified freely forever:
One day He's coming—O glorious day!

One day the grave could conceal Him no longer,
One day the stone rolled away from the door;
Then He arose, over death He had conquered;
Now is ascended, my Lord evermore.

Living, He loved me; dying, He saved me;
Buried, He carried my sins far away;
Rising, He justified freely forever:
One day He's coming—O glorious day!

One day the trumpet will sound for His coming,
One day the skies with His glory will shine;
Wonderful day, my beloved ones bringing;
Glorious Savior, this Jesus is mine!

Our Walk in the Body of Christ (Romans to Philemon)

Walk in the steps of the faith of our father Abraham (Rom. 4:12)

Walk in newness of life (Rom. 6:4)

Walk not after the flesh, but after the Spirit (Rom. 8:1)

Walk not after the flesh, but after the Spirit (Rom. 8:4)

Walk honestly (Rom. 13:13)

Walk by faith (2 Cor. 5:7)

Walk in the Spirit (Gal 5:16)

Walk in the Spirit (Gal. 5:25)

Walk worthy (Eph. 4:1)

Walk not as the Gentiles walk (Eph. 4:17)

Walk in love (Eph. 5:1)

Walk as children of light (Eph. 5:8)

Walk circumspectly, not as fools, but as wise (Eph. 5:15)

Walk by the same rule (Phil. 3:16)

Walk so you have us as ensamples (Phil. 3:17)

Walk worthy of the Lord (Col. 1:10)

Walk ye in him (Col. 2:6)

Walk in wisdom toward them that are without (Col. 4:5)

Walk worthy of God (1 Thess. 2:12)

How ye ought to walk and to please God (1 Thess. 4:1)

Walk honestly toward them that are without (1 Thess. 4:12)

Some which walk among your disorderly, working not at all (2 Thess. 3:11)

Appendix

Why I Use the King James Bible

There are several reasons why I use the King James Bible. If you are new to the KJB, I hope that you will allow me to get you excited about putting out the extra effort it takes to get used to this Bible. Many people have urged me to use other versions of the bible such as the NKJV, ESV, NASB or NIV. I agree that it is possible for God to use these "easy to read" modern bible versions to save a soul. But God wants us also "to come unto the knowledge of the truth" (1 Tim. 2:4). Easier and popular is not always better.

I have come to understand that it is not only a matter of simply "taking out the thees and thous" but also that the changes in the modern bible versions are both textual and doctrinal. I hope you will realize that I have your best interest in mind and that I am only trying to bless you. After reading my reasons for using the King James Version of the Bible, I hope that you will understand its benefits and welcome the challenge. That you will apply yourself to enjoying it. Here are some of the reasons:

- The King James Bible cuts me to the heart and convicts my soul like no other Bible does. Try it for yourself, take any passage of Scripture and read it in various Bible translations, which one speaks to you?

- Although the original autographs no longer exist, God has preserved His word perfectly by exact copies of the originals. I believe that the KJB is the precise 100% accurate word of God. I believe God has kept His promise and preserved His word. I believe that He oversaw every step of the preservation of His word from the inspiration of Holy men moved by the Holy Spirit to write it, to the collection, translation (by 47 men who had the Holy Ghost in them), to the printing and publication.

- The Old Testament in the 1611 King James Bible is based on the Hebrew Masoretic Text, manuscripts carefully copied by hand by the Jewish scribes using strict rules to help prevent errors and departures from the original autographs. A small part of the Bible is in Aramaic, such as portions of the book of Daniel.

- In 1516 and 1522 Erasmus published his collection of the best Greek New Testament manuscripts, called the Textus Receptus "received text." He gathered this from the Byzantines who fled to Europe after the

Turks invaded what had been the Eastern Roman Empire in 1453. The King James New Testament, Martin Luther's German New Testament, and the Textus Receptus (King James Greek New Testament) are the only Bible versions which do not have any words of God omitted.

- Over time and after a great deal of research I have come to understand that almost all modern bible versions are based on the corrupt Alexandrian texts, the Codex Vaticanus and the Codex Sinaiticus. These few texts have been eclectically (a little bit of this and a little bit of that) brought together into a "Critical Text" assembled (or concocted) by two unbelieving men, Westcott and Hort in 1881. Nestle-Aland/UBS (United Bible Society) also used the Westcott and Hort corrupt Greek New Testament. They included a Jesuit priest, Carlo Martini, on their Bible Committee. Higher Criticism, which swept over Germany and other parts of Europe after Martin Luther died, also denied the deity of Jesus.

- For those new to the King James Bible it is valuable to know some of its features. The King James Bible is a word for word (formal equivalence) rather than a thought for thought (dynamic equivalence) translation. "Every word of God is pure" (Proverbs 30:5).

- It is well worth it to get used to the pronouns used in the KJB because they are more specific than the general pronoun "you." If it has a "T" such as in "thee" and "thou" it is singular; if it has a "Y" as in "ye" and "you" it is plural. Thus: "I said unto thee [Nicodemus], Ye [plural you, meaning the nation of Israel] must be born again" (John 3:7).

- The KJB does not capitalize the pronoun names for God. To do so can be presumptive and it is left up to the reader to interpret the one referred to in the Bible with the help of the Holy Spirit. So please realize that although I capitalize words which pertain to God the KJB may have these words in lower case. Be prepared that British English in the KJB has a slightly different spelling than American English in words such as Saviour. In addition, the suffix "eth" indicates ongoing present tense such as "worketh."

- The King James Bible (1611) does not use quotation marks, but capital letters begin a conversation. The spelling was updated in 1769.

- The 47 King James Bible translators italicized words which they included for clarity but were not in the original manuscripts. Here is an example "I am *he*" (John 8:28). This lets the reader see at a glance what is written in the original word of God.

- The cross references between the Old and the New Testament and other verses are easily accessed in the King James Bible. God's word is precise and concise. He uses similar words and phrases so we can compare them and understand more of His word. For more information, go to kjvtoday.com or get the excellent book *Bible Per-VERSIONS* by Eric and Lonna Neumann available on Amazon.

- The KJB uses the precise identical word or phrase for easy cross reference between the Old and the New Testament. For example, "the father of many nations" is found in Gen. 17:3, 4 and Rom. 4:17, 18. Furthermore, the KJB contains a unique number code.

- After the KJB was published in 1611 most people acquired this book rather than the very popular Geneva Bible because of its formal equivalence to the word of God and beautiful poetic language.

- Satan has been attacking God's word from the beginning: "Yea, hath God said, Ye shall not eat of every tree of the garden?" (Gen. 3:1). But God has promised to preserve His word. "The words of the LORD are pure words: as silver tried in a furnace of earth, purified seven times. Thou shalt keep them, O LORD, thou shalt preserve them from this generation for ever" (Psalms 12:6, 7).

- God gave His Word through 40 different Jewish men over 1,600 years written in three different languages: Hebrew, Greek, and Aramaic. God preserved the Bible down through the centuries through dedicated copyists who meticulously copied it by hand. Yet this collection of 66 books fit together perfectly to reveal one continuous and complete blueprint of who God is, what He has done, and will do in heaven and on earth. This perfect continuity could only occur if God told these men what to write. The fulfilled prophecies confirm that God is the author.

The majority of all ancient Bible texts found (over 5,000), agree with the KJB. An excellent DVD documentary on how we got the King James Bible and Church history is *A Lamp in the Dark: The Untold History of the Bible* (A Chris Pinto Production) find it on Youtube or their website adullamfilms.com.

I used the NKJV for 15 years before I understood the problems with it. A good video on the NKJV problems on Youtube is the "New King James PerVersion." The New King James follows the Jehovah's Witness Bible in places calling Jesus a Servant instead of the Son of God. The subtle changes, omissions, and footnotes in the NKJV will not only weaken a person's faith, it takes a person away from the powerful true word of God found only in the King James Bible. Another excellent source for more information is Gail Riplinger's "New Age Bible Versions" seminar on Youtube.com.

The NKJV does not use the same manuscript as the KJB. The NKJV uses the corrupt Stuttgart edition of the Old Testament Hebrew Text (ben Asher) not the Hebrew (ben Chayyim) used in the King James Bible. The NKJV omits the word "blood" 23 times; "Lord" 66 times; "God" 51 times; "heaven" 50 times; "repent" 44 times; "hell" 22 times; the following words are completely omitted "new testament, damnation, devils, JEHOVAH." The NKJV ignores the KJB Textus Receptus over 1,200 times. This information is taken from the website: Messiah Congregation oneinmessiah.net/njkv.htm.

Please notice how a very important verse for right division is changed in the New King James Version (NKJV) compare the following:
Rom. 15:8 (KJB) Now I say that Jesus Christ WAS a minister of the circumcision for the truth of God, to confirm the promises made unto the fathers.
Rom. 15:8 (NKJV) Now I say that Jesus Christ HAS BECOME a servant to the circumcision for the truth of God, to confirm the promises made to the fathers.
Christ was (NOT as the NKJV says: has become) a minister to the circumcision (Israel) when He was on earth, as Paul explained.

Here is an example of a doctrinal change in the New King James Version:
1 Cor. 1:18 (NKJV) For the message of the cross is foolishness to those who are perishing, but to us who are BEING SAVED it is the power of God.
1 Cor. 1:18 (KJB) For the preaching of the cross is to them that perish foolishness; but unto us which ARE SAVED it is the power of God.
Notice how the NKJV changed the doctrine of salvation to a progressive salvation, rather than a one-time instantaneous event saying we "are BEING SAVED" in 1 Cor. 1:18. No one can be secure if they are "being saved," instead of "are saved." The NKJV is a counterfeit bible, not the KJV.

The New International Version (NIV) is missing 16 entire verses. Try finding Acts 8:37 in the NIV. Here is the list of missing verses (some newer NIV bibles have these verses in the footnotes, but they belong in the text):
Matthew 17:21; 18:11; 23:14.
Mark 7:16; 9:44; 9:46; 11:26; 15:28.
Luke 17:36; 23:17; John 5:4.
Acts 8:37; 15:34; 24:7; 28:29.
Romans 16:24 and 1 John 5:7 (this verse is missing words).

Philo (AD 25 BC–50), a Jewish man, tried to unite Greek philosophy (Plato) with the Jewish Old Testament. <u>Origen</u> **(AD 185-254) did much damage to God's word by changing it in Alexandria, Egypt. The true line of Bibles came from the Antioch line. Paul says that "after my departing shall grievous wolves enter in among you, not sparing the flock. Also of your own selves shall men arise, speaking perverse things" (Acts 20:29, 30a). Paul also writes, "For we are not as many which** <u>corrupt</u> **the word of God" (2 Cor. 2:17). See if this verse is quoted correctly in your Bible: "God was manifest in the flesh" (1 Tim. 3:16, some bibles leave out "God"). Satan is taking the true word of God away from Christians and many are unaware of what is happening.**

There is evidence that Vaticanus (that includes the Apocrypha) was one of the fifty Greek Bibles Constantine commissioned Eusebius the bishop of Caesarea (an admirer of Origen) to prepare for the bishop Constantinople in AD 331.

The KJB translators primarily used the Bishop's Bible correcting any errors and the Greek texts of Stephanus 1550 and Beza 1598. <u>**I believe the King James Bible is the true word of God in the English language, perfectly based on the true Greek and Hebrew texts which God has preserved.**</u> **There are really only two Bibles in the world today those based on God's preserved texts like the KJB, and all the others based on corrupt texts. "How firm a foundation He has laid for us all in His excellent word." We need to use the most accurate text in our Bible study. For all these reasons I believe that I would be wasting your time and mine if I use any other Bible version.**

God does not want His word changed in any way, NOT added or subtracted to: ". . . If any man shall <u>add</u> **unto these things, God shall add unto him the plagues that are written in this book: And if any man shall** <u>take away</u> **from the words of the book of this prophecy, God shall take away his part out of the book of life, and out of the holy city, and from the things which are written in this book" (Rev. 22:18, 19).**

Satan used the Catholic church to keep the Bible from the common people. The inferior Alexandrian text (Vulgate) was kept in a dead language which few could read (Latin) shut up for the 1,000-year Dark Ages (AD 500-1500).

But Martin Luther hatched the egg that Erasmus had laid by translating the Textus Receptus which Erasmus had collected so that people could read it.

William Tyndale (1494-1536) was the first to translate the Greek (TR) and Hebrew Bible into English. The King James Bible Old Testament is 76 percent the New Testament is about 90 percent the work of Tyndale (Bere, Michael *Bible Doctrines for Today*, A Beka Book, Pensacola, FL 1996, page 79).

Remember, the modern bible versions hide (obscure) the revelation of the "mystery" given to Paul. But the mystery is evident in the King James Bible for those who study the Bible rightly divided.

Proving the superiority of the King James Bible is simple and easy: the KJV exalts the Lord Jesus Christ more than any other Bible on the planet. The true scriptures testify of Jesus Christ and exalt Him.

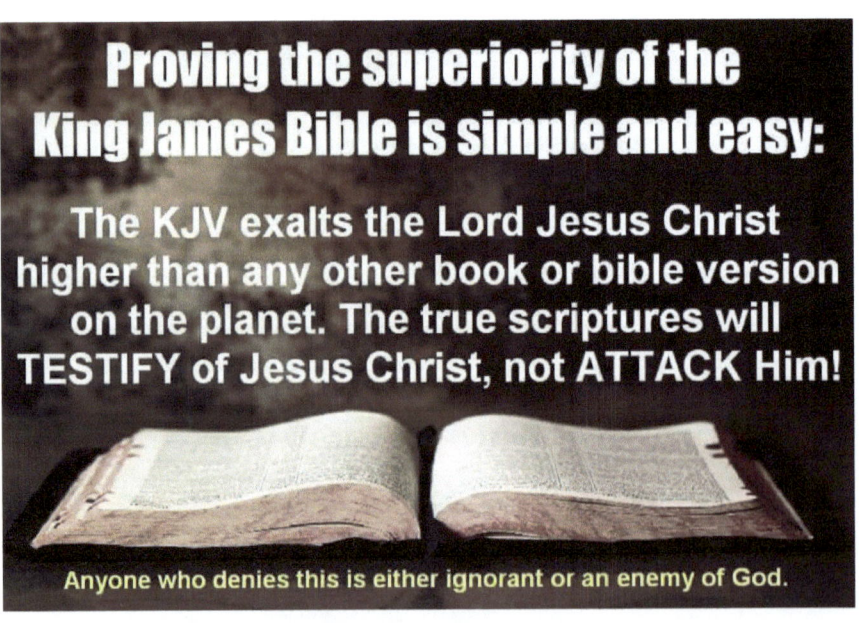

The KJB (also known as the KJV) is a masterpiece inspired and preserved by God the Holy Spirit. The Lord Jesus Christ, the Word (John 1:1-4) said that His words are eternal "heaven and earth shall pass away, but MY WORDS SHALL NOT PASS AWAY" (Matt. 24:35).

Now I not only use the King James Bible, but believe it is God's perfect word.

About the Author

She was saved in 1990. She became, not only a King James Bible user, but a King James Bible believer in 2014. She has more than twenty-five years of experience teaching the Bible, eighteen of those years were with the AWANA clubs where she earned her Citation Award for Bible memorization. In 2015, she was introduced to Pauline dispensational truth by watching Les Feldick on YouTube. After learning the basics of "rightly dividing the word of truth" (2 Timothy 2:15), she learned more from the Bible and Richard Jordan and his Grace School of the Bible. A retired nurse midwife, she has devoted the rest of her life "to make all men see what is the fellowship of the mystery" (Eph. 3:9). She teaches a Bible study in her home which is available on Facebook and YouTube (mariannemanley.com). Her joy after understanding the Bible better led her to edify the body of Christ by writing **God's Secret** in 2017. **Romans: A Concise Commentary**, **First Corinthians: A Commentary, Second Corinthians: A Commentary, Galatians: A Commentary, Treasure Hunt Volume I** (Romans to Galatians), **Ephesians A Commentary, Philippians, Colossians, Philemon Commentary, Treasure Hunt Volume II** (Paul's Prison Epistles), **Why was the Earth without Form, Void, and Dark?**, *Just as God Said* for children, *The Certainty of the Pre-Tribulation Rapture* (First and Second Thessalonians Commentary), **Paul's Pastoral Epistles** (First and Second Timothy, Titus, and Philemon Commentary), **Treasure Hunt Volume III** (Paul's T Books), **Acts of the Apostles Commentary Part 1, 2, 3, Missed the Rapture? Read this Commentary on Hebrew!** and **How to be Saved Made Simple, Why the King James Bible is the Holy Bible**, and the **Rightly Dividing Study Guides**. Many people have all her books!

Other Books by Marianne Manley

God's Secret A Primer with Pictures for How to Rightly Divide the Word of Truth (on Amazon in color or black and white or in Spanish **El Secreto de Dios**).

Why the King James Bible is the Holy Bible
Rightly Dividing COLOSSIANS and PHILEMON Study Guide
Rightly Dividing PHILIPPIANS Study Guide
Rightly Dividing EPHISIANS Study Guide
Rightly Dividing GALATIANS Study Guide
Rightly Dividing SECOND CORINTHIANS Study Guide
Rightly Dividing FIRST CORINTHIANS Study Guide
Rightly Dividing ROMANS Study Guide
Romans: A Concise Commentary (also in a Black and White Edition)
First Corinthians: A Commentary
Second Corinthians: A Commentary
Galatians: A Commentary
Ephesians A Commentary
Philippians, Colossians, Philemon Commentary
The Certainty of the Pre-Tribulation Rapture (First and Second Thessalonians)
Paul's Pastoral Epistles (Timothy Letters, Titus, and Philemon Commentary)
Treasure Hunt Volume I (Commentary only Romans to Galatians)
Treasure Hunt Volume II (Commentary only on Paul's Prison Epistles)
Treasure Hunt Volume III (Commentary on Paul's T Books)

Why was the Earth without Form, Void, and Dark?
Just as God Said
Acts of the Apostles Commentary Part One, Two, Three
Missed the Rapture? Read this Commentary on Hebrews!
How to be Saved Made Simple (This booklet is perfect for our lost loved ones.)
Could God Have a 7,000 Year Plan for Mankind? (also in Black and White and
AD 34 The Year Jesus Died for All (same content as Could God, in 9x6 size)

The author may be contacted by e-mail at mariannemanley@sbcglobal.net
Please visit her website: www.mariannemanley.com (free .pdf files)
Follow her on Facebook at facebook.com/marianne.manley.7 and God's Secret Facebook Page at facebook.com/GodsSecretAPrimerwithPictures
Find her on YouTube (Just type in her name and find her teaching the Bible, a-chapter-at-a-time) or on Salvation, Rightly Dividing, and the Rapture her YouTube channel or Truth Be Told, or call (858) 273-2049.